OBSESSION

BYRON YORK

REGNERY
PUBLISHING
A Division of Salem Media Group

Regnery® is a registered trademark of Salem Communications Holding Corporation

Cataloging-in-Publication data on file with the Library of Congress

ISBN 978-1-68451-106-8
eISBN 978-1-62157-936-6
Library of Congress Control Number: 2020936163

Published in the United States by
Regnery Publishing
A Division of Salem Media Group
300 New Jersey Ave NW
Washington, DC 20001
www.Regnery.com

Manufactured in the United States of America

10 9 8 7 6 5 4 3 2 1

Books are available in quantity for promotional or premium use. For information on discounts and terms, please visit our website: www.Regnery.com.

To Tom and Helen York

CONTENTS

The Long Campaign

In early December 2019, a reporter asked House Speaker Nancy Pelosi why she was rushing to pass articles of impeachment against President Donald Trump. "One of the biggest criticisms of the process has been the speed at which the House Democrats are moving," the reporter noted.

"The speed?" Pelosi replied, with a touch of indignation. "It's been going on for 22 months, okay? Two and a half years, actually. This was two and a half years ago they initiated the Mueller investigation. It's not about speed. It's about urgency."

Pelosi's words attracted little attention among Democrats, but they were a bolt of lightning for Republicans. In one brief moment, the Speaker confirmed what Trump's defenders had always believed about the Democratic campaign to impeach the president and remove him from office: it had been going on for a long time. It didn't start with Ukraine. It didn't start with a phone call between Trump and Ukrainian President Vlodymyr Zelensky. It didn't start with a hold on U.S. aid to Zelensky's country. No, the drive to remove the president from office was underway well before that. It reached back into the 2016 campaign and then, just a few months into the Trump presidency, to the appointment of Trump-Russia special counsel Robert Mueller. It was going full-bore, in the form of the Trump-Russia investigation, until it morphed, nearly seamlessly, into an investigation over alleged improprieties with President Trump's phone call with the Ukrainian president, and then, finally, into impeachment. There were different battles, but they were all part of one long campaign.

And now Pelosi seemed to concede the point.

"She is finally recognizing that what we've been saying for the last two years is true," Republican Congressman Chris Stewart of Utah wrote in his journal that evening. (Stewart, a member of the Intelligence Committee, kept a diary—non-classified—during the most intense battles over Trump.) "She's always known it was true," Stewart continued. "And she's going to regret expressing it, honestly. But it is true. They've been trying to impeach and remove him literally from the day before he was inaugurated."

"It was vindication for those of us who said the whole thing started with tears in Brooklyn," recalled Georgia Congressman Doug Collins, the top Republican on the House Judiciary Committee. "Tears in Brooklyn" was Collins's way of saying the Democratic effort to remove Trump actually began on a weepy election night at Hillary Clinton's campaign headquarters in Brooklyn on November 8, 2016. "For me, it was vindication," Collins repeated. "It was: 'See, we've been saying this all along, you've been lying about it all along, at least now you're admitting it.'"

Pelosi's statement was so important to Republicans because it confirmed that the investigations that inundated the Trump administration—the Russia-focused FBI investigation called Crossfire Hurricane; the investigation by the House Intelligence Committee; the investigation by the Senate Intelligence Committee; the Mueller investigation; the House Intelligence Committee Trump-Ukraine impeachment investigation; then the House Judiciary Committee investigation; and finally the Senate impeachment trial—were really *all* about impeachment. The fact that the investigating had been going on so long, and in so many iterations, suggested to Republicans that the real goal was to get Trump rather than get to the bottom of whatever controversy dominated the news of the day.

Now, with the perspective of time, the Democratic effort to remove Trump, and the president's struggle to defend himself, appear less a rushed impeachment than a long and agonizing political civil war: The presidential campaign and transition were a prelude, a time of growing tension; 2017 saw the formal start of the war, with the appointment of a special counsel, and a sense of hope—at least on the president's side—that hostilities might be wrapped up quickly; 2018 was a stalemate, as each side, optimism gone, dug in for a long battle; 2019 saw what at first appeared to be the end of action—Mueller's last stand—only to see the conflict flare up again in one more desperate Democratic attack as the 2020 elections approached.

This is the story of that long campaign, from the first shot—the appointment of Mueller—to the final gasp in the Senate impeachment trial.

CHAPTER ONE

James Comey, Russia, and the Road to Mueller

"His instincts were that Comey was no good"—
"Six ways from Sunday"—Pulling a J. Edgar Hoover—
"It's bullshit"—The Comey Campaign—The Last Straw—
"You are not able to effectively lead the Bureau"—
Eight Days in May—A Glimpse of a Terrible Future

If any single day marked the official kickoff of the Democratic campaign to remove President Trump, it was May 17, 2017. On that day, Robert Mueller, the former FBI director, was appointed special counsel to investigate the Trump-Russia affair. But also on that day—less noted—came the first formal call for Trump's impeachment in the House of Representatives, when Democratic Representative Al Green of Texas announced, "This is where I stand. I will not be moved. The president must be impeached."

From that point on, the two processes—investigation and impeachment, a legal battle and a political one—were intertwined.

The two were always dependent on each other. Mueller had the power to investigate and prosecute anyone associated with the Trump campaign, but it was widely understood that he could not indict the president himself. The House had limited authority to investigate—nothing like the full law enforcement powers Mueller had—but it had the sole constitutional authority to impeach the president. So, if any action against the president were to result from Mueller's work, it would have to be undertaken by the House.

What that meant was that Mueller's team, as well as being prosecutors, also served as the *de facto* investigative arm of the House of Representatives. Democratic lawmakers, then in the minority, could not impeach the president, but they could crack the door open and wait to see what Mueller found. If the special prosecutor turned over material that could be used against Trump, Democrats could apply pressure for impeachment. If they could win a majority in the House, they could initiate impeachment themselves. But in any scenario, their strategy depended on the prosecutor.

The symbiotic relationship between investigator and lawmaker had been noted back in the 1980s, when the old independent counsel law was in effect. That law—a post-Watergate reform intended to check the power of the presidency—required an independent counsel, upon completion of his investigation, to write a report to Congress presenting his findings. Congress could then decide whether to use those findings to impeach the president. In *Morrison v. Olson*, a case challenging the constitutionality of the law (in which the Supreme Court upheld its constitutionality by a 7–1 vote), the lone dissenter was Justice Antonin Scalia, who observed that appointing an independent counsel was, in actual practice, a step toward removing the president; as he put it, the law was "acrid with the smell of threatened impeachment."

The independent counsel law survived that Supreme Court challenge, but it did not survive the fallout from the impeachment of Bill Clinton, in which the law functioned precisely as Scalia predicted. And before the law bit Democrats on the backside during Clinton's presidency, it wounded Republicans during the Reagan-era Iran-Contra scandal. Unappy lawmakers from both parties allowed it to expire in 1999.

But official Washington still believed there had to be some mechanism to investigate a president and other top officials accused of wrongdoing. So that same year, 1999, the Justice Department adopted regulations for what became known as special counsels, who would have many of the same powers as the old independent counsels, but who were not required to present a report to Congress. The idea was that if Congress did not receive a report that could serve as a roadmap to impeachment, the opposition party would be less tempted and less able to impeach the president. But what the drafters of the regulations did not contemplate was that, in the white-hot political atmosphere of an investigation—say, the Trump-Russia probe— there might not be much practical difference between an independent counsel and a special counsel. In such a high-profile case, the special counsel could not present a brief summary of his investigation to the Justice Department, decline to charge anyone, and be done with it. The opposition party in Congress would inevitably want to get involved, see the special counsel's findings, and keep open the option of impeachment. So, starting in May 2017, Mueller was effectively the investigator for the House, just as Kenneth Starr, the independent counsel who investigated Bill Clinton, had been before him.

Trump was not prepared for what lay in store. Perhaps no president could have been. But the special counsel process could leave the target— in this case, the president—remarkably in the dark about the most basic things. In the days after the appointment of Mueller, for example, Trump's lawyers could not be sure whether the president himself was formally under investigation. It is hard to believe in retrospect, but at the time they didn't know.

In addition, Trump did not understand the central role a single person—FBI Director James Comey—played in his worsening predicament. It was clear, of course, that Trump's decision to fire Comey on May 9, 2017, led to the appointment of Mueller. What Trump could not know at the time was that Comey, in ways hidden from the public and from many others in government, had orchestrated the events that led to the special counsel probe, and to the greatest crisis of Trump's presidency. And Trump did not have the perspective to see that perhaps the most consequential decision of his first year was the decision *not* to fire the FBI director immediately upon taking office. Trump kept Comey on the job for a variety of reasons: perhaps naiveté, perhaps a belief that he could win Comey over, perhaps something else. But when Comey was allowed to stay at the FBI past the Trump inauguration, his behind-the-scenes machinations set in motion a conflict that would blow up Trump's presidency. The story of the beginning of the Mueller investigation—the formal effort to remove the president from office—is the story of the relationship between Donald Trump and James Comey.

"His instincts were that Comey was no good"

Trump was never entirely comfortable with the FBI director. "His instincts were that Comey was no good," said John Dowd, who was Trump's lawyer in 2017 and 2018. "And he hung that initially on the way Comey handled Hillary Clinton." Even though Trump was running against Clinton in 2016, and even though he benefited from Comey's mishandling of the Clinton email case—prematurely exonerating her in July 2016 and then re-opening the investigation just eleven days before the presidential election—Trump was wary of Comey. "His gut and instincts were, there's something wrong with this guy," Dowd recalled.

That was precisely what Trump's friend and adviser Rudy Giuliani was telling the candidate during the campaign and transition. "I advised him to fire Comey," Giuliani recalled. "Every time we talked about Comey, I said the guy's gonna turn on you. There's something wrong with him."

Dowd and Giuliani were not alone. During the transition, there were others, including Senator Jeff Sessions, a key campaign adviser who would become attorney general, who recommended that Trump fire Comey right away—as quickly after Inauguration Day as possible. It wasn't because they were offended on behalf of Clinton, although they felt Comey's handling of the email matter was erratic and unprofessional. The important thing for the Trump team was that Comey's behavior in the Clinton affair might foretell how he would act in a Trump administration. Looking forward, Comey at the helm of the FBI could mean another disaster, only this one involving President Trump.

"If he stays, and he's a loose cannon like that while Obama's in office, why would we think he'd be any different when President Trump was in office?" asked New Jersey Governor Chris Christie, who spoke to Trump about Comey on a number of occasions. Even before the election, the two men discussed what Trump, if he were elected, should do with the FBI director. Christie, a former U.S. attorney, believed President Trump would have sufficient grounds to fire Comey, but if he did, he should do it quickly. "I said to him, 'You have to either develop a trusting relationship with Comey or you need to get rid of him right at the beginning if you don't trust him,'" Christie recalled. "'Once you take the oath, if you keep him, he's yours.'"

The president famously ended up firing Christie from the transition, but like many who leave the official circle, Christie stayed in touch with Trump. And Comey's future was a regular topic of conversation. Each time, Christie's message was the same: "In my view, there was plenty of reason to relieve Comey of his duties, so I said to the president-elect: 'Don't own it. If you want to get rid of him, get rid of him now.'"

At the same time, there were others, including some senior Republicans on Capitol Hill, who vouched for Comey. Vice President-elect Mike Pence was not keen to fire Comey, either. Most important, Trump himself wanted to make the relationship with Comey work. Many people who have dealt with Trump over the years say that he has always felt, throughout his life, that if he can meet and talk to someone, if he can get to know them, then they will like him. It is something he believes he can do through the sheer force of his personality. Some call it naiveté, but it was a confidence Trump brought to Washington, where it lasted through years of vicious partisan warfare. During the transition, the president-elect wanted to win over the director of the FBI. He decided not to fire Comey.

There was one last factor working in Comey's favor. Some Trump team members who did not particularly like Comey nevertheless believed the new president should follow a strict process in firing him. The FBI director reported to the deputy attorney general, who reported to the attorney general, who reported to the president. On Inauguration Day, only the president was in place. Jeff Sessions had not yet been confirmed as attorney general, and no one had any idea who the deputy attorney general would be. There was no one to fire Comey. Some advised Trump to wait until he had the structure in place to get rid of the FBI director. Trump accepted their advice.

Then came January 6, 2017.

"Six ways from Sunday"

By early January, the Intelligence Community had finished its assessment of Russian efforts to interfere in the 2016 election. The assessment, which was written in both classified and unclassified versions, focused mostly on the evidence that the Russian government used various methods—hacking the emails of the Democratic National Committee and top Clinton campaign aide John Podesta, plus employing a content farm to disseminate divisive political messages on social media—in an attempt to sow discord in the United States during what was an extremely contentious presidential election.

The final weeks of 2016 were filled with news reports, based on leaks, that the Intelligence Community had concluded that Russia had not only interfered with the election for the purpose of destroying Americans' confidence in the system—it had interfered for the specific purpose of electing Donald Trump. While there was unanimous agreement in the intelligence world that Russia had interfered, there was disagreement among intelligence experts on Capitol Hill—a debate unknown to the public at the time—about whether that interference was explicitly intended to elect Trump. Nevertheless, the leaks led to endless discussion on cable TV and pronouncements from the president-elect's adversaries that he owed his election to Vladimir Putin.

President-elect Trump reacted by sniping at the Intelligence Community. He was never happy about the assessment, not because he believed Russia was innocent but because he believed the Putin-helped-Trump storyline, heard every day in the media, would undermine the legitimacy of his election and hamper his ability to govern. So, when the *Washington Post* reported on December 9, 2016, that the Intelligence Community had concluded Russia specifically favored Trump, Trump fired back.

"These are the same people that said Saddam Hussein had weapons of mass destruction," the Trump transition team said in a statement. "The election ended a long time ago in one of the biggest Electoral College victories in history. It's now time to move on and 'Make America Great Again.'" The statement made clear that Trump believed the Russia talk was designed to undercut his authority as president-elect. To him, it was a fight about politics, not intelligence.

Meanwhile, the drafting of the assessment continued in December. Unbeknownst to Trump or to anyone else in the public, top intel officials were debating whether to include allegations from a sensationalist dossier compiled by a former British spy, Christopher Steele. The public did not know it at the time, but the Clinton campaign and the Democratic National Committee had secretly used a friendly law firm to pay for Steele's research. The result was a collection of serious, damaging, and, as it turned out, false allegations against Donald Trump.

The Steele dossier claimed there was a "well-developed conspiracy" between Trump and Russia, in which Trump campaign chief Paul Manafort used a short-term, low-level foreign policy adviser, Carter Page, as an intermediary to the Russians in a plot to weaken the Clinton campaign. It also claimed that during a July 2016 trip to Moscow, Page met with Igor Sechin, head of the Russian energy giant Rosneft and a close associate of Vladimir Putin, who offered Page a huge bribe, amounting to perhaps billions of dollars, to persuade Trump, should he become president, to end U.S. sanctions on Russia. And it described something that became known as the "pee tape," which was said to be a video, supposedly made by Russian spies, of businessman Donald Trump watching as prostitutes performed a kinky sex act—a "golden showers" routine—in a Moscow hotel room in 2013, which could supposedly be used to blackmail Trump.

The bottom line was that the dossier purported to be proof of what became known as "collusion" between the Trump campaign and Russia. Comey's FBI was so impressed that in fall 2016, while the presidential campaign was underway, it agreed to put Steele on its payroll to continue the work.

But none of the allegations were verified, even though during the transition FBI agents worked furiously—and unsuccessfully, it was later learned—to corroborate Steele's work. Nevertheless, there was a lot of discussion within the FBI over whether to make the unverified material part of the Intelligence Community Assessment. Comey, along with top deputy Andrew McCabe, wanted the Steele allegations to be included. On December 17, 2016, Comey wrote an email to top FBI aides describing a conversation he had the night before with Director of National Intelligence James Clapper. "During a secure call last night on this general topic, I informed the DNI that we would be contributing the [Steele] reporting (although I didn't use that name) to the IC effort…I told him the source of the material, which included salacious material about the president-elect."

Comey was the one who wanted to give the dossier wider exposure by including it in the assessment. The CIA opposed using the Steele material; the agency's view was that it was "internet rumor." In the end, the CIA won—mostly. The Steele material was left out of the main body of the assessment, but a brief summary was included in an appendix. Later, the CIA was proven correct when intelligence investigators concluded that Steele's work was almost entirely garbage. The "well-developed conspiracy" allegation fell apart, as did the Page-Rosneft charge. And when FBI agents located Steele's primary source on the Moscow hotel prostitutes allegation, he said it was "jest," that it was "rumor and speculation," and expressed surprise that Steele, or anyone else, ever took it seriously. It had all been a joke.

But James Comey took it very seriously. As December 2016 ended and January 2017 began and Trump was preparing to take office, Comey and other top intelligence chiefs planned to brief the president-elect on the assessment. At the same time, a series of leaks appeared in the media supporting and building the collusion storyline. Trump, of course, struck back on Twitter. On January 3, he tweeted: "The 'intelligence' briefing on so-called 'Russian hacking' was delayed until Friday, perhaps more time needed to build a case. Very strange."

The tweet prompted the top Democrat in the Senate, Minority Leader Charles Schumer, to issue a warning that would later become something of an epigraph to the entire Trump-Russia affair. The Intelligence Community was "very upset with how [Trump] has treated them and talked about them," Schumer said on MSNBC. "Let me tell you, you take on the Intelligence Community, they have six ways from Sunday at getting back at you. So even for a practical, supposedly hard-nosed businessman, [Trump] is being really dumb to do this."

Could anything have been more prescient? Three days later, on January 6, Comey and the intel chiefs traveled to New York, where they would brief Trump in his Trump Tower headquarters. They would soon show they really did have six ways from Sunday of getting back at the president-elect.

"Pulling a J. Edgar Hoover"

For Comey, the meeting had a double purpose. Yes, the FBI director was one of the intelligence leaders briefing the president. But secretly, the FBI was also investigating the Trump campaign, based on the dossier allegations and more. The Trump Tower session was a way to conduct what amounted to an ambush interview of a key subject—the president-elect himself—in the guise of a security briefing. And the subject wouldn't even know it.

Comey and top FBI officials prepared meticulously for the moment. The director held a planning meeting with McCabe, chief of staff James Rybicki, general counsel James Baker, and the top supervisors of Crossfire Hurricane, which was the name FBI officials had given to their Trump-Russia investigation. They came up with a plan for Comey to broach the Moscow hotel story to Trump privately, apart from the other intel officials, and then gauge his response. According to a report later done by the Justice Department inspector general, Michael Horowitz, the FBI planners "agreed that the briefing needed to be one-on-one, so that Comey could present the 'salacious' information in the most discreet and least embarrassing way."

The FBI team worried about Trump's reaction. After all, here was the director of the Federal Bureau of Investigation, in his first face-to-face meeting with the president-elect, delivering a message that amounted to: we know about you and those hookers in Moscow. The FBI team worried that Trump might "perceive the one-on-one briefing as an effort to hold information over him like a 'Hoover-esque type of plot,'" the Horowitz report concluded—a reference to the FBI's notorious founding director, J. Edgar Hoover, who relished keeping (and using) embarrassing secrets on top political leaders.

Still, the FBI group hoped that, once Comey hit Trump with the Moscow hotel story, the president-elect might "make statements about or provide information of value to the pending Russia interference investigation," according to Horowitz. Perhaps it might even be something self-incriminating. Given that hope, Comey made plans, once the meeting was over, to dash out of Trump Tower and immediately write down everything he could remember from the meeting. It might be evidence someday.

All went as planned. Sitting around a conference table in a room that had been transformed into a SCIF, or Sensitive Compartmented Information Facility, the intel chiefs, including Comey, briefed Trump and a few top aides on the broader aspects of the Intelligence Community Assessment. Then, as the meeting ended, Comey said, "Can I have a few minutes alone with the president-elect?" Trump's team, taken by surprise, looked at each other. What's this? they thought. It didn't seem quite right. Someone asked Trump if he was okay meeting with Comey alone. Trump said, "Sure. I'm fine." So everyone except Comey and the president-elect left the room.

According to Comey's memoir, Trump said some nice things to Comey, saying he had a "great reputation" and that the people at the FBI "really like" him as a leader. Trump said he hoped Comey would stay on as director. Trump's remarks were both a manifestation of his make-people-like-me personality and an indication that Trump had sided with the transition advisers who argued that Comey should not be fired.

At that point, Comey related the Moscow hotel room story, straight out of the Steele dossier. Trump, surprised, immediately denied it. Then Comey, according to his memoir, "explained that I wasn't saying the FBI believed the allegations. We simply thought it important that he know they were out there and being widely circulated."

The news came out of nowhere to Trump. What's this story about prostitutes and Moscow, and why is the director of the FBI telling me this? Trump protested to Comey that he, Trump, had been unfairly accused of all sorts of things in the past. But Comey and the FBI team anticipated that Trump would react negatively to the news. "There was a real chance that Donald Trump, politician and hardball deal-maker, would assume I was dangling the prostitute thing over him to jam him, to gain leverage," Comey wrote later. "He might well assume I was pulling a J. Edgar Hoover."

Trump might make that assumption because that was precisely what Comey was doing. Still, Comey looked for some way to "reassure" the president-elect that the FBI wasn't going after him. "The bit about 'pulling a J. Edgar Hoover' made me keen to have some tool in my bag to reassure the new president," Comey recalled. "I needed to be prepared to say something, if at all possible, that would take the temperature down. After extensive discussion with my team, I decided I could assure the president-elect that the FBI was not currently investigating him." Trump, the hope went, would then relax and lay off the FBI.

When the moment came, when Trump was growing increasingly concerned, defending himself and saying the Moscow hotel story was not true—which, of course, it was not—Comey stuck to his plan. "As he began to grow more defensive and the conversation teetered toward disaster, on instinct, I pulled the tool from my bag," Comey wrote. "'We are not investigating you, sir.' That seemed to quiet him." The meeting ended.

Comey dashed out of Trump Tower and into a government SUV idling nearby. "Comey said he had a secure FBI laptop waiting for him in his FBI vehicle and that when he got into the vehicle, he was handed the laptop and 'began typing as the vehicle moved,'" the inspector general's report said. Comey worked on his account as the FBI car took him to the New York field office, where aides had set up a secure video teleconference with top aides and the "Crossfire Hurricane" team.

"It's bullshit"

Trump, meanwhile, knew he had just been set up for something, although he did not know quite what. After Comey left, Trump walked out of the room to talk with aides, who had stood out in the hallway waiting for the Trump-Comey one-on-one to end. "It's bullshit," he said, relating that Comey wanted to talk about some out-of-the-blue allegation (at the time, no one knew about the dossier) that might be added to the end of the Intelligence Community Assessment.

People who were there described Trump as somewhat angry, but perhaps more bewildered. What was going on? "He was agitated that the FBI was screwing around with him," one aide remembered. "It may have been another alert to him that perhaps these people were not on the up-and-up.

"A lot of us immediately dismissed the crazy stuff, the golden show-ers," the aide recalled. "I knew Trump pretty well, not just from the campaign. That's not even conceivable. There are a lot of things about Trump that are wild, but that's not possible. I know this guy. He wouldn't do that stuff. He washes his hands 20 times a day. I knew that was phony."

"He thought the whole thing was strange and ridiculous," recalled Chris Christie. "He said, 'Can you believe this stuff?'"

Trump saw Comey's gambit as a blunt effort to gain control over a new president. "In my opinion, he shared it so that I would think he had it out there," Trump said in an interview six months later with the *New York Times.*

"As leverage?"

"Yeah, I think so."

If Trump believed he was being set up on January 6, he believed it more strongly just four days later, on January 10, when CNN reported some sensational breaking news: "CNN has learned that the nation's top intelligence officials provided information to President-elect Donald Trump and to President Barack Obama last week about claims of Russian efforts to compromise the president-elect." The report went on to say that "compromising personal" information about Trump came from "a former British intelligence operative whose past work U.S. intelligence officials consider to be credible."

Of course, the "compromising personal" information Comey provided to Trump was not credible at all. But the story consumed cable news—especially so when, a short time later, the online publication BuzzFeed published the Steele dossier in its entirety. All of Christopher Steele's false allegations flooded into public view at once, made possible by the news of the Trump Tower briefing. It was an extraordinarily damaging moment for a new president who hadn't yet taken the oath of office.

The headlines were terrible. "Trump Was Told of Claims Russia Has Damaging Details on Him," read the *New York Times*. "Trump Told Russia Has Dirt on Him," read *USA Today*. The cable news commentary followed along those lines, but with less nuance.

Trump was beside himself but could do nothing about it. On the night of the CNN report, he tweeted "FAKE NEWS—A TOTAL POLITICAL WITCH HUNT!" Early the next morning, January 11, he tweeted, "Intelligence agencies should never have allowed this fake news to 'leak' into the public. One last shot at me. Are we living in Nazi Germany?" (In retrospect, Trump's "one last shot" reference was perhaps the most inaccurate prediction he ever made. There would be many, many, many more shots to come.)

Meanwhile, some Trump aides were scrambling to find out the story behind the dossier. They would not learn until much later that it was paid for by the Clinton campaign and the Democratic National Committee. They were just trying to find out what was behind the allegations. Where did they come from? Were any of them true? They believed Trump entirely on the Moscow hotel room story. But what about the rest? Were some true, or partially true?

They zeroed in on something that, it appeared, could easily be proven true or false. The dossier said that Trump lawyer and fixer Michael Cohen had met Russian officials in Prague in August 2016 to arrange secret payments to the Russian hackers who attacked the Clinton campaign. A threshold question seemed simple enough: Had Cohen ever been to Prague? "I asked him a million questions about where were you on this date," recalled one Trump aide. "Were you ever in the Czech Republic? Where's your passport? I want to see your passport." Cohen said that he had never been in Prague, had never been in the Czech Republic, and that the story was entirely false. He left Trump Tower to go to his apartment, returning with his passport, which showed no evidence of such a trip. Trump aides were convinced that Cohen was telling the truth, and the false Prague story gave them something about the dossier to criticize in a round of media appearances.

Things were moving quickly. On January 11, Trump held a long news conference at Trump Tower. "I think it was disgraceful that the intelligence agencies allowed any information that turned out to be so false and fake out," he said. "I think it's a disgrace, and I say that—and that's something that Nazi Germany would have done and did so. I think it's a disgrace that information that was false and fake and never happened got released to the public."

A reporter asked the president if he trusted U.S. intelligence officials. Trump responded: "Intelligence agencies are vital, and very, very important." He then noted that he would soon be appointing his own choices to top intel jobs. The one thing he did not say was that he trusted U.S. intelligence officials, at least the ones then in office.

That same day, Trump called Comey. What happened? Who leaked? Comey tried to sidestep the president-elect's concerns. "Comey said that, among other things, he remembered telling Trump that the source of the information was 'not a government document, and it's not classified,'" the inspector general's report said. "Comey also remembered telling Trump that to 'speak of it as a leak doesn't make sense' because 'a lot of people in Washington had [the information],' and Comey said he told

Trump that he had previously warned Trump that it might soon be published by the media."

It was all double-talk. A leak can do terrible harm whether it involves classified information or not; the Steele material was not classified, but it was very damaging. And yes, some people in Washington did have the dossier; Steele had told several journalists about it in the desperate hope they would report it before the election. But news organizations, which of course could not verify the allegations any more than the FBI could, did not report it. They needed a news hook to do that. And they got it with the leak that the intelligence chiefs had briefed the president-elect on the dossier. If the dossier was important enough for the nation's top intelligence officials to tell the president-elect, then wasn't it important enough for the public to know, too? That was news. And so the leak of the Trump Tower briefing led directly to the publication of the entire dossier. Trump had been played, and he knew it.

The Comey Campaign

Comey seemed to believe it was quite clever to assure Trump that he was not under investigation, even as the investigation continued apace. Comey later wrote that telling Trump, "We are not investigating you, sir" was "literally true" because the FBI "did not have a counterintelligence case file open on him." But Comey was hairsplitting, and other FBI officials warned him that what he said was misleading. Baker told Comey as much in a pre-meeting planning session. Of course Trump is under investigation, Baker argued. His conduct might well be "within the scope of an investigation looking at whether his campaign coordinated with Russia."

But Comey was now on the record with Trump saying that the president-elect was *not* under investigation. And not surprisingly, after January 6, Trump was even more uncomfortable with the FBI director. "I think the president was suspicious of Comey since that meeting [in

Trump Tower], wasn't sure what he could do about it, or whether he could install his own director or whether he should keep Comey," one former senior aide said. "That was constantly swirling."

Complicating matters was that the FBI director, unlike most other political appointees, had a ten-year term. Comey was then in his fourth year. He did not have to be replaced. At the same time, there were hundreds of important jobs in the various cabinet departments that did have to be filled. Transition days were filled with discussions about them. And then came the inauguration. The decision on Comey had still not been made, and Trump was now president. What to do? Trump felt he needed to know more before making a choice. "He said, 'Maybe I should meet with Jim and talk to him,'" the former aide said. "So we set up a dinner with Comey and the president. The president says, 'Let's just talk to the guy. I'll talk to him alone.'" Trump would have a discussion with Comey one-on-one—the way Comey had done at Trump Tower.

The dinner took place on January 28 in the Green Room. With the exception of servers who came in and out, Trump and Comey were alone. Comey never expressed any objection to meeting with the president alone. In a wide-ranging conversation, Comey again told Trump that he was not under investigation. Trump brought up the Moscow hotel story and said that he was deeply troubled by the possibility that his wife, Melania, might think it was true. Trump brought up the possibility of the FBI's investigating the matter, "to prove it was a lie," as Comey recounted in a contemporaneous memo of the talk.

"I replied that it was up to him, but I wouldn't want to create a narrative that we were investigating him," Comey wrote at the time, "because we are not and I worried such a thing would be misconstrued."

"Because we are not"—that was yet another highly nuanced statement from Comey. Did the FBI have a case file with "Donald J. Trump" at the top? No. Was it investigating the Trump *campaign*, of which then-candidate Trump was the most important part? Yes—no matter what Comey assured the president.

So just a week into his presidency, Trump knew that Comey was (again) telling him the FBI was not investigating him, even as it seemed to be investigating him.

The dinner did not resolve the question in Trump's mind about what to do with Comey. And in the next two weeks, there was yet another complicating factor, when Comey was centrally involved in the case of Michael Flynn, the president's new national security adviser who was fired on February 13. Flynn was accused of lying about a conversation he had with the Russian ambassador during the transition. He was later indicted for making false statements to investigators. Comey was behind it all, first circumventing standard procedure to send FBI agents to interview Flynn in the White House, and then assuring Congress that the agents did not think Flynn had lied to them and that any action against Flynn was unlikely. The episode gave Trump more evidence of his FBI director's troubling behavior.

The problem was, Trump had not fired Comey when he had the chance. And he was still in the dark about most of what Comey was doing. So he kept trying to draw Comey in, to bring him around. On February 14, the day after the Flynn firing, Trump invited Christie to lunch at the White House. Also attending was Jared Kushner, the president's son-in-law. To no one's surprise, Comey was again on Trump's mind. "He asked me if I was still friendly with Comey," Christie recalled. "I said yeah. And he said, 'Well, listen, tell him I think he's a good guy and tell him I want him to be part of the team.'" Trump repeated his request near the end of the lunch.

Christie ignored Trump's appeal. "I just didn't think it was the right thing to do, and I didn't think it was in the president's interest," he recalled. But that moment, more than a month after Comey blindsided Trump with the false dossier allegation, showed how strongly Trump believed he could win people over to his side. "He thinks once people meet him and know him…they're going to like him," Christie said. "I think, quite frankly, it's a little naive. Certainly at that time—prior to three years in Washington—I thought he felt that way."

Trump's classic businessman approach caused him to repeatedly misjudge the intentions of rivals in Washington, especially in the critical early months of his presidency. Some of those rivals were out for blood, not a relationship. Failing to fully understand that sometimes made Trump more sanguine about his prospects than the facts warranted. That was apparent—again—during the lunch with Christie when Trump brought up the firing of Flynn the day before.

"He said, 'Now that I've fired Flynn, this whole Russia thing will be over, because he was the guy with the Russia problem,'" Christie recalled. "And I laughed. He said, 'Why are you laughing?' And I said, 'Mr. President, we're still going to be talking about this on Valentine's Day of next year, if not the year after.' And Jared said, 'That's nuts.' And I said, 'Let me tell you, man, I've done these investigations. And I know they get a life of their own, and people just keep digging and digging and digging. I know the way it works. And it's going to go on for a long time.'"

But Trump, not fully appreciating the threat Comey and the Russia investigation posed, kept hoping to develop a working relationship with the FBI director. And Comey kept playing games with the question of whether the president was under investigation. Not long after, during appearances before the House and Senate in early March, Comey privately told lawmakers that the president was *not* under investigation.

Comey's talk to the Senate, to the Judiciary Committee specifically, left lawmakers frustrated and angry. Not only did Comey say the president was not under investigation, he also indicated that the White House would likely have no trouble with Michael Flynn. Senator Charles Grassley, the committee's chairman, did not go public with that frustration until 2020, when he wrote that, "I received a briefing from then-Director Comey on March 15, 2017. In that briefing, Director Comey stated that the FBI agents that interviewed Lt. Gen. Flynn 'saw nothing that led them to believe [he was] lying,' and he led us to believe that the Department was unlikely to prosecute Flynn for false statements. Later, during Comey's book tour, he denied any memory of those comments."

Comey's words were secret at the time; Senate rules forbade members discussing them publicly. But then, just days after talking to Grassley, Comey spoke in public—with an entirely different story.

In a widely-reported appearance before the House Intelligence Committee on March 20, 2017—at that point, Trump had been in office for all of two months—Comey made a bombshell announcement. "I have been authorized by the Department of Justice to confirm," he said, "that the FBI, as part of our counterintelligence mission, is investigating the Russian government's efforts to interfere in the 2016 presidential election, and that includes investigating the nature of any links between individuals associated with the Trump campaign and the Russian government and whether there was any coordination between the campaign and Russia's efforts."

One obvious question presented itself immediately: Did "individuals associated with the Trump campaign" include Donald Trump himself? Was the president under investigation? But when Democratic Representative Eric Swalwell asked Comey, "Was Donald Trump under investigation during the campaign?" Comey replied, "I'm not going to answer that." When Swalwell asked, "Is [Trump] under investigation now?" Comey said, "I'm not going to answer that."

The clear impression for anyone to draw was that yes, the president was under investigation. Who would believe the FBI was investigating the Trump campaign but somehow scrupulously avoiding Trump himself?

Grassley was appalled. Hadn't Comey just told him the opposite? The Judiciary Committee chairman tweeted, "FBI Dir Comey needs to be transparent + tell the public what he told me about whether he is or is not investigating @POTUS." What Grassley, still bound by Senate rules, could not say was that Comey had already told him that Trump was *not* under investigation. The plainspoken senator from Iowa was disgusted that the FBI director was saying one thing in private and another in public.

The day after Comey's House testimony, Trump got a preview of how an investigation can hinder a president's ability to govern. On March

21, Senator Schumer called on the Senate to delay the confirmation of Trump Supreme Court nominee Neil Gorsuch until after the Russia investigation was resolved. Republicans had stalled consideration of President Obama's candidate for the Supreme Court, Merrick Garland, for nearly a year, Schumer said, but now they were "rushing to fill the seat for a president whose campaign is under investigation by the FBI."

"You can bet if the shoe were on the other foot and a Democratic president was under investigation by the FBI, the Republicans would be howling at the moon about filling a Supreme Court seat in such circumstances," Schumer said. It would be "unseemly" for the Senate to confirm Gorsuch as long as the "cloud" of an FBI investigation "hangs over the presidency."

Schumer's ploy outraged fellow lawmakers who knew what Comey had told the House and Senate. "Mr. Comey didn't just tell the president, Senator Feinstein, and me that the president was not under investigation," said Grassley. "He also had told the Gang of Eight. Of course, the Gang of Eight includes the Senate Minority Leader, Senator Schumer. But even after Mr. Comey told the Gang of Eight that the president was not under investigation, [Schumer] told the media he was. That helped feed the media hysteria. The minority leader even tried to say that the Senate shouldn't vote on the Supreme Court nomination because the president was under investigation. And the whole time, he knew it wasn't true."

Not long after, Comey assured the president for a third time that he was not under investigation. In a March 30, 2017, phone conversation, Trump again told Comey that the Moscow hotel story was a "cloud" over his life—it appeared he meant his marriage more than his presidency—and asked if Comey could do something to remove it. "I reminded him that I had told him we weren't investigating him and that I had told the Congressional leadership the same thing," Comey wrote in another contemporaneous memo. "He [Trump] said it would be great if that could get out and several times asked me to find a way to get that out." But Comey would never let that get out. He had created a house of mirrors in which Trump could not tell what was true and what was not.

The Last Straw

By the beginning of April, Trump still could not decide what to do with Comey. The FBI's Trump-Russia investigation had been going since long before the election. Sensational headlines appeared nearly every day. Cable TV talked and talked. If Trump were to fire the FBI director amid all the Russia speculation, it would be widely perceived as an effort to quash the investigation. Firing Comey, a reasonable option on Day One of the presidency, became fraught with risk.

Trump called Christie to talk things over. "He asked me at one point, did I think he should fire Comey?" Christie recalled. "I said to him, 'I think that's very problematic for you right now, because of the ongoing Russia thing. That's why I told you before I thought if you're going to get rid of him, just tell him during the transition his services would no longer be needed on January 20. But now that you've gotten this far into it, no matter what, people are going to say you fired him in an attempt to impede, derail, discourage the investigation into Russian collusion. I think it's a really difficult thing for you to do.'"

Christie said Trump should be prepared to endure enormous blow-back if he fired Comey. He did not advise Trump to do one thing or another, just to be ready for a huge controversy if he took action.

At that point, Trump still did not appear to have made a decision. "He was just listening," Christie explained. "When he has his mind made up, he will argue back to you, if you're recommending something that is contrary to what he wants to do. He'll get into a back-and-forth with you. In this instance, he just listened. That's why I was pretty convinced when I got off the phone with him that day that he had not yet made up his mind, that he really was looking for counsel and not just for affirmation of what he may have been inclined to do."

Trump took no action in April. Then, on May 3, Comey testified before the Senate Judiciary Committee. Democratic Senator Richard Blumenthal went perhaps farther than any other Democrat in trying to create the impression that the president was under investigation.

"You have confirmed, I believe, that the FBI is investigating potential ties between Trump associates and the Russian interference in the 2016 campaign, correct?" Blumenthal asked the director.

"Yes," said Comey.

"And have not, to my knowledge, ruled out anyone in the Trump campaign as potentially a target of that criminal investigation, correct?"

"Well, I haven't said anything publicly about who we've opened investigations on," replied Comey. "I briefed the chair and ranking on who those people are. And so I can't—I can't go beyond that in this setting."

"Have you ruled out anyone in the campaign that you can disclose?"

"I don't feel comfortable answering that, senator because I think it puts me on a slope to talking about who we're investigating," replied Comey.

"Have you—have you ruled out the president of the United States?"

"I don't—I don't want people to over-interpret this answer," said Comey. "I'm not going to comment on anyone in particular, because that puts me down a slope of—because if I say no to that, then I have to answer succeeding questions. So what we've done is brief the chair and ranking on who the U.S. persons are that we've opened investigations on. And that's—that's as far as we're going to go, at this point."

"But as a former prosecutor, you know that when there's an investigation into several potentially culpable individuals, the evidence from those individuals and the investigation can lead to others, correct?"

"Correct," said Comey. "We're always open-minded about—and we follow the evidence wherever it takes us."

"So potentially," Blumenthal continued, "the president of the United States could be a target of your ongoing investigation into the Trump campaign's involvement with Russian interference in our election, correct?"

"I just worry," Comey said. "I don't want to answer that—that seems to be unfair speculation. We will follow the evidence, we'll try and find as much as we can and we'll follow the evidence wherever it leads."

Given the context of the conversation, and given the ubiquity of media coverage suggesting that collusion did in fact happen, would any reasonable listener take away any impression *other* than that the president was under investigation?

So each time Comey privately reassured Trump that he was not under investigation, Trump became more frustrated by the conflict between those confidential reassurances and Comey's refusal to say the same thing in public. And then there was the more fundamental question of whether Comey was telling the truth at any time. The whole while, Trump veered between a desire to win Comey's allegiance and frustration at Comey's behavior. It was an exercise in futility; anyone who knew what was going on would have concluded that Comey was jerking the president around.

The May 3 appearance before the Senate was the last straw. On May 9, Trump fired the FBI director. "While I greatly appreciate you informing me, on three separate occasions, that I am not under investigation," Trump wrote, "I nevertheless concur with the judgment of the Department of Justice that you are not able to effectively lead the Bureau."

Eight Days in May

Trump's dismissal of Comey set off an old-fashioned, hair-on-fire, 24/7 firestorm. It led to a new flood of leaks, a raging controversy over Trump's motive, and condemnation of the process he used to sack the FBI director.

On the process, there was no doubt it was mess. A few days before the firing, Trump, outraged at Comey's performance in front of the Senate, went to his golf resort in Bedminster, New Jersey, to contemplate what to do. The president had top aide Stephen Miller draft a letter firing Comey. Many top White House officials, including chief of staff Reince Priebus and counsel Don McGahn, were involved in conversations with the president, mostly trying to talk him out of firing Comey. Trump would not be moved. Angry at Attorney General Jeff Sessions, who had two months earlier recused himself from the Russia investigation, Trump ordered Deputy

Attorney General Rod Rosenstein to come up with a rationale for firing Comey that focused on Comey's handling of the Clinton investigation—which had, after all, been a matter of legitimate concern during the transition. Rosenstein did as instructed. Finally, Trump put together a brief letter firing Comey with Rosenstein's longer memo and gave it to Keith Schiller, who essentially served as Trump's private security man, to deliver in person to Comey. But no one had checked to see if the director would be in his office. In fact, Comey was traveling in California, and Trump ended up firing him long distance. Once news got out and the storm erupted, the White House was poorly prepared—actually, totally unprepared—to explain what the president had done.

It was an indisputably chaotic process. And a frustrating one. Given the secrecy involved, no one could talk about the real reason for the firing: Comey's record of duplicity in multiple encounters with the president.

Trump did not hide from the press, even as the storm consumed the White House. As was often the case, he had no confidence in his communications team and decided he could tell his story better than anyone else. On May 11, he sat for a long interview with NBC's Lester Holt. "When I decided to just do it, I said to myself, I said, 'You know, this Russia thing with Trump and Russia is a made-up story,'" Trump told Holt. "It's an excuse by the Democrats for having lost an election that they should have won."

For the president's opponents, that was an aha moment. There it was: Trump admitting he fired Comey to end the Russia investigation. Exhibit A for an obstruction of justice charge against the president.

But in that same interview, Trump also said he knew firing Comey would set off a huge controversy and possibly result in *lengthening* the investigation, which in any event would continue. "Let me tell you, as far as I'm concerned, I want that thing [the Russia probe] to be absolutely done properly," Trump said. "When I did this now, I said I probably, maybe will, confuse people. Maybe I'll expand that—you know, I'll lengthen the time because it should be over with. It should—in my opinion, should've been over with a long time ago because it—it is an excuse. But I said to myself, I might even lengthen out the investigation. But I have to do the right thing for the American people. He is the wrong man for that position."

As Trump spoke, a wave of leaks, all suggesting dark motives for the Comey firing, began to appear. On May 10, the day after the firing, the *Wall Street Journal* reported that Trump had fired Comey because the FBI was closing in on collusion. The bureau's Russia probe was "heating up," the *Journal* said, and Comey was devoting more and more time to it. "Mr. Comey started receiving daily instead of weekly updates on the investigation," the paper reported, saying Comey "was concerned by information showing possible evidence of collusion."

The story cited "people with knowledge" of the Russia probe. What became clear in the hours and days after the firing was that Comey himself was leaking repeatedly, or had authorized repeated leaks, in an effort to discredit the president. It was six ways from Sunday, again.

On May 11, just forty-eight hours after the firing, the *New York Times* reported that Trump had "demanded loyalty" from Comey during a private dinner early in the administration. (Missing from the story was the important context, unknown to the public at the time, of Comey's "pulling a J. Edgar Hoover" on Trump during the transition. Was it crazy for a president to seek reassurances of loyalty from a top official who did something like that?) The paper said Comey had "told associates" about the private dinner. Its description of the event echoed a secret contemporaneous memo Comey had written about the dinner.

A few days later, on May 16, the *Times* revealed the existence of Comey's memo, and others written by him, in a story reporting that, in another conversation, Trump had asked Comey to go easy on Michael Flynn. "Mr. Comey wrote the memo, detailing his conversation with the president immediately after the meeting, which took place the day after Mr. Flynn resigned, according to two people who had read the memo," the *Times* said. "It was part of a paper trail Mr. Comey created documenting what he perceived as the president's improper efforts to influence a continuing investigation." Lest anyone suspect that Comey might have some ulterior motive, or might not have recounted the conversations accurately, or in any way be less than trustworthy, the *Times* added, "An FBI agent's contemporaneous notes are widely held up in court as credible evidence of conversations."

Thus began the story of Comey's memos. There were seven in all, written between January 6, 2017, and April 11, 2017. Each memorialized some Comey interaction with the president. The FBI treated them as top-secret classified documents, even though, with the exception of a few small excerpts, they were not classified at all. Once the *Times* story came out, lawmakers investigating the Trump-Russia affair, both House and Senate, Democrat and Republican, clamored to see the memos. In a letter dated May 17, 2017—the day after the *Times* report—Grassley and Judiciary Committee subcommittee chairman Lindsey Graham joined ranking Democrats Dianne Feinstein and Sheldon Whitehouse to ask the FBI to "produce all such memos, if they exist." Other committees made similar requests.

The FBI rejected all of them. The contents of the Comey memos were known to no one—except Comey, the top FBI officials he had showed them to, and the journalists he had leaked them to. Members of Congress, of both parties, were kept in the dark. And of course, the public was, too.

The Senate Intelligence Committee scheduled Comey to make a post-firing appearance on June 8, 2017. Lawmakers hoped to have seen the memos by then and be able to question him about them. But the FBI, and Comey, too, refused to provide the memos to the committee, so the senators had to question Comey without knowing what he had written.

Still, Comey revealed a lot. Perhaps the biggest revelation was his confession—not really a confession, since he seemed somewhat proud of it—that he wrote the memos with the intention of leaking them and setting off a storm that would result in the appointment of a special counsel to investigate Trump. Comey arranged to give some of the memos to a friend, Columbia University law professor Daniel Richman, so that Richman could leak them to the *New York Times*.

"I asked a friend of mine to share the content of the memo with a reporter," Comey told the Senate. "Didn't do it myself, for a variety of reasons. But I asked him to, because I thought that might prompt the appointment of a special counsel. And so I asked a close friend of mine to do it."

Within hours of Comey's testimony, a bipartisan group at the Senate Judiciary Committee fired off a letter to Richman asking for the memos Comey sent him. Richman refused. He wouldn't even say if he still had any of the memos. A few months later, the committee asked Richman to come in for an interview. He refused. Later, he claimed to be one of Comey's attorneys, with the suggestion that their interactions were privileged.

In his memoir, Comey wrote that he acted because he did not trust the Justice Department to do "the right thing" on the question of a special counsel and came up with his leak plan as a way to force the issue. "I decided I would prompt a media story by revealing the president's February 14 direction that I drop the Flynn investigation," Comey wrote. "That might force the Department of Justice to appoint a special prosecutor.... And, although I was banned from FBI property, I had a copy of my unclassified memo about his request stored securely at home."

In explaining his behavior, Comey stressed that he had not leaked any classified material. "To be clear, this was not a 'leak' of classified information no matter how many times politicians, political pundits, or the president call it that," Comey wrote in his memoir. It turned out Comey's defense was not true, because classifying authorities found that some of what Comey wrote should have been classified at a low level. But it was minor stuff; given the small scale, the Department of Justice decided not to prosecute him.

Comey did far more damage by leaking highly sensitive law enforcement material. He was an FBI employee and subject to rules requiring that he keep such information confidential. Yet he leaked the memos in hopes of leveraging them into an investigation of the president of the United States. That was a big deal. When Horowitz, the Justice Department inspector general, examined Comey's behavior, he concluded that the director had set a "dangerous example" for everyone at the FBI.

"By not safeguarding sensitive information obtained during the course of his FBI employment, and by using it to create public pressure for official action, Comey set a dangerous example for the over 35,000 current FBI employees—and the many thousands more former FBI employees—who similarly have access to or knowledge of non-public information," Horowitz wrote in an investigative report. "Comey's closest advisers used the words 'surprised,' 'stunned,' 'shocked,' and 'disappointment' to describe their reactions to learning what Comey had done," the report noted.

It would be hard to imagine a more complete repudiation of Comey's performance. And yet, in the days after his firing on May 9, 2017, no one on the outside knew what Comey was up to—which was, in essence, choreographing the craziness that gripped Washington in the wake of his firing. And the craziness ended precisely the way Comey wanted it to, eight days later, on May 17, 2017, when Rosenstein announced the appointment of Comey's immediate predecessor as FBI chief, Robert Mueller, as special counsel to investigate the president. The most momentous turn in the young Trump presidency had been engineered by the vengeful FBI director.

A Glimpse of a Terrible Future

Trump learned that a special counsel had been appointed during a meeting in the Oval Office. The news hit him like a bolt out of the blue. "Oh, my God, this is terrible," Trump said. "This is the end of my presidency. I'm fucked."

Those words, quoted in the Mueller report, were not made public until 2019. When the report was released, there was widespread speculation that Trump's exclamation revealed a consciousness of guilt, that deep inside, he knew he was guilty of some terrible offense and would soon be caught. But the reality was simpler than that. The fear Trump was expressing was of watching his presidency disappear into an ugly and familiar Washington sinkhole: the ever-expanding, never-ending investigation.

The Trump White House did not include a lot of veterans of the George W. Bush administration. But many of the people there had some earlier connection with the Bush White House and remembered the last big special counsel investigation, a CIA leak case.

It was a strange, convoluted affair rooted in the nasty partisan fight over the Iraq War. In his January 28, 2003, State of the Union address, making the case for invasion, Bush said, "The British government has learned that Saddam Hussein recently sought significant quantities of uranium from Africa." That was two months before the start of the war. A few months into the war, on July 6, 2003, a former diplomat named Joseph Wilson published an op-ed in the *New York Times* saying that in early 2002 he had been sent by the CIA, allegedly at the behest of Vice President Dick Cheney, to Africa to check on the claim that Saddam Hussein had sought radioactive material there. He found nothing, Wilson wrote, and he told the CIA that. Therefore, the Bush administration knew before the State of the Union that Bush's brief statement was untrue. An intense debate followed over what became known as the "16 words."

The White House, particularly Cheney's office, was dumbfounded. Who is this guy? they asked about Wilson. In the search to find out who Wilson was and why he went to Africa, someone discovered that Wilson's wife, a CIA employee named Valerie Plame, had suggested him for the assignment. A week after Wilson's op-ed, the influential conservative columnist Robert Novak published a piece saying that Plame, "an agency operative on weapons of mass destruction," suggested Wilson for the job. Novak sourced that information to two senior administration officials.

Novak's naming of Plame led to an uproar when a left-wing journalist, David Corn, reported in the *Nation* that Plame was an undercover agent. Her identity as an agent was classified, and whoever outed her had committed a crime. "So where's the investigation?" asked Corn.

On the way, as it turned out. With Corn cheerleading, Senator Schumer called for the FBI director—yes, it was Robert Mueller—to investigate what became known as the CIA leak affair. Then Schumer led the charge for the appointment of a special counsel to find the leaker.

A troubled Bush Justice Department finally gave in to pressure. Attorney General John Ashcroft recused himself because of his ties to the administration. That left the question to the deputy attorney general, a man named James Comey, who appointed a special counsel—a friend of his, Patrick Fitzgerald, who was the U.S. attorney in Chicago. Fitzgerald started his investigation on December 30, 2003.

What was not known to the public at the time, and would not become known for years, was that Fitzgerald learned the identity of the leaker almost as soon the investigation began. It was a State Department official named Richard Armitage, who privately came forward to investigators with the information. Armitage was never charged with anything. Although there were rumors about him all along, his identity as the leaker remained secret until September 2006. At that point, the *Washington Post* reported, "some have questioned... why Fitzgerald spent two years appearing to chase a question that had already been answered."

In those years, Fitzgerald's unnecessary investigation tormented the Bush White House and created an enormous distraction for both President Bush and his top aides. Fitzgerald called Karl Rove, the president's closest adviser, before a grand jury a total of five times. He took possession of all of Rove's, and Rove's wife's, computers and phones, plus reams of other records, in an attempt to prove that Rove lied to the grand jury about a conversation with a reporter. The investigation took a heavy toll on Rove—he wrote an anguished account of it in his memoir—and on the White House, as well. It does nothing to promote the smooth and efficient running of a White House when a top official is in his office talking to FBI agents or agonizing over whether he is about to be indicted.

In the end, Fitzgerald did not charge Rove with anything. The only person to be charged was Lewis "Scooter" Libby, who was Cheney's chief of staff. And Libby was not charged with leaking anything but rather with lying to investigators. Libby's life, and the work of the vice president's office, was similarly disrupted; Libby was later found guilty of perjury and obstruction of justice.

Fitzgerald served as special counsel for more than three years. In that time, he never charged anyone with an underlying crime, and never charged anyone beyond Libby with anything at all. He spent most of that time investigating a leak when he already knew the leaker, creating the possibility of so-called process crimes like perjury by repeatedly questioning people on a complex series of events that did not amount to a crime. In the process, he did enormous damage to the Bush White House.

"It was dreadful," said one former Bush aide, thinking back to those days. "I may be over it by now. Maybe."

It was all an enormous waste that gripped Washington for years. It destroyed reputations. So, when President Trump faced the prospect of a special counsel, there was plenty of reason to fear that the investigation would stretch for years, distract top aides (not to mention the president himself), and overshadow the presidency. It would have been unduly optimistic to think anything else.

And ominously, some of the same people who made a mess of the CIA leak investigation were reprising roles with the Trump-Russia probe. In 2003, Comey appointed the special counsel; years later, he schemed for the appointment of a special counsel. In 2003, Mueller, the FBI director, began the CIA leak probe; years later, he became the Trump-Russia special counsel. In 2003, Schumer led the charge for a special counsel; years later, he did the same thing. In 2003, David Corn agitated for an investigation; years later, he was given an early look at the Steele dossier and agitated for an investigation again. And in 2003, Fitzgerald was the special counsel; years later, as a friend of Comey's, he was one of the people to whom Comey sent his secret memos in the effort to spark the appointment of a Trump-Russia special counsel. Even Scooter Libby showed up again, when he was pardoned by Trump in April 2018, after the painful similarities between the Fitzgerald and Mueller investigations had become apparent.

President Trump knew enough history to be deeply concerned about the prospect of a Mueller investigation. And he knew that the special counsel regulations would inevitably lead to talk of impeachment. He could see well enough what lay ahead. And at that moment in the Oval Office, May 17, 2017, he entered a fight that would consume the rest of his term in office.

Did it have to happen? Is it possible to imagine another scenario? If Trump had fired Comey immediately, would events have taken a different course? Would an FBI under new leadership have continued the Russia investigation only to find, as Mueller ultimately did, that it could not establish conspiracy or coordination between the Trump campaign and Russia—that there was, as Trump often said, "no collusion"? Given the toxicity of the political atmosphere in 2017, could that possibly have been the end of things? And might such an outcome have occurred absent Comey's malign influence? It is impossible to say. But it is possible to say that Trump's two decisions on James Comey—first, not to fire him, and later, to fire him—changed the course of his presidency.

By then, of course, matters were far out of his control—in the White House, in the law enforcement and intelligence agencies, and, increasingly, on Capitol Hill.

CHAPTER TWO

Impeachment 1.0: The Search for a Crime

A Weird Day at the Electoral College—Impeachment before Inauguration—"I will not be moved"—The Search for Grounds: Emoluments? Charlottesville? The NFL? — Fifty-Eight Votes

At nearly the same moment on May 17, 2017, that President Trump slumped at his desk in dread at the appointment of Mueller, Representative Al Green, a Democrat from Texas, stepped to the floor of the House to deliver the first formal call for the president's impeachment.

"I rise today with a heavy heart," Green said. "I rise today with a sense of responsibility and duty to the people who have elected me, a sense of duty to this country, a sense of duty to the Constitution of the United States of America. I rise today, Mr. Speaker, to call for the impeachment of the President of the United States of America for obstruction of justice."

At the time, Democrats were in the minority in the House and had no power to impeach anybody, even if they all agreed on it. Green was an early leader, perhaps *the* early leader, in calling for impeachment. But how many supporters did he have? At least at first, it appeared he had almost none. Which is why, when he spoke on May 17, Republicans did not pay much attention.

"I don't think anybody on our side took it seriously," recalled Republican Representative Doug Collins, a member of the Judiciary Committee.

Why not? "Because it was Al Green. I don't mean that disrespectfully, but Al had been threatening to do it for several weeks."

So, to Republicans, impeachment seemed to be kooky fringe stuff. Still, GOP lawmakers did notice something in those first few months of 2017 that struck them at first as notable, and later as troubling. Democrats seemed to have an extraordinary level of animosity against the new president—an animosity that went far beyond normal partisan opposition, even intense partisan opposition. Something was going on among House Democrats that Republicans would only fully appreciate years later. It started on the House floor before Donald Trump even became president.

A Weird Day at the Electoral College

January 6, 2017, should have been a day for formality and celebration in the House. On the celebration side, it was the day members were sworn in for service in the 115th Congress. On the formality side, it was the day a joint House and Senate session would certify the results of the Electoral College for the 2016 presidential election. Congress would finally, formally, recognize Donald Trump's victory.

The session began with members of the Senate walking into the House chamber, along with Vice President Joe Biden, who would preside over the certification. Two senators and two representatives had been appointed "tellers" who would announce the electoral votes from each state and declare that the vote total "seems to be regular in form and authentic." When the ceremony began, seconds after the results from Alabama—nine votes for Trump—were announced, Jim McGovern, a Democratic representative from Massachusetts, rose to protest.

"I object to the certificate from the State of Alabama on the grounds that the electoral votes were not, under all of the known circumstances, regularly given, and that the electors were not lawfully certified, especially given the confirmed and illegal activities engaged in by the government of Russia that were designed to interfere with our election," McGovern said as Republicans began to boo from the other side of the chamber. Even though there had been news reports that Democrats hoped to persuade Trump electors to defect, McGovern's objection during the certification caught the ears of some Republicans. Were they really doing this?

Yes, they were. Biden, having been briefed beforehand, was ready to respond. "Sections 15 and 17 of Title 3 of the United States Code require that any objection be presented in writing, signed by a Member of the House of Representatives and a Senator," he said to McGovern, reading from piece of paper on the desk. "Is the objection in writing and signed not only by a Member of the House of Representatives but also by a Senator?"

"Mr. President, the objection is in writing and is signed by a member of the House of Representatives but not yet by a member of the United States Senate," McGovern said.

"In that case, the objection cannot be entertained," Biden answered.

Republicans applauded as the process got back on track: Alaska... Arizona...Arkansas...California...Colorado.... Then, when the roll call got to Florida, another Democrat, Jamie Raskin of Maryland, stood to protest.

"I have an objection because 10 of the 29 electoral votes cast by Florida were cast by electors not lawfully certified because they violated Florida's prohibition against dual office voting," Raskin said.

"Debate is out of order," Biden countered, asking whether the complaint was signed by a senator.

"Not as of yet," Raskin said.

"In that case, the objection cannot be entertained," Biden said.

The session was going according to a script that few on the Republican side had expected. Just the day before, a left-wing activist group called Americans Take Action had distributed a lengthy report outlining how Democratic representatives might challenge the proceedings (including by making objections based on obscure issues like "dual office voting"). The group even offered a sample script—just fill in the name of a state here—for House Democrats to use when they rose to object.

After Florida, the clerk moved on to Georgia. At that moment, Democratic Representative Pramila Jayapal of Washington State rose. "I object to the certificate from the State of Georgia on the grounds that the electoral votes were not…"

Biden was becoming impatient. "There is no debate," he said. "There is no debate."

Jayapal plowed ahead. "Mr. President, even as people waited hours in Georgia…"

"There is no debate," Biden repeated. "There is no debate. If there is not one signed by a senator, the objection cannot be entertained."

"Mr. President, the objection is signed by a member of the House, but not yet by a member of the Senate," Jayapal said.

"It is over," Biden snapped, slamming down the gavel.

Then-Speaker of the House Paul Ryan, sitting behind Biden on the dais, began to laugh and applaud. Republicans joined in. After a moment, the process started and moved normally for a few states, until the roll call came to Michigan. At that point, Democratic Representative Barbara Lee of California rose to speak.

"Mr. President, I object because people are horrified by the overwhelming evidence of Russian interference in our elections," she said.

Lee barely got out the word "horrified" before Biden began banging the gavel. "Section 18, title 3 of the United States Code prohibits debate in the joint session," he began.

Lee continued. "Mr. President, even with the malfunction of 87 voting machines at predominantly African…"

Biden cut her off again, banging the gavel.

"There is no debate in order," Biden said. "Is it signed by a senator?"

Biden kept banging the gavel. Republicans booed. "The objection cannot be entertained," Biden ruled.

Moments later, yet another Democrat, Representative Sheila Jackson Lee of Texas, rose. "Mr. President, I object on the massive voter suppression that included counting ballots that were provisional that denied individuals access to polling places."

"The gentlewoman will suspend," Biden said, before reading the rules one more time. Another bang of the gavel and the count moved on.

Democrats interrupted the proceeding five more times, including when Barbara Lee objected "on behalf of the millions of Americans, including members of the Intelligence Community, who are horrified by evidence that the Russians interfered in our election." The process took far longer than necessary, but finally ended when Trump, with 304 electoral votes, was declared president.

"The purpose of this joint session having been concluded," Biden said with a little weary laugh, "the chair declares the joint session dissolved." As Republicans applauded, Biden turned to shake Ryan's hand and said, "God save the Queen." It was unclear precisely what he meant, but it seemed to be a mild joke to ease the tension of one of the strangest Electoral College certifications ever.

What had the day meant? For many Americans, it didn't even make the news. But for some GOP lawmakers, it was a disconcerting experience. They had no idea what was coming in the months and years ahead, but the anger and vehemence they saw on the Democratic side disquieted them.

"It was one of the biggest moments for me," said Collins, who nearly three years later would be ranking Republican as the Judiciary Committee debated impeachment. "I didn't know where it was headed, because of course we controlled the House and Senate, but it struck me as more than just odd that there was that much vitriol on a day that should have been a formality of just doing the Electoral College, pass that and be done with it. So I took notice."

"This had always been a perfunctory exercise," said Representative Steve Scalise, the Republican whip. "Calling the roll of the electors has always been something that nobody paid attention to, because it was just the final step of a foregone conclusion. And yet leading up to this you saw the left trying to identify electors in every state and convince them to change their vote. I had never seen anything like that before. It got pretty intense."

Republican Congressman Jason Chaffetz of Utah, who was first elected in 2008, went to the certification of President Barack Obama in 2009. Back then, he and his fellow Republicans had a feeling they were watching history. "The tone of this one was very different," Chaffetz recalled. "They were mad, they were angry, they were self-righteous, and they were already convinced that something had been stolen from them. All we could hear was Russia, Russia, Russia."

Impeachment before Inauguration

The first mention of impeachment on the House floor came on February 2, 2017, less than two weeks into the Trump presidency. "Mr. Speaker, it is only day 13 of the Trump administration, and we are already faced with yet another round of questions about President Trump's potential conflicts of interest over his business holdings," Wisconsin Democratic Representative Mark Pocan said in a floor speech. Pocan demanded that the new president divest his business holdings, make public his tax returns, and rescind his executive order banning some citizens of a few Muslim countries from entering the United States. "Short of that," Pocan said, "we will have to take other actions, including legislative directives, resolutions of disapproval, even exploring the power of impeachment."

As early as he was in the House, Pocan was actually behind the game in the public discussion of impeachment. It is impossible to say who first suggested President Trump be impeached, but the discussion began months before there was a President Trump.

Certainly there was talk around Washington in spring 2016, after candidate Trump did not, as some expected, collapse in the Republican primaries. Anti-Trump Republicans who had failed to take his candidacy seriously as he led the polls throughout 2015 realized that it was too late to stop him once primary voting began.

On April 17, 2016—immediately after the Wisconsin Republican primary, won by rival Ted Cruz in the last gasp of GOP challenges to the frontrunner—*Politico* published a piece entitled "Could Trump Be Impeached Shortly after He Takes Office?" The publication admitted it was "highly improbable"—the most improbable part was Trump's getting elected in the first place—but legal scholars and political types were said to be "speculating about it."

Some thought Trump might be removed for overstepping his authority in executive orders. Some thought he might be removed for some sort of unsavory business dealings in his past. Some thought he would just do something to convince both Democrats and Republicans in Congress to take action against him. But since none of them thought Trump would actually win, the impeachment scenarios were mostly for amusement.

Then came the night of tears in Brooklyn, and the question of removing Trump from office became a real-life exercise.

On November 11, 2016—the Friday after Trump won on Tuesday night—the *New York Times*' David Brooks devoted his entire column to the possibility of removing Trump from office. "Trump's bigotry, dishonesty and promise-breaking will have to be denounced," Brooks wrote. "We can't go morally numb. But he needs to be replaced with a program that addresses the problems that fueled his ascent. After all, the guy will probably resign or be impeached within a year. The future is closer than you think."

"We're not going to have to suffer through four years of Donald Trump," the left-wing filmmaker Michael Moore predicted. "We must organize the apparatus that will bring charges against him...and then we must remove him from office."

A University of Utah professor named Christopher Peterson got some media attention by pushing a theory that Trump could be impeached immediately upon taking office for alleged offenses committed *before* becoming president. Another professor, Robert Kuttner, who was also co-editor of the progressive journal the *American Prospect*, published

"Impeaching Trump: The Process Begins Now" on January 1, 2017, nearly three weeks before Trump was sworn in.

To be fair, not all agreed with the idea of impeaching Trump. Some dissenters felt he should be removed from office via the 25th Amendment. On November 16, *The Atlantic*'s David Frum tweeted: "Twenty-Fifth Amendment to the Constitution. Article IV. We're all going to be talking a lot more about it in the months ahead."

While the possibility of impeachment was "remote," *Washington Post* columnist Richard Cohen argued on January 9, the chances of removal under the 25th Amendment were far better. Under its provisions, the cabinet could essentially vote the president out of office, provided it had the approval of Congress. "Maybe the only thing that will constrain him is his own cabinet," Cohen wrote.

And so on. The talk about removing Trump continued right up until the moment he was sworn in. So it is not entirely clear whether the *Washington Post* was late or early when, on Inauguration Day, January 20, 2017, at 12:19 p.m., it published a story headlined, "The Campaign to Impeach President Trump Has Begun." At that moment, Trump had been president for nineteen minutes.

"I will not be moved"

After Mark Pocan's speech, there were few mentions of impeachment on the House floor in the first few months of Trump's presidency. On March 1, Democratic Congressman Hakeem Jeffries of New York, who would later become an impeachment manager, said Congress confronted a situation similar to that of Richard Nixon in 1973, which "concluded with impeachment proceedings and the ultimate resignation of a president in disgrace." On March 29, Democratic Representative Maxine Waters of California delivered a long floor speech about Trump's alleged ties to Russia, as well as his business connections. She called for Congress to create "a comprehensive, independent, bipartisan commission to expose the full truth of Trump's ties to Russia." The investigation would expose the president's "Kremlin Klan," Waters said, and then "we will find that there was collusion." At that point, "Republicans in Congress will have no choice but to put country ahead of party—I say impeach Donald Trump."

There was nothing much beyond that until May 17—Mueller Day, when everything changed. The appointment of a special counsel brought on a wave of agitation about impeachment among House Democrats, a wave that would not crest until the end of 2019. The existence of a special counsel—the House's *de facto* investigative office—turbocharged Democratic hopes that impeachment might become a real option. The appointment of Mueller was the fuel that got the Democratic impeachment machine up and running, even when Democrats were a minority in the House.

When Al Green rose to propose impeachment, no one had ever taken to the floor to actually make a case for removing Trump. Green did, basing his argument on alleged obstruction of justice. Trump was "a president who fired the FBI director who was investigating the president," Green said. Further, Trump, in the Lester Holt NBC interview, "let us know that he considered the investigation when he fired [Comey]." It all added up to obstruction of justice, Green said, citing polls reporting that a plurality of Americans supported impeachment. "This is where I stand," Green said. "I will not be moved. The president must be impeached."

Democratic Representative Adriano Espaillat of New York gave brief remarks supporting Green, as did Sheila Jackson Lee. The next day, Democratic Congressman Jamie Raskin of Maryland took the floor with Lee and Pramila Jayapal—all members of the Judiciary Committee who would later play roles in impeachment—for a long discussion of the issue. They called for immediate hearings. Lee returned a week later to do it again.

On June 7, Democratic Representative Luis Gutierrez of Illinois, another Judiciary Committee member, rose in favor of impeachment hearings. "Robert Mueller...will not be able to indict him while he is president no matter what he uncovers," Gutierrez said, previewing an issue that would become a very hot topic two years later. "Most legal scholars argue a sitting president cannot be indicted in criminal court. So it is the Judiciary Committee that will bring charges if there is evidence of 'treason, bribery, or other high crimes and misdemeanors....'"

The next day, Representative Raskin commanded an hour of time for the Progressive Caucus. "Imagine that this had happened under the Obama administration," he said. "Obama had made a similar demand of FBI Director Comey, who was investigating, after all, Hillary Clinton's emails," and then used "the full trappings of his office and his influence to try to get the FBI director to drop the investigation."

On July 12 came House Resolution 438, the first on-paper impeachment proposal, from Green and Representative Brad Sherman of California, proposing that President Trump be impeached for a variety of alleged actions outlined in the Comey memos, all related to the Russia investigation. Trump, it said, "sought to use his authority to hinder and cause the termination of such investigation(s) including through threatening, and then terminating, James Comey."

No one had any idea how much support impeachment had among the Democratic conference. Since the momentum began with the firing of Comey and the appointment of Mueller, most impeachment calls focused on those events, along with prior developments in the Russia investigation. But as 2017 went by, some Democrats began coming up with new reasons to remove the president. It started, improbably enough, with football.

The Search for Grounds:
Emoluments? Charlottesville? The NFL?

On September 22, 2017, the president spoke at a rally in Alabama. He touched on the subject of former National Football League quarterback Colin Kaepernick, who had set off a wave of controversy by refusing to stand for the national anthem. "Wouldn't you like to see one of these

NFL owners, when somebody disrespects our flag, to say, 'Get that son of a bitch off the field right now,'" Trump said. "He is fired. He's fired!" The president's comment started an ugly debate in the media. It also spurred Al Green to change his approach to impeachment.

"Mr. Speaker, I rise today as a proud American: a person who believes in his country, who salutes the flag, says the Pledge of Allegiance, and sings the national anthem," Green said on the House floor September 26. "I rise today to defend, denounce, and announce."

What followed was an almost surreal glimpse inside Green's impeachment reasoning. The "defend" part of his speech was to "defend any mother who has been called a dog because her son engaged in peaceful protest." It was also to "defend any son who is called a dog because he is engaged in peaceful protest." The "denounce" part was Green's denunciation of the president, who has "brought discourse to a new low." And the "announce" part was this: "I rise to announce that next week I will bring a privileged resolution before the Congress of the United States of America. I will stand here in the well of the Congress, and I will call for the impeachment of the President of the United States of America."

Green's decision to use a "privileged resolution" caught the ear of Republican leadership. Basically that meant that Green, if he were persistent enough—and he showed every sign of being quite persistent—would ultimately be able to force the House to take a vote on his resolution. At some point or other, Republicans were going to have to confront the simmering Democratic movement to impeach the president, as embodied by Al Green.

For the next few days, Green lectured the House on the finer points of impeachment, especially his view that a president need not have committed an actual crime to be impeached. He planned to offer his impeachment resolution on October 2. But the night before that, on October 1, came the Las Vegas shooting, in which a gunman killed fifty-eight people and wounded 413 at a music festival on the Las Vegas Strip. On October 2, Green announced that it was a time to mourn, and he was postponing his resolution.

Nine days later, on October 11, Green was ready to go. He read his proposal, House Resolution 646, aloud on the floor. It contained four articles of impeachment. They represented a complete change from Green's earlier call for impeachment on obstruction of justice. They were, in fact, unlike any articles anyone could have contemplated. Right from the start:

> Article I: That Donald John Trump, President of the United States of America, unmindful of the high duties of his office and the dignity and proprieties thereof, and the harmony, respect, and courtesies, which ought to exhibit and be maintained in American society, has under the inane pretext of dispensing with political correctness, produced a demonstrable record of inciting white supremacy, sexism, bigotry, hatred, xenophobia, race-baiting, and racism by demeaning, defaming, disrespecting, and disparaging women and certain minorities. In so doing, Donald John Trump, President of the United States of America, has fueled and is fueling an alt-right hate machine and its worldwide covert sympathizers engendering racial antipathy, LGBTQ enmity, religious anxiety, stealthy sexism, and dreadful xenophobia, perfidiously causing immediate injury to American society....

Green listed the evidence to support his charge. It started with Trump's NFL attack ("He disrespected, disparaged, and demeaned mothers of professional football players") and went on to Trump's reaction to the hurricane in Puerto Rico; the "Muslim ban" executive order; and the executive order to end transgender service in the military. And then:

> Article II: That Donald John Trump, President of the United States of America, unmindful of the high duties of his high office and the dignity and proprieties thereof, and of the harmony and courtesies which ought to exist and be maintained

within American society, did betray his trust as president and
bring shame and dishonor to the office of the presidency by
associating the majesty and dignity of the presidency with causes
rooted in white supremacy, bigotry, racism, anti-Semitism, white
nationalism, and neo-Nazism....

Green based Article II entirely on Trump's widely reviled and often
misinterpreted "very fine people" statement after the white supremacist
rally in Charlottesville, Virginia. And then:

Article III: Donald John Trump, President of the United States
of America, unmindful of his high duties of his high office
and the dignity and proprieties thereof, and of the harmony
and courtesies which ought to exist and be maintained in
American society, did engage in perfidy by making the widely
reported claim that 3 to 5 million people voted illegally in the
2016 presidential election, and, further, expending tax dollars
to establish a commission to investigate his claim....

The explanation for Article III went into detail about the establishment of Trump's voter fraud commission, particularly the controversies
that ensued when some states denied the commission routinely available
voter data. And finally:

Article IV: "Donald John Trump, President of the United States
of America, unmindful of the high duties of his high office and
of the dignity and proprieties thereof, and of the harmony and
courtesies which ought to exist and be maintained in American
society, while aware of the widely reported history of unlawful
abuses and brutality perpetrated by many, not all, police officers against innocent persons in the United States of America,
did betray his trust as president, bringing shame and dishonor
to the office of the presidency by encouraging law enforcement

officials to violate the constitutional rights of suspects in their custody and control....

Green supported Article IV by citing a speech Trump gave in July 2017 about law enforcement in which he discussed "thugs being thrown into the back of a paddy wagon" and urging police to, "Please, don't be too nice." Green claimed Trump's speech represented a violation of the president's oath of office.

So there they were: four articles of impeachment. To Republicans, they seemed entirely nuts. Impeach a president for *that*? Surely no Democrat would support this craziness.

The fact was, as Republicans began to realize, some Democratic lawmakers were simply changing before their eyes. "The reputation of Al Green was actually pretty good back then," remembered Jason Chaffetz. "He was an exceptionally nice guy; he gave an incredible speech—you never wanted to speak after him. He was an important person in the Congressional Black Caucus. But the vitriol that was spewing—it was almost a race as to who was going to be the most aggressive and the first to market in bringing out all these sensational allegations."

Chaffetz also saw a transformation in Representative David Cicilline, a Democrat from Rhode Island who would serve on the Judiciary Committee in impeachment. "He was a super-nice guy—until Donald Trump won," Chaffetz said. "And he just turns like I've never seen before, with so much venom. I mean, he could not have been a nicer guy, somebody I was friends with. And then, as soon as Donald Trump was in place—wild, crazy assertions. It's like they got in a room and totally convinced themselves that it's time to get the pitchforks out and we're going to take this guy down no matter what."

There was more to come. On November 15, Democratic Representative Steve Cohen of Tennessee, who would serve on the Judiciary Committee for impeachment, introduced another set of new articles. Like Green, Cohen, acting along with several other Democrats, went beyond the old impeach-Trump-for-Russia model.

Cohen included five articles. The first proposed to remove Trump for obstruction of justice related to the Russia investigation—nothing new there. The second proposed impeachment for alleged violation of the Constitution's Foreign Emoluments Clause, that is, accepting payments from foreign states. The third article proposed impeachment for alleged violations of the Domestic Emoluments Clause, that is, accepting money from federal or state officials. The fourth article proposed to remove Trump for "undermining the independence of the federal judiciary and the rule of law." And the fifth article proposed to remove him for "undermining the freedom of the press."

The articles were based mostly on news reports. The Foreign Emoluments Clause article cited reports outlining Trump's income from foreign countries at his hotels and resorts. The article used as an example a dinner, thrown by a group that supported stronger Turkish-American relations, at the Trump International Hotel in Washington. The group paid $95 per person for 190 guests, and then, the next day, spent more than $30,000 for breakfast, dinner, and drinks, including a 24 percent "Banquet Event Service Charge." The Domestic Emoluments Clause article was also based on media accounts, focusing mostly on Trump's practice of spending weekends at his properties, sometimes in Florida, sometimes in Virginia, and sometimes in New Jersey. The article cited the president's companies' acceptance of $73,000 from the Secret Service for use of golf carts at his resort, and his companies' acceptance of $1,092, also from the Secret Service, for lodging at Trump's Palm Beach club, Mar-a-Lago.

The article concerning the federal judiciary was based on Trump's reaction to judicial opposition to his so-called "Muslim ban," which was in fact a ban on entry for some people from a small number of mostly Muslim countries. The article cited Trump for calling U.S. District Judge James Robart, who issued a restraining order against the ban, a "so-called judge." The article also cited candidate Trump's criticism of U.S. District Judge Gonzalo Curiel, in which Trump noted that Curiel was Hispanic and "a very hostile judge to me."

Finally, the article concerning freedom of the press proposed to remove Trump for "repeatedly" calling press organizations "fake news." It cited Trump tweets attacking newswomen Megyn Kelly and Mika Brzezinski, and also a statement by Trump that the media's behavior was "disgusting." The article noted that in January 2017, Trump's transition team "considered a plan to relocate the press corps from the White House press room to the White House Conference Center near Lafayette Square or to space in the Old Executive Office Building." For such offenses, the lawmakers concluded, Trump "warrants impeachment and trial, and removal from office."

Taken together, the Al Green and Steve Cohen articles represented two emerging sides of the attack on Trump. One focused on Russia and the follow-the-money allegations Democrats were making on a regular basis. The other focused on the cable news outrages of the day during Trump's first year in office. To Republicans, it seemed beyond belief that anyone thought that any of those things would be grounds for impeaching and removing the president of the United States. Perhaps Democrats didn't believe it either. But here they were.

"I just thought it was a nutty idea that would stay within the fringe of the Democrats in the House," Steve Scalise recalled. "It would stay tightly confined to the fringe elements in the House that just hated the president since the day he came down the escalator."

Fifty-Eight Votes

The only way to find out for sure how much support impeachment had was to take a vote. Al Green had been pushing for months for a privileged resolution to consider his impeachment articles. Republicans knew that, even though they were in the majority, Green would eventually get his vote. So on December 6, 2017, they gave it to him. Since GOP leaders had come to believe that Green would ultimately force a vote anyway, they decided to get it over with sooner rather than later.

It was not a vote on the more conventional articles of impeachment—Russia and emoluments—as sponsored by Cohen. Rather, it was on Green's attempt to impeach the president for his statements about the NFL, the Charlottesville riots, and "fueling an alt-right hate machine." In other words, Republicans allowed a vote on the fringiest of proposals to remove the president.

And fifty-eight Democrats voted for it. That was about 30 percent of the entire Democratic conference. The number included a few prominent Democrats, like Representative John Lewis of Georgia and Representative James Clyburn of South Carolina, a top member of the party leadership. It was well short of a majority—the final vote was 364 against, 58 for—but still a pretty significant number. Republicans who thought the supporters would just be Al Green and Jamie Raskin and Maxine Waters and perhaps a few others were dumbfounded.

"I was shocked that it was that high," remembered Scalise. Looking back, Scalise still couldn't believe the football article. "When the president criticized NFL players who kneeled during the pledge—they actually had that as an article of impeachment! And many Democrats voted for it. Many. Like, over 50 Democrats voted to impeach the president over criticizing NFL players." A tone of incredulousness remained in Scalise's voice, years after the fact.

To other amazed Republicans, the vote was a suggestion that the effort to impeach and remove Trump wasn't really about high crimes and misdemeanors, as prescribed in the Constitution. It was about ousting Trump by whatever means were at hand. It is hard to overstate how surprised some Republicans were that fifty-eight of their colleagues had voted "Aye" on Green's articles.

Who else was amazed? Al Green. "Mr. Speaker, yesterday 58 persons voted to impeach Donald John Trump, President of the United States," Green said on the floor the next day. "Mr. Speaker, that is 57 more than a good many people anticipated."

The number was so high that some of the 126 Democrats who voted against impeachment felt the need to distance themselves from the result.

Nancy Pelosi, then the minority leader, issued a statement stressing that investigations of Trump "should be allowed to continue" before any action to remove him. "Now is not the time to consider articles of impeachment," she said. There was a special counsel investigating the president, Pelosi noted, and the House should wait to see what he finds.

But the impeachers knew they were on to something. Yes, fifty-eight votes were not enough. But it was just the beginning. "It's a process, and this is another step in the process," Green told reporters after the vote. "Just stay tuned. I assure you, that's not the last vote to impeach."

CHAPTER THREE

The Search for Collusion

A Blind Start—Trump's Choice: Attack or Cooperate?—
"I don't let any grass grow under me"—A Collusion
Goose Chase—The Bitter End of the Beginning

After the initial shock of the Mueller appointment, two questions settled in for the president and his legal team: Who is Robert Mueller, and how do we deal with him?

Mueller was not, of course, an unknown quantity. He had been a U.S. attorney, head of the Justice Department's Criminal Division, acting deputy attorney general, and director of the FBI from 2001 to 2013. (Comey was his successor.) Since leaving the FBI, Mueller was a partner at the white-shoe WilmerHale law firm in Washington. Through it all, he had a reputation as a sharp, no-nonsense, upright man. He was all business, and he expected those who worked for him to be all business, too.

Although it is the sixth-largest metropolitan area in the country, Washington can feel like a small town to those who work in the world of politics, law, lobbying, and media. People knew Mueller. His career had some indisputable low points—like his bungling of the post-9/11 anthrax case—but overall, he had a good reputation. He was known as someone to respect. His appointment to investigate the Trump-Russia matter prompted a wave of bipartisan praise.

"Robert Mueller is [a] superb choice to be special counsel," tweeted former House Speaker Newt Gingrich. "His reputation is impeccable for honesty and integrity. Media should now calm down."

"There is no better person who could be asked to perform this function," said Senator Dianne Feinstein of California, at the time ranking Democrat on the Judiciary Committee. "He is respected, he is talented, and he has the knowledge and ability to do the right thing."

"I commend [the Department of Justice] for bringing in an independent voice to help bring clarity to this situation," said Republican Senator Orrin Hatch of Utah, also a veteran of the Judiciary Committee.

Democrats were happy because there would be a special counsel. Republicans were not happy, but they were at least satisfied because, if there had to be a special counsel, Mueller had the potential to do the job fairly. Less discussed at the time was the possibility—probability, actually—that regardless of his well-known sense of rectitude, Mueller would fall victim to the immutable laws of special counsel investigations. They go on too long, they branch out in unanticipated directions, and they end in murky and often disputed conclusions. Why would Mueller, despite his reputation, be any different?

A Blind Start

First, the president needed lawyers. He of course had the White House counsel to represent the office of the presidency. But a formal special counsel probe meant that Trump needed not just an outside lawyer, but also an outside legal team. He approached some of the biggest names in Washington's legal world and was turned down. So almost immediately after Mueller was appointed, in May 2017, Trump began the team with Mark Kasowitz, his longtime personal lawyer from New York, and Michael Bowe, a lawyer with Kasowitz's firm. A short time later, he added Jay Sekulow, a Washington lawyer who had argued for many conservative causes. Sekulow, who had appeared before the Supreme Court a dozen times, came in with a very specific assignment:

He was to make the case in the media, and also to work on constitutional issues in preparation for what would become known in the office as "the moment." "The moment" was shorthand for the time, thought to be inevitable, when the special counsel would request—or demand—the president's testimony. It was a question that was not urgent in the first months, but everyone knew it was coming. It could well become the most important episode of the entire investigation, both for Mueller and for Trump.

At nearly the same time as he brought on Sekulow, the president hired his lead lawyer, John Dowd, who had defended Senator John McCain in the "Keating Five" investigation in the late 1980s and who conducted the investigation by Major League Baseball into allegations of gambling by Cincinnati Reds star Pete Rose. Dowd was eminently qualified by any estimation, but he had another appeal as well: a veteran of the Justice Department, he knew and had worked with Mueller. In addition, he was, like Mueller, a former Marine. There was a feeling on the team that the two men, Dowd and Mueller, might be able to work with each other.

In July, Trump added another veteran Washington attorney, Ty Cobb, who would help lay the groundwork for the early relationship between the Trump and Mueller camps. As a spokesman, the team hired Mark Corallo, who had worked for Republican investigators on Capitol Hill and in the Justice Department in the George W. Bush administration.

The first task was to figure out what Mueller was up to, which was harder than it sounded. News reports each day were filled with talk about Mueller investigating this or Mueller investigating that, but on the inside, the Trump legal team did not know what was going on.

"You have to understand, at that time, it was unclear to us what Mueller was doing," recalled Michael Bowe. "Comey testifies [Trump] was not under investigation at the time Comey was fired. If he wasn't under investigation when Comey was there, why would he be under investigation the day after Comey got fired? Now, we know there was a massive, two-year investigation of the president, but at that point in time we didn't even know if Mueller was authorized to investigate the president, and we certainly weren't aware of any facts that would justify that."

To start with, Trump's lawyers pored over the public version of Rosenstein's letter to Mueller outlining the scope of the investigation. Here was the heart of it:

> The special counsel is authorized to conduct the investigation confirmed by then-FBI Director James B. Comey in testimony before the House Permanent Select Committee on Intelligence on March 20, 2017, including:
> 1) Any links and/or coordination between the Russian government and individuals associated with the campaign of President Donald Trump; and
> 2) Any matters that arose or may arise directly from the investigation; and
> 3) Any other matters within the scope of 28 CFR 600.4(a).
> If the Special Counsel believes it is necessary and appropriate, the Special Counsel is authorized to prosecute federal crimes arising from the investigation of these matters.

What, precisely, did that mean? First, the investigation confirmed by Comey during that memorable appearance before the House was, in Comey's words at the time, a counterintelligence probe into "the Russian government's efforts to interfere in the 2016 presidential election." Did that mean Mueller would continue the counterintelligence investigation into the Russians? That was something the Trump team saw as unrelated to the president or his campaign. But Mueller's scope also included, as Comey said, "investigating the nature of any links between individuals associated with the Trump campaign and the Russian government and whether there was any coordination between the campaign and Russia's efforts."

That meant Mueller was authorized to extend the investigation into what the FBI had already been probing, including possible links to the Trump campaign. In addition, he was empowered to look at "any matters" that might arise "directly" from the investigation. That could mean virtually anything, depending on Mueller's discretion and his definition of the word "directly." And finally, the reference to "28 CFR 600.4(a)" was a reference to the criminal code section on obstruction of justice, meaning Mueller could pursue possible charges for things like making false statements, destroying documents, and other examples of impeding the investigation.

What the president's legal team did not understand was precisely where Donald Trump fit into all of that. They knew the feds were investigating Russian meddling. They knew the Justice Department had initially pursued Michael Flynn. They knew the Christopher Steele dossier played some role in it all. And they knew the press was on fire over a theory of collusion. What they did not know was how that might translate, in the new Mueller investigation, into an investigation of President Trump himself.

Would the investigation focus on collusion? On obstruction? Mostly on Trump? Mostly on Russia? For the legal team, May 2017 marked a blind start to the most consequential investigation of the Trump presidency.

Trump's Choice: Attack or Cooperate?

From the very beginning, even as they tried to figure out what the special counsel was doing, the Trump team, and especially the president himself, had conflicting impulses on how to deal with Mueller. Should they attack him or try to cooperate with him? Ultimately, Trump chose to do both, and he had different teams of people for each job. For the cooperation, he used his formal legal team. For the attacks, he relied on a group of outside confidants who could go on television and take shots at the special counsel. But in the beginning, the president chose to emphasize cooperation over confrontation. The first six months of the investigation saw Trump mostly refrain from personal, full-scale attacks on Mueller.

Trump had a number of objections to the Mueller appointment. First, he was completely blindsided by it—Rosenstein had engineered the whole thing to shock the president, and it did. Second, Mueller had personal connections and had made decisions that convinced the president he had too many conflicts to do the job fairly.

One such conflict was an old dispute between Trump and Mueller over Mueller's membership in the Trump National Golf Club in Sterling, Virginia. Mueller joined the club in 1994, when he lived in suburban Virginia. In 2011, having moved to the District of Columbia, Mueller wrote a letter to the club, saying he and his wife could "no longer make full use" of its facilities. The Muellers inquired whether they would be "entitled to a refund of a portion of our initial membership fee." The club responded that they would be placed on a waiting list for a possible refund. That was the last the Muellers ever heard from Trump National; there would be no refund.

After Mueller's appointment, Trump claimed that lingering bad blood over the golf club issue constituted a conflict for Mueller. Trump's top aides did not believe his complaint had much merit—senior adviser Stephen Bannon called it "ridiculous and petty"—but Trump felt it was a conflict. His objection went nowhere when, on May 23, 2017, a week after Mueller was appointed, Justice Department ethics officials pronounced him fit to serve. (Later, Mueller's prosecutors briefly pursued a theory that, by claiming a conflict over the golf club, Trump obstructed a federal investigation. They questioned aides about the issue and included a brief discussion of it in the Mueller report.)

Trump also had more substantial objections to Mueller. One was Mueller's relationship with Comey, whose firing, by Trump, led to a secret Comey scheme to spur the appointment of a special counsel.

Mueller and Comey were friends. In 2013, before Trump came on the scene, *Washingtonian* magazine published a feature headlined, "Forged Under Fire—Bob Mueller and Jim Comey's Unusual Friendship." The piece described the two men as having been "brothers in arms" in the days after the September 11, 2001, terrorist attacks, when Mueller was the newly arrived director of the FBI and Comey was, first, United States attorney for the Southern District of New York, and later, deputy attorney general. "The two men are deeply alike, sharing a background and core principles," *Washingtonian* wrote, noting that Mueller and Comey were "close partners and close allies."

In the Trump-Russia investigation, the two were together again— Mueller as the investigator and Comey as the star witness. Indeed, for many of President Trump's critics, the firing of Comey was Exhibit A in the case for obstruction of justice they hoped Mueller would build. Comey's testimony would be critical. That, for Trump defenders, raised a question: Should a prosecutor pursue a case in which his close friend is both main witness and alleged victim?

"It's somewhat ironic, no?" asked an anonymous Capitol Hill lawyer at the time. "I mean, the whole purpose of the special counsel is to have a prosecutor from outside the government and outside of the normal chain of command because inherent conflicts render the Justice Department incapable of handling it. So, now the special counsel is a close friend with the star witness, who by his own admission leaked the memos at least in part to engineer the appointment of a special counsel. Only in Washington."

Beyond the Comey friendship, Trump also objected to Mueller's staff hiring decisions. In the first weeks and months of operations, Mueller hired seventeen prosecutors, mostly from the Justice Department. Press reports found that thirteen were Democrats and none were Republicans. No fewer than ten had contributed at least $200—the minimum amount that requires federal disclosure—to Democratic candidates. An analysis by Politifact found that five of them had contributed to Hillary

Clinton's 2016 campaign. One, Jeannie Rhee, gave $5,400, and another, James Quarles, gave $2,700. The new Mueller staff had given to other Democrats as well—Rhee gave $11,950 in federal races, Andrew Weissmann gave $6,600, Greg Andres and Andrew Goldstein gave around $3,000, and four others gave less than $1,000. All went to Democrats. And that was just in federal races; the Mueller team had also given thousands in state and local races—again, all to Democrats. The biggest donor of all, Politifact found, was Quarles, who gave over $35,000. He was the only Mueller hire who had given even a small amount—$2,750—to Republicans.

Most Americans, even if they are partisans, don't give to political campaigns. A tiny number—the Center for Responsive Politics estimated it to be 0.52 percent of the population—contributes more than $200 to federal candidates. And yet Mueller managed to assemble a team in which the majority of prosecutors had contributed a significant amount of money to campaigns—all of it, with the exception of Quarles's $2,750, to Democrats.

Finally, Mueller's top deputy, Andrew Weissmann, who was sometimes referred to as the special counsel's "pit bull," attended Hillary Clinton's 2016 election-night event at the Javits Center in New York. According to the campaign's plan for that night, thousands of pieces of confetti that looked like shards of glass would be dropped when Clinton's victory was declared. It was supposed to be symbolic of Clinton's breaking the "glass ceiling" that kept a woman from becoming president. Instead, the night dragged on with no victory announcement and steady reports of Trump's winning state after state. The crowd Weissmann joined was crushed. And now Weissmann was playing a top role in investigating Donald Trump, the man who made that night in the Javits Center so miserable. (In 2020, after the investigation was over, Weissmann participated in a fundraiser for Democratic presidential candidate Joe Biden.)

It's no surprise that given all that, Trump felt the investigation was tilted against him. What is remarkable is that the president, who could reach tens of millions of followers in an instant via Twitter, held his tongue, or mostly held his tongue, for months afterward.

On May 18, at a little before 8:00 a.m. on the morning after Mueller was appointed, Trump tweeted, "This is the single greatest witch hunt of a politician in American history!" About an hour later, he tweeted, "With all of the illegal acts that took place in the Clinton campaign & Obama Administration, there was never a special counsel appointed!" The two tweets were an alarming start for those who wanted the president to lay off Mueller, but for most of May, Trump said nothing about the new investigation.

The subject of whether to attack Mueller came up several times in the president's discussions with his team. "The heart of my role was reminding [Trump] that if you want these guys to be even more aggressive, go after Bob Mueller personally," recalled Mark Corallo, who worked with Mueller in the Bush Justice Department and who admired the new special counsel. Yes, it was legitimate to point out that so many of Mueller's aides were partisan Democrats. And yes, it was legitimate to criticize his actions. But don't get personal. "I would say to him, 'Mr. President, just don't attack Bob Mueller by name. Don't attack him. It's okay for us to disagree with his tactics. It's okay for you to question things that he is doing. But don't go after him personally—his integrity, his reputation. Leave that alone. There's no point. It doesn't help you. It doesn't help us get through the investigation.' And all the lawyers agreed with that."

Trump mostly took his team's advice, although there were times when he could not resist the temptation to strike back. One month into the investigation, on June 14, the *Washington Post* published a story headlined, "Special Counsel is Investigating Trump for Possible Obstruction of Justice, Officials Say." The story, citing "five people briefed on the interview requests," reported that Mueller was questioning "senior intelligence officials" to determine whether Trump obstructed justice. "Trump had received private assurances from then-FBI Director James B. Comey starting in January that he was not personally under investigation," the paper said. "Officials say that changed shortly after Comey's firing."

The news, which the *Post* called a "major turning point" in the Trump-Russia investigation, set off a barrage of tweets from Trump. "You are witnessing the single greatest WITCH HUNT in American political history—led by some very bad and conflicted people!" the president tweeted on June 15, the day after the story appeared. "I am being investigated for firing the FBI Director by the man who told me to fire the FBI Director! Witch Hunt!" Trump tweeted the next day. "MAKE AMERICA GREAT AGAIN agenda is doing very well despite the distraction of the Witch Hunt," he tweeted June 18.

On June 22, Trump went on Fox News to make his case that Mueller should withdraw from the investigation. "Well, he's very, very good friends with Comey, which is very bothersome," Trump said. "Look, there has been no obstruction. There has been no collusion. There has been leaking by Comey, but there's been no collusion, no obstruction, and virtually everybody agrees to that. So we'll have to see. I can say that the people that have been hired are all Hillary Clinton supporters."

Subsequent stories set off even more "witch hunt" tweets from Trump. Such talk, though mild compared to what would come from Trump and his allies in 2018 and 2019, was heard loud and clear at the special counsel's office. "Initially, in the summer, Bob was annoyed by the president's teeing off," recalled John Dowd. "I explained to him that it's political. He's got a political role. And Bob seemed to understand that. But he said, 'What I'm worried about is that it will discourage cooperation.' And I said, 'Hell, we'll fix that. We've told everyone to cooperate, and we'll do it again.... Bob appreciated that."

In the big picture, though, Trump, for all the "witch hunt" talk, held back from declaring war on the new special counsel. He did not mention Mueller by name in a single tweet in the rest of 2017. None. Why? For one, that's what his team was advising him to do. But it was also yet another manifestation of Trump's belief that he could, through the sheer force of his personality, make people like him. He tried it with Comey. And now, facing a new special counsel, he tried it again with Mueller.

"I don't let any grass grow under me"

Trump and his team began the Mueller investigation by believing that 1) they could build a good working relationship with Mueller, and 2) it would be all over by the end of 2017, just six months away.

"The president wanted it over yesterday," recalled Michael Bowe. "I believe he felt like any client wrongly accused: he thought he had nothing to hide and could end it by just walking down there, looking Mueller in the eye, and saying 'I didn't do anything. Tell me what you think I did.' Or by finding the right person who Mueller trusted to say the same thing." Trump was particularly upset by the effect the investigation—a topic of intense interest around the globe—was having on his ability to deal with foreign leaders. Presidents and prime ministers wanted to know what was going on in the United States and whether President Trump would remain in office and have the same influence as a president not under investigation. Trump told his team continually that the investigation was interfering with his ability to deal with foreign governments. He wanted it done with.

To do that, Trump sought to open up communications with Mueller almost instantly. "We were sort of being pushed to go talk to Mueller before Mueller ever wanted to talk to us," Bowe said. "Our first conversation occurred before he had his first office." It was an unusual start to that kind of investigation. Normally, the new prosecutor would open up, begin work, and months would go by before he would get in touch with the subject of his investigation. But Trump wanted his team talking to Mueller right away because he believed he did nothing wrong and wanted to confront and resolve any uncertainty immediately. "We were the ones banging on their door," Bowe recalled.

As always, Trump believed differences could be talked out, adversaries could be charmed, and a deal could be made. But, as he soon discovered, that approach worked neither in Washington's deeply partisan political culture nor in its highly politicized legal culture. As a businessman, Trump had been involved in many, many lawsuits. But he had never been under criminal investigation before. And he had certainly never been involved in a criminal investigation like the Mueller probe.

A meeting with Mueller was set for June 16, roughly a month after the special counsel was appointed. The idea was that Dowd, the former Marine, would have a good eye-to-eye talk with Mueller, the former Marine. "I kept making the point that Bob knows John," said Mark Corallo, recalling a White House strategy session. "They're not best friends or anything, but he knows him and respects him as a lawyer, and that's important for Mueller."

Trump was happy. "He is all about relationships," Corallo said. Trump gave his blessing to a cooperative start. If the Mueller relationship could get off to a good beginning, maybe it could all be over sooner rather than later.

The meeting was held at Mueller's temporary offices. The Trump team came with an offer: the president wanted the investigation completed quickly. Mueller wanted a lot of evidence from the White House. Trump would offer virtually unlimited cooperation in the production of evidence in order to get things over quickly. Doing so might avoid the long, grinding fights over access and privilege that often marked special counsel investigations.

"We made a bargain," Dowd said, recalling the meeting. "Bob said to me, 'I have no bias at all,' and we accepted that. I told him that we had a lot of issues with Rosenstein and where this had come from, and the fact that the president was blindsided by his appointment. And we had problems with conflicts that they had. But we were putting that aside, we were not going to object. The president wants to get you the facts, but we'll only do that if you'll get it done."

"And he said to me, 'John, I don't let any grass grow under me.' We reached across the table, we shook hands, and I said, 'Bob, we're going to get you everything.'"

"They said they were going to move expeditiously," Jay Sekulow recalled. "They had no desire to drag this out and put the country through a long process."

Mueller said the sort of things that one says in get-started meetings. He said his door would always be open, and that he understood how the investigation was affecting the country and the president. With that, it was over.

The team then reported back to Trump. The lawyers told Trump they had confidence in Mueller, that they made their concerns known to him, that he understood them, and that he sought to reassure them about the partisan appearance of his lawyers. "I'm in charge," Mueller told them. He, and not some headstrong Democratic partisan prosecutor, would be making decisions. "We all said we trusted Bob to ride herd on his staff," Corallo recalled.

In the next few weeks the two sides hammered out how, precisely, the cooperation agreement would work. (It was never written down—just a handshake deal.) Certainly, many documents that Mueller would want to see would be covered by executive privilege, or some other privilege. Why would Trump just turn them over? On the other hand, Mueller would not want to fight hand-to-hand over each document, which would take years.

Seeking to balance both sides' interests, Trump and Mueller reached an informal understanding by which the White House would give documents to the special counsel without claiming privilege, but Mueller would limit the ways he used the material. The thinking was this: Mueller was in the executive branch. The White House was in the executive branch. The White House would hand over the material, one executive branch entity to another, without claiming any privilege—provided Mueller would agree that, if he intended to use the material outside the executive branch—say, to give it to Congress—he would first consult the White House.

The Trump team based its idea on a July 15, 2008, memo written by Michael Mukasey, at the time attorney general under George W. Bush.

In 2008, Democrats had taken control of the House and were demanding that the administration turn over documents from the Valerie Plame CIA leak investigation that bedeviled the Bush White House from 2003 to 2007. The administration did, in fact, turn over a lot, but drew the line at interviews with the president and vice president. (House Democrats had made a particular villain of Vice President Dick Cheney and were hot to have information on him.) In the memo, Mukasey noted the long tradition of White Houses cooperating with criminal investigations—but not with Congress, a separate branch of government. Mukasey warned that while White House cooperation with the criminal investigation—the Patrick Fitzgerald probe—was good, submitting to Congress's demands would be a bad idea.

"Were future presidents, vice presidents or White House staff to perceive that such voluntary cooperation [with a criminal investigation] would likely be made available to Congress (and then possibly disclosed publicly outside of judicial proceedings such as a trial)," Mukasey wrote, "there would be an unacceptable risk that such knowledge could adversely impact their willingness to cooperate fully and candidly in a voluntary interview."

The Trump response to Mueller ran along similar lines. "The key was Mueller was within the executive branch and could be within privilege," Dowd added. "So we had our protected pipeline to speed information to the office of special counsel."

Under Trump's proposal, the White House would not have to go through each document page-by-page looking for privileged material— provided Mueller agreed to the White House's conditions. "You can imagine what a nightmare it would be to take document by document and assert the privilege, because most of it was within [executive] privilege, and indeed the White House communications privilege," said Dowd. "I thought it was a great idea. Ty Cobb got Bob's and [top deputy James] Quarles' promise that if they needed to use any of it publicly, they would come back to the White House."

The deal led to an extraordinary transfer of documents and information to the special counsel's office. For example, a White House official named Annie Donaldson, who was White House Counsel Don McGahn's chief of staff, took detailed, extensive notes on meetings that involved the president and the counsel's office. Donaldson's notes were a vivid, real-time look at what the president and his advisers said in key meetings that touched on the subject matter of Mueller's investigation. They were voluminous—it would have taken hours to read them all—and they most certainly covered areas over which a president might legitimately claim privilege. Trump turned them over to Mueller. McGahn himself sat for more than thirty hours of interviews with the Mueller team. That's a lot for investigators to demand from a high-ranking White House official, but McGahn did it because Trump did not object to the interviews going forward. Reince Priebus, Hope Hicks, Steve Bannon, K. T. McFarland, Jared Kushner, and others talked to the Mueller prosecutors at great length.

"Bob said on several occasions that he had never seen such cooperation," Dowd recalled. "But that was the idea. We're all pros. We all know each other. And the president, every time we gave them something, he blessed it. This wasn't just one shot. We reported to him regularly, and he said, 'Give it to them, we've got nothing to hide.' We knew we were within the executive privilege pipeline."

The president made sure that Mueller's prosecutors never forgot that they should hold up their end of the deal. In the meetings between teams, the Trump side would often bring a message from the president, and each time it went something like this: I respect what you are doing, but it is imposing on my ability to govern, particularly in foreign relations. They would recount an anecdote, sometimes containing sensitive information, of the investigation causing the president problems in dealing with foreign leaders. The conclusion was always the same: this needs to end as quickly as possible.

The arrangement represented Trump and his team's placing an enormous amount of trust in Mueller and his prosecutors. After all, it was a fundamentally adversarial relationship. Mueller's prosecutors might use the material to subpoena the president or even to indict him—that was, of course, against Justice Department policy, but it was publicly discussed at the time—or to create a road map for Congress to impeach him. Trump's willingness to hand over evidence was a leap of faith.

"There was more trust in our relationship than in any in my entire career," said Dowd.

The question of trust—that is, could Mueller and his team of prosecutors be trusted—was perhaps the most discussed issue on the Trump side in the early days. Not everyone agreed on Mueller's worthiness of such trust. One of the skeptical was Jay Sekulow. "It wasn't a personal thing," he recalled. "I didn't have the relationship with Mueller. I had met him probably three times in my life. This was John's call. John had the experience and the relationship with him."

On the other hand, Corallo, a Mueller fan from the Bush years, strongly supported the trust strategy. He even staked his position on it. "When I took this job, I said, 'I won't be a part of any personal attacks on Bob Mueller,'" Corallo recalled telling his colleagues on the legal team. "He's a friend. I'm loyal. And I believe he's going to do the right thing."

Corallo paused a moment. "Now in hindsight," he continued, "maybe I was wrong." Others would come to think that, too, as the investigation wore on.

A Collusion Goose Chase

The cooperation deal, while enormously important at key points in the investigation, did not play a big role in the beginning. That was because the material Trump had to offer mostly concerned events in the White House and was thus relevant mostly to allegations of obstruction of justice. What Mueller pursued right at the beginning, though, was collusion, the accusation that the Trump campaign conspired or coordinated with Russia to fix the 2016 election.

The case for collusion, repeated daily on anti-Trump media outlets, boiled down to five people and incidents. First, there was a trip that Carter Page, a short-term, low-ranking member of the Trump campaign foreign policy advisory board, took to Moscow in July 2016. Second, there was an allegation that during the Republican National Convention that same month, the Trump team "gutted" the GOP platform position on Ukraine to make it more palatable to Vladimir Putin. Third, there was the case of Michael Flynn, the short-tenured national security adviser accused of lying about a phone conversation with the Russian ambassador during the transition. Fourth, there was the case of George Papadopoulos, another short-term, low-ranking Trump campaign foreign policy figure, whom conspiracy theorists wrongly believed might have had foreknowledge of the Russian hack of the Democratic National Committee. And fifth, there was the June 9, 2016, Trump Tower meeting, in which Trump's son Donald Trump Jr., campaign chairman Paul Manafort, and son-in-law Jared Kushner met with a Russian lawyer who had promised dirt on Hillary Clinton but was actually seeking to persuade them to end U.S. sanctions on Russia.

The Trump team was able to follow what Mueller was doing. They knew which witnesses Mueller was calling, and re-calling, to testify. And they knew that in the early days of his investigation—May, June, and July 2017—Mueller was chasing the collusion theory. Trump's lawyers watched it happen in real time. And they could see what Mueller was, and wasn't, discovering.

First, Carter Page. Although a minor figure in the campaign, he was an extraordinarily important figure in the earliest collusion theories; the Steele dossier had claimed that campaign boss Paul Manafort used Page as the vehicle to further a "well-developed conspiracy" between Trump and Russia. The dossier also alleged that during Page's 2016 trip to Moscow, a close Putin associate offered Page a huge bribe to convince Trump to rescind U.S. sanctions on Russia.

Before Mueller was appointed, the FBI had interviewed Page five times in March 2017. Once up and running, Mueller went after other witnesses to learn more about what Page might have been up to in Moscow. On June 9, 2017, Mueller's prosecutors interviewed one of the officials at the Moscow school at which Page gave a speech during his 2016 visit. On July 28, they interviewed another school official. On June 19, they interviewed Corey Lewandowski, who headed the Trump campaign at the time of the Page trip. On October 3, they interviewed Sam Clovis, a Trump campaign official who had some dealings with Page. Mueller also had the results of the FBI's wiretap of Page, the warrant for which was granted under dubious circumstances in October 2016. That surveillance allowed investigators to not only listen to Page's voice communications going forward, but to read his electronic communications going back in time to his dealings with the Trump campaign.

After all that, on November 17, 2017, the Mueller team questioned Page in front of a grand jury. They pushed him hard but failed to confirm any of the collusion theories. "Basically it's like Guantanamo Bay detention camp in a lot of ways," Page said of his time in the grand jury. "But I actually would have enjoyed being in Gitmo more than what I went through with these people." Page did not know it at the time, but the grand jury appearance would be the last time he heard from Mueller's prosecutors. The testimony appeared to close the book on the theory that Carter Page was a major player in a grand collusion scheme between Russia and the Trump campaign. Page was never charged with any wrongdoing.

Second, there was the convention episode. Mueller's prosecutors talked to everyone who was involved in crafting the platform at the GOP gathering in Cleveland in July 2016. The story—it was a persistent rumor, actually—stemmed from an article in the *Washington Post* with the headline, "Trump Campaign Guts GOP's Anti-Russia Stance on Ukraine." The headline was false; no one took anything out of the party's original draft platform on Ukraine and Russia. A single delegate to the convention, a Texas woman named Diana Denman, proposed language pledging a tougher U.S. stance against Russia. Officials added most of the toughening language Denman suggested, but rejected her proposal that the U.S. provide "lethal defensive weapons to Ukraine's armed forces," instead writing that the U.S. would support "increasing sanctions...against Russia unless and until Ukraine's sovereignty and territorial integrity are restored." The platform also pledged that the U.S. would support "providing appropriate assistance to the armed forces of Ukraine and greater coordination with NATO defense planning." The GOP platform, far from being "gutted" actually ended up stronger on Ukraine than it had originally been. The story was not only wrong, but 180 degrees wrong.

Nevertheless, Mueller chased it. His prosecutors interviewed Rachel Hoff, a GOP official who played a role in drafting the platform, on May 26, 2017, which was during Mueller's first ten days in office. They interviewed Diana Denman on June 7. They interviewed the Trump campaign's director of national security, J. D. Gordon, on August 29. They interviewed another GOP official, Matt Miller, on October 25. By the fall of 2017, Mueller knew there was nothing to the platform story. No one was charged with any wrongdoing related to it.

Then there was Flynn. It was not known until the Mueller report came out, but in the late summer of 2016, the FBI opened a counterintelligence investigation of Flynn, who became candidate Trump's top national security aide, and then, in the transition, the incoming national security adviser. It is still not known precisely why the FBI opened the probe. It's possible that agents acted because Flynn attended a December 2015 dinner in Moscow for the tenth anniversary of the media outlet Russia Today (RT). Flynn, who occasionally appeared on RT as an analyst, was seated next to Vladimir Putin. As a former top U.S. intelligence official, he told U.S. authorities about the trip beforehand and briefed those authorities on it after he returned. Whatever the reason, by Election Day 2016, Flynn was under FBI investigation.

In late December 2016, as Flynn was preparing to take office, the Obama administration levied sanctions on Russia, expelling diplomats in retaliation for Russia's interference in the presidential election. In a phone call with the Russian ambassador, Sergey Kislyak, Flynn asked that Russia not escalate the dispute but instead respond in a "reciprocal" manner. There was nothing wrong with an incoming White House official's talking to an official from a foreign government, nor was there anything wrong with Flynn's suggesting that Russia hold off from taking any big actions for three weeks or so until the new administration was in office.

Nevertheless, Obama Justice Department officials, who had a recording of the Flynn-Kislyak call picked up by American intelligence community wiretaps, theorized that Flynn might have violated the Logan Act. It was an audacious theory, in large part because the Act—which forbade private citizens from conducting foreign policy—was passed in 1799 and had never, in 217 years, been successfully prosecuted. It was, for all intents and purposes, a dead letter. In addition, many legal experts thought that even if it were in effect, it was unconstitutional. But acting on the suspicion that Flynn might have violated the Logan Act, the FBI came up with a scheme to go to the White House on January 24, 2017—just four days into the new administration—and question Flynn about the call with Kislyak.

The FBI agents who would interview Flynn debated how to handle the questioning. "What is our goal?" they wrote in notes preparing for the interview. "Truth/Admission or to get him to lie, so we can prosecute him or get him fired?" They decided not to show Flynn the call transcript to refresh his memory. They also chose to dispense with protocol like clearing the interview with the White House counsel's office. "We just decided, you know, screw it," Comey said, according to a memoir published by a former aide.

When they arrived at the White House, the agents "asked Flynn if he recalled any conversation with Kislyak in which the expulsions were discussed, where Flynn might have encouraged Kislyak not to escalate the situation, to keep the Russian response reciprocal," according to the agents' notes of the interview. Flynn's response, according to the notes was, "Not really. I don't remember."

The FBI agents did not detect any signs that Flynn was deliberately lying to them. No action was taken against him. Meanwhile, the Flynn story, leaked to the press, became part of the daily stream of Russia news. Vice President Mike Pence asked Flynn about the issue, and White House officials came to believe that Flynn lied to Pence. Flynn had become a red-hot liability. The president fired him on February 13, 2017.

In March, Comey told senior lawmakers on Capitol Hill that the agents who questioned Flynn did not believe he had deliberately lied and that he, Comey, did not expect any charges to be brought against Flynn. That is where things stood until May, when Mueller was appointed. At that point, everything changed. The special counsel's new prosecutors pulled the Flynn case off the shelf and threatened to prosecute Flynn to compel his cooperation with the new investigation.

On December 1, 2017, Flynn pleaded guilty to lying to the FBI about the Kislyak phone call. Mueller's prosecutors pressed, but they never charged Flynn with conspiracy or coordination with Russia to influence the 2016 election.

Also that summer, Mueller repeatedly questioned K. T. McFarland, who had been Flynn's deputy during the transition and Flynn's brief time in the White House. McFarland had just finished a workout when, on August 29, 2017, without any prior notice, two agents called her at her home in Southampton, Long Island, to tell her they were waiting outside the house and would like to question her. McFarland allowed them in and answered their questions without an attorney present. "We sat at my dining room table, the agents in their white shirts, dark suits, and ties, me in my gym clothes and sneakers," McFarland wrote in a memoir.

The agents asked McFarland questions about events months ago for which she had no chance to prepare. (Among many things, they asked her about the Logan Act.) They assured her she was not a target of the investigation—what had she done wrong?—but returned to interview her two more times. Then they made McFarland come to Washington for a fourth round of questioning. Finally lawyered up, McFarland learned that Mueller was considering charging her with making false statements during her first three interviews. In the end, Mueller did not act. McFarland viewed the episode as a perjury trap that she was lucky to escape. Mueller and his prosecutors did not accuse her or Flynn of anything involving conspiracy or coordination with Russia.

The fourth example of alleged collusion was Papadopoulos. The FBI claimed that Papadopoulos was the reason the bureau started the Crossfire Hurricane investigation on July 31, 2016. It was then that agents had heard from the Australian government that several months earlier Papadopoulos supposedly admitted that he knew about the Russian DNC hack ahead of time. He didn't. In fact, Papadopoulos, based in London, was the subject of all sorts of international intrigue by people who may or may not have been working for Russia, and was under secret surveillance and recording by the FBI. In particular, Papadopoulos was said to have told a mysterious Maltese professor, Joseph Mifsud, that the Russians had "dirt" on Hillary Clinton, and in fact had "thousands" of emails.

But the bureau quickly discovered Papadopoulos was a dry hole. In October 2016, a confidential FBI source covertly taped a discussion in which the source tried to lead Papadopoulos into confessing knowledge of collusion.

"You don't think anyone from the Trump campaign had anything to do with the fucking over the, at the DNC?" the source asked.

"No," said Papadopoulos. "I know that for a fact."

"But you don't think anyone would have done it, like under, undercover or anything like that?" the source said.

"No, I don't think so," Papadopoulos answered. "There's absolutely no reason. First of all, it's illegal, you know, to do that shit."

That was October 2016. The FBI did not get around to interviewing Papadopoulos until January 27, 2017. After questioning, agents came to believe he lied to them about when he had his discussion with Mifsud. Papadopoulos had said it was before he joined the Trump campaign, when in fact it was after.

Like the Flynn case, the FBI did not do a lot with Papadopoulos after that January 27 interview. But once Mueller was appointed, the special counsel's prosecutors moved quickly. On July 27, 2017, just a couple of months into the investigation, Mueller's agents arrested Papadopoulos when he was getting off a flight at Washington's Dulles Airport. He was kept in a jail cell overnight. They pressed him for information about collusion, threatening to indict him for lying to agents back in January.

Mueller's prosecutors interviewed all the participants in a March 31, 2016, meeting in which candidate Trump met—for the only time— with his foreign policy advisory board, including Papadopoulos (but minus Carter Page, who never met Trump). They also interviewed Trump campaign official Sam Clovis, who had had some dealings with Papadopoulos on October 3. Agents re-interviewed Papadopoulos in August and September of 2017.

On October 5, 2017, Papadopoulos pleaded guilty to making false statements to investigators. He cooperated with Mueller and was eventually sentenced to fourteen days in prison, of which he served twelve days. He was never charged with any crime alleging that there was a conspiracy or cooperation between the Trump campaign and Russia. The Papadopoulos case did not advance the theory of collusion, and Mueller knew it by the fall of 2017.

Fifth, and finally, there was the Trump Tower meeting, the event the president's opponents, especially those in the media, believed to be Exhibit A of collusion.

On July 8, 2017, just weeks into Mueller's investigation, the *New York Times* published a story headlined "Trump Team Met with Lawyer Linked to Kremlin during Campaign." It described a meeting on June 9, 2016, not long after candidate Donald Trump had clinched the Republican nomination, in which three top campaign figures—chairman Paul Manafort, son Donald Trump Jr., and son-in-law Jared Kushner—met with a group of Russians who had gotten the meeting by promising Trump Jr. damaging information on Hillary Clinton.

"While President Trump has been dogged by revelations of undisclosed meetings between his associates and Russians," the paper reported, "this episode at Trump Tower on June 9, 2016, is the first confirmed private meeting between a Russian national and members of Mr. Trump's inner circle during the campaign."

The story began on June 3, 2016, when a British music promoter named Rob Goldstone, who had worked a bit with the Trump Organization during the Miss Universe pageant in Moscow in 2013, sent an email to Trump Jr. At the time, Goldstone was representing Emin Agalarov, a Russian singing star who employed Goldstone as a publicist. Emin Agalarov was the son of Russian billionaire Aras Agalarov, who was Donald Trump's partner in staging the 2013 pageant.

In the email, Goldstone told Trump Jr. that a powerful Russian had "offered to provide the Trump campaign with some official documents and information that would incriminate Hillary and her dealings with Russia and would be very useful to your father."

"This is obviously very high level and sensitive information," Goldstone continued, "but is part of Russia and its government's support for Mr. Trump—helped along by Aras and Emin."

Russia and its government's support for Mr. Trump—to some analysts, those were the key words of collusion, along with Trump Jr.'s response: "Seems we have some time and if it's what you say I love it."

It seemed simple, almost cut-and-dried—until investigators started looking into it. Goldstone was a longtime public relations man. He was good at something he called the "publicist's puff," by which he meant the art of using inflated phrases and enticing language to lure his target to accept a meeting. In this case, Goldstone said later, "I puffed it and used some keywords that I thought would attract Don Jr.'s attention. I mean, publicist puff is how they get meetings." Goldstone was happy to talk to investigators about it—not just Mueller's prosecutors, but Senate investigators as well—because he knew the whole thing came to nothing.

When Trump Jr. agreed to the meeting, it turned out the Russians who came to Trump Tower had no dirt on Hillary Clinton but were instead there to advocate repeal of the Magnitsky Act, a 2012 law that imposed tough financial and travel sanctions on Russian officials. Vladimir Putin had retaliated for the Magnitsky Act by banning American adoptions of Russian children, and opponents of the Act often cited the adoption ban in arguing that the Act should be repealed. Indeed, at the meeting, Natalia Veselnitskaya, a Russian lawyer who did much of the talking, gave a lobbyist-like pitch for repeal. That should not have been a surprise, since an American law and lobbying firm, BakerHostetler, was playing a role in this particular anti-Magnitsky campaign.

There is no evidence that anyone proposed a deal: Russian help in the election in exchange for Trump's help in repealing the Magnitsky Act. Instead, the Russians got in the door, began making their pitch, and immediately bored the Trump team to death. As the Russians talked, Kushner texted Manafort—who was sitting in the room with him—the simple message: "waste of time." Kushner also sent a message to two assistants asking them to call him so he would have an excuse to leave. Manafort looked at his iPhone. Less than twenty minutes into it, Trump Jr. told the Russians there was nothing the campaign could do, and perhaps the subject could be addressed later.

When investigators asked Anatoli Samochornov, the man the Russians brought to the meeting to serve as a translator, what Trump Jr. meant by that, he said, "Frankly, if you are asking for my reaction, it was a very polite way of saying, 'Thank you very much. It's time for you to go. The meeting's over.'"

And indeed it was. Veselnitskaya left the meeting disappointed, while the three Trump officials were unhappy that twenty minutes of their time had been wasted. A year later, when news of the meeting broke, it became the most important twenty minutes of the Trump-Russia investigation.

Mueller began probing the Trump Tower meeting as soon as the special counsel's office got up and running. His prosecutors interviewed Samochornov on July 13, 2017. The translator was thought to be the most reliable source of what was said: he was in the room for the entire meeting, he was not affiliated with either side, and he understood what the Russians were saying in Russian and what the Americans were saying in English.

Samochornov was a bust. He did not remember anyone bringing up Goldstone's original email promising dirt on Clinton. He did not remember Trump Jr., Manafort, or Kushner asking any of the Russians any questions. He did not remember anyone mentioning that any sort of information might be provided in the future. He did not remember anyone mentioning Hillary Clinton, or negative information on Hillary Clinton. He did not remember anyone discussing a future meeting. In addition, he testified about a lunch the Russian participants had immediately before the Trump Tower meeting, and he did not remember anyone mentioning Hillary Clinton at that either.

It wasn't a hopeful start for the Mueller team. After Samochornov, prosecutors interviewed two other participants, Rinat Akhmetshin and Irakly Kaveladze, on November 14, 2017, and November 16, 2017, respectively. Mueller also had the written testimony of Veselnitskaya. He had Manafort's notes of the meeting. He had all of the documents and emails surrounding preparations for the meeting and the meeting itself. When the story broke in the press, Donald Trump Jr. publicly released his emails on the matter. The Mueller report later noted that the younger Trump "declined to be voluntarily interviewed" by prosecutors. But Trump Jr. did testify before the Senate Intelligence Committee, the House Intelligence Committee, and the Senate Judiciary Committee, and Mueller had all that testimony. Mueller did not immediately interview Paul Manafort because the special counsel's office was prosecuting Manafort on unrelated financial charges. But Mueller did get to question Manafort after Manafort pleaded guilty to some charges and entered a brief cooperation agreement in September 2018. Mueller interviewed Jared Kushner on April 11, 2018.

Mueller never charged anyone with any wrongdoing of any sort in relation to the Trump Tower meeting.

So, there were the five key examples of "collusion." To the list, Mueller made one addition—an accusation of obstruction arising from press coverage of the Trump Tower meeting—that many saw as a stretch even for a prosecutor determined to find wrongdoing. On July 8, 2017, when the *New York Times* was about to report the meeting, the president, traveling in Europe for the G20 summit, strategized about how his son, Don Jr., should respond. The elder Trump ended up dictating nearly all of a statement to the *Times*, attributed to his son:

> It was a short introductory meeting. I asked Jared and Paul to stop by. We primarily discussed a program about the adoption of Russian children that was active and popular with American families years ago and was since ended by the Russian government, but it was not a campaign issue at the time and there was no follow up. I was asked to attend the meeting by an acquaintance, but was not told the name of the person I would be meeting with beforehand.

White House officials denied Trump had dictated most of the statement. Mark Corallo was unhappy with the statement and was quoted in the *Times* to the effect that the Trump Tower meeting might have been a setup orchestrated by Fusion GPS, the opposition research firm that helped create the Steele dossier and was also working against the Magnitsky Act. Infighting ensued that led Corallo to resign a few weeks later. The bottom line was that the president's actions involved making a statement to a news organization. The statement was accurate, although it did not mention the Goldstone email that started the whole thing. But even if the statement were entirely a lie, it was a statement given to the *New York Times*, not made under oath to prosecutors. It was simply not an act of obstruction of justice. The whole statement episode was a curious footnote to the search for collusion.

As the final months of 2017 approached, Mueller had looked for collusion in all of the obvious places. Not only could he not connect any Trump figures to collusion, he could not establish that collusion had occurred at all. The foundation for the entire investigation—the allegation of conspiracy or coordination between the Trump campaign and Russia—collapsed on itself.

The Trump team, of course, knew that. And that is one reason the two top defense lawyers, Dowd and Cobb, told the president they expected Mueller to be finished by the end of the year. Others were skeptical—"I didn't think it would end quickly," said Jay Sekulow—but word got out that Trump, listening to his team, agreed that it would be over in a matter of months. Cobb even went public. "I'd be embarrassed if this is still haunting the White House by Thanksgiving, and worse if it's still haunting him by year end," he told Reuters on August 18, 2017. "I think the relevant areas of inquiry by the special counsel are narrow."

But the inquiry was not at all narrow, and the investigation was not over by Thanksgiving. It wasn't over by Christmas. Instead, it was taking a new course.

The Bitter End of the Beginning

The change began in the fall of 2017. It was becoming clear to all involved that Mueller and his prosecutors were failing in the search for collusion and were shifting the investigation to a search for obstruction of justice. That meant the investigation would not only not be over by the end of 2017, but might go on for a very long time. Trump's team remembered Mueller's promise not to "let any grass grow under me" even as they watched the grass begin to grow under the special counsel.

The president himself was deeply concerned, and he continued to fret about the effect a continuing investigation would have on his ability to conduct world affairs. For example, on October 27, AP reported that "Anders Fogh Rasmussen, the former NATO chief and adviser to Ukraine's leader, said Russian President Vladimir Putin 'must be laughing right now' at how successfully he's undermined Western democracy." The next night, October 28, Cobb sent an email to Dowd and

Sekulow. "Client just called," Cobb said, referring to Trump. "TV saying Russia must be laughing—it's killing him."

It was just one more indication of how the investigation and surrounding publicity were diminishing Trump's international influence and ability to govern effectively. "We have to keep this moving," Sekulow responded to Cobb a few minutes later. "Keep letting Bob know there are consequences for the country. I know you all keep stressing that. It is real."

A short time later, Dowd emailed the AP story to James Quarles. "Please pass to Bob," Dowd wrote. "I know you are doing your best but this is what the president is putting up with ahead of his critical trip to Asia. Let me know if there is anything I can do to help accelerate your work."

Three weeks later, Dowd sent Quarles another news story, "Russia Vetoes Independent UN Committee Probe of Syria Chemical Attacks." Dowd added the message, "Jim, the President wanted you and Bob to know about this veto by Russia and there has been another chemical attack which will require action." The message was clear each time: This probe is hampering the president. Prolonging it will make things worse. Please wrap it up.

What made the situation more bitter for the Trump team was that they could see that the collusion investigation was going nowhere. "By the end of November, first week of December, Bob was done," recalled John Dowd. "He had exhausted all of the evidence and the witnesses. We knew it, and they knew we knew it. We knew all the facts, and we knew all the witnesses and all the documents. There was absolutely nothing there."

"I think they knew early on they had no case," said Jay Sekulow. "They were just fishing. It was obvious to us they had nothing. So they were going after these rather one-off events so that maybe they could concoct a story with a timeline. That just never materialized, because it didn't happen."

A meeting was scheduled for December 21. The Trump team's position toward Mueller was going to be: it's time for you to wrap this up. But that was not what Mueller had in mind.

"We can do the 21 December and hope we can talk about concluding this inquiry of the President," Dowd wrote to Quarles on December 8. "From what we know, the facts demonstrate this cloud should be removed from his Presidency. He needs to do a full court press on the grave Russian threat without any question about his authority as the leader of this country on the world stage."

Defense notes in preparation for the meeting began with the heading "Purpose: Conclusion of your inquiry of the President," in bold and underlined. Later, there was a sub-heading, "End Game," followed by two notations. The first was "Completion of witness interviews by December 22, 2017," and the second was "Meeting with the SC [special counsel] before end of December 2017." After that, "there is no basis to continue this inquiry and handicap this president," the notes said.

When the meeting began, Dowd outlined the team's position. "We said, 'look, we kept our end,'" Dowd recalled telling Mueller, "'Are you going to hold up your end?'"

The next moment marked an enormous change in the course of the investigation. "Well, you know, if we're going to square our corners," Mueller replied, according to Dowd, "we ought to really talk to the president."

A probe into collusion was one thing—an investigation into the actions of people affiliated in some way with the campaign. But a probe into obstruction of justice was something else—it was an investigation into the intentions of the president of the United States. The next year of the investigation was basically a fight over the president's testimony.

Dowd started the defense right there on the spot. A 1997 District of Columbia Circuit Court ruling known as the *Espy* case—named for Mike Espy, who was Bill Clinton's secretary of agriculture—held that prosecutors could not burden a president with questioning about just anything; they had to show that the information they sought from the president was both important and not available from any other source. Dowd remembered asking Mueller and his team what questions they had that only the president could answer, that met the standard under *Espy*.

"I never got an answer to that question," Dowd said. "I probably put it to him nine times. But I never got an answer...."

The phrase "square our corners" stuck in Dowd's mind. "That's when I first knew we were going to get the stall," he continued. "And we were fucked."

For Dowd, as for the president, the meeting marked the end of the extraordinary level of trust the team had placed in Mueller. They had had a deal. Trump would turn over reams of potentially privileged information to Mueller, saving the special counsel months and possibly years of fighting over access. In return, Mueller would not drag out the investigation as others had done in previous Washington probes.

"We really relied on Mueller's word," Dowd recalled. "And he absolutely busted his word and played all sorts of games from then on. It was stunning to watch."

The end of 2017 marked a "turning point," Sekulow agreed. "It kind of put to bed the whole theory that this was going to end quickly."

CHAPTER FOUR

War

1505 and 1001—The List—The Client—Blow Up—
Rudy Giuliani and the "Public-Private Defense"—The Rest
of the Story—"Holy crap, what's wrong with Bob?"

The Trump team could first see the shift in the interviews. In the summer and early fall of 2017, Mueller questioned witnesses about alleged acts of collusion—the going theory at the time—but by later in the fall and the beginning of winter, he appeared to be moving toward questioning witnesses on alleged acts of obstruction of justice.

As time went on, the witnesses were increasingly from the White House, where Mueller was looking for obstruction. On October 13, prosecutors interviewed Reince Priebus, the former White House chief of staff. On October 16 and 17, they interviewed Sean Spicer, the former White House spokesman. On October 24, they interviewed Jared Kushner, the president's son-in-law who was deeply involved in nearly everything at the White House. On October 31, close White House aide Stephen Miller. On November 1, Kushner again. On November 6, Annie Donaldson, the McGahn aide who had taken such extensive notes on White House meetings. On November 8, they questioned Corey Lewandowski. On November 15 and 16, James Comey. On November 21, Uttam Dhillon, another deputy of McGahn's. On November 30, they interviewed McGahn himself for the first time; he was back for more on

December 12 and 14. On December 7 and 8, they questioned Hope Hicks. On December 14, Stephen Miller was back again.

With the exception of Lewandowski—and also of Comey, the alleged victim of Trump's alleged obstruction—all had worked in the White House during the turbulent months between the inauguration and Comey's firing. That did not mean Mueller did no interviews that touched on the dying collusion allegation. During the same time period, the Mueller team followed up on previous work done on the Trump Tower meeting, on the Republican convention episode, on Carter Page, on George Papadopoulos, and on Michael Flynn. (There was a flurry of activity in late November on Flynn, leading up to his guilty plea on December 1, 2017.) Indeed, much later in the investigation, in late 2018 and 2019, Mueller would go off on one last collusion goose chase involving Trump associate Roger Stone. But by the beginning of 2018, the collusion investigation had mostly become an obstruction investigation. And everyone on both sides of the case knew that an obstruction investigation could last a very, very long time.

It wasn't because of the change of topic, *per se*. It was because a collusion investigation and an obstruction investigation were such different things. Mueller already had all he needed to declare that he was unable to establish conspiracy or coordination—collusion—between the Trump campaign and Russia. But an obstruction investigation would focus on the president's actions and, more important, his intent. What was he thinking when he did X or Y? Mueller said he needed to interview Trump himself to discern intent, while Trump's defenders maintained that the president had already turned over enough evidence for Mueller to conclude that Trump did not obstruct. That disagreement was the source of the battle over Trump's testimony that would consume all of 2018.

Perhaps it was unreasonable to expect that a special counsel investigation could be done in six months, no matter how much the president cooperated, and no matter the faith that most of Trump's legal team put on Mueller's sense of fairness. Things just don't work that way in Washington, particularly in a wildly partisan atmosphere. But Trump's side had something more to fear than just the dynamics of special counsel investigations. What some had come to suspect, but could not know for sure at the time, was that it was not just the direction of the investigation that was changing. There might be something about the special counsel himself that was changing too.

1505 and 1001

In the period after the December 21, 2017, meeting between the president's legal team and the special counsel prosecutors, two numbers became critical to the investigation. The first was 1505, which was shorthand for the federal law, 18 USC 1505, that covered obstruction of justice. The Justice Department's Criminal Resource Manual wrote that the law "forbids anyone from corruptly, or by threats of force or by any threatening communication, influencing, obstructing, or impeding any pending proceeding before a department or agency of the United States, or Congress." The manual further defined the term "corruptly" as "acting with an improper purpose, personally or by influencing another, including making a false or misleading statement, or withholding, concealing, altering, or destroying a document or other information."

The other number, 1001, referred to the law, 18 USC 1001, that covered false statements. The Criminal Resource Manual noted that the law applied to "whoever, in any matter within the jurisdiction of the executive, legislative, or judicial branch of the Government of the United States, knowingly and willfully 1) falsifies, conceals, or covers up by any trick, scheme, or device a material fact; 2) makes any materially false, fictitious, or fraudulent statement or representation; or 3) makes or uses any false writing or document knowing the same to contain any materially false, fictitious, or fraudulent statement or entry." (The defense team sometimes referred to 1001 along with another part of the code, 18 USC 1623, which specifically covered false statements to federal courts and grand juries.)

By the December 21 meeting, it was clear to the Trump defense team that Mueller's prosecutors were zeroing in on 1505 and 1001. Having failed to establish that a conspiracy or coordination existed between the Trump campaign and Russia, they were now focusing on 1505, or obstruction of justice. And they wanted to interview Trump so that, if they failed to establish that obstruction occurred, they might allege a 1001 violation, that is, making a false statement in the interview.

The morning after the December 21 meeting, Dowd sent a note to the team with a few assignments. He asked Sekulow to review cases from the U.S. Circuit Court of Appeals for the District of Columbia on the meaning of "corruptly"—the key word in 1505. He also gave his thoughts on the definition of the word "proceeding" as it appeared in 1505. Dowd had taken the position that the Mueller investigation did not fit under the definition of a "proceeding" in the law and subsequent cases.

"In our negotiations, on the obstruction issue, we win on the law," Dowd wrote. "There was nothing to obstruct since an FBI investigation/ Counter Intel inquiry is not a 'proceeding' within 1505." Dowd quoted from an earlier brief, which included a passage from a law professor, Elizabeth Price Foley, who wrote, "In the almost 120 years since Section 1505 and its predecessor have been on the books, no court appears to have ever held that an ongoing FBI investigation qualifies as a 'pending proceeding' within the meaning of the statute. Instead, Section 1505 applies to court or court-like proceedings to enforce federal law."

"Accordingly," Dowd argued, "the president should not be required to answer any allegations of obstruction." He then asked for a list of people the special counsel had interviewed and re-interviewed; a look at all of the president's tweets on Flynn and the Comey firing; and the text of Comey's congressional testimony. And then he concluded:

> I am still concerned about elevating P's [President Trump's] status from zero to a testifying witness and exposing him to 1001 and/or perjury trap. (Comey v. Trump on whether he said, "I hope you can see your way clear to letting this go, to letting Flynn go. He is a good guy. I hope you can let this go,"

which the President denies saying) so they turn an obstruction case into a 1001/1623 case because he testified about an investigation which is not a "proceeding" as a matter of law.

Makes no sense to me to walk him into that fire. I am bothered that RM [Mueller] is soooo anxious to get him under oath when he has no case to begin with. I say let RM report that there is no obstruction case as a matter of law and no basis to question.

Let the boss testify about no collusion.

That last line pointed to an intriguing but probably impossible option. What if an agreement could be reached under which Trump would be questioned only about allegations of collusion, or some very specific subset of the collusion question, and not about allegations of obstruction? Would Mueller agree to it? Even more important, would Mueller's prosecutors abide by it?

In an early morning exchange of emails on Christmas Eve, Dowd asked Cobb, "I need your view on no obstruction/not a proceeding as a basis to decline testimony."

"Do you have something short on it I could review?" Cobb asked in return. "We need bullets to whittle down the interview but we have to do an interview. I've been explaining that to him for months. No tape though. Insult after Hillary and will leak. Right?" The "insult after Hillary" reference was to the fact that Hillary Clinton's FBI interview in the email investigation was not recorded on audio or video.

Dowd sent some of the arguments from a previous email and added, "RM seemed unprepared on question of P testimony until I reminded him of Espy case. Then he said he could inquire into 'corrupt intent' (not aware it is an element) and the conflict in recollection in the hope conversation. Given the Flynn and Papadopoulos charges RM is too hungry for my money."

"Too hungry for my money." That was how the Trump team was starting to feel about Mueller as 2017 ended.

The List

The new year, 2018, got off to a contentious start. The two sides agreed to hold a conference call on January 8. As it happened, very early that morning, NBC News reported that "initial talks" were underway about a Trump interview with Mueller and that both sides were discussing "potential options for the format." No date had been set, but NBC said it could come "within weeks."

The call included Dowd and Sekulow from the Trump team and Quarles and Goldstein from the Mueller team. Defense notes from the call show that it was nearly all about whether the president would testify, and if he did, under what conditions. For the Trump lawyers who had been thinking about what Mueller had said back on December 21 about "squaring the corners," the call was confirmation that the subject of obstruction of justice and of Trump's mindset had come to dominate the investigation.

The two sides talked hypothetically about a Trump interview. If there were one, where would it be? Trump did not want to go to Mueller, but he also did not want Mueller to come to the White House. There was some discussion about Camp David, possibly at the end of January. There was talk about logistics—White House chief of staff John Kelly was consulted—but the idea never got terribly far. ("We sure as hell weren't going to Camp David," Dowd recalled.) It appears that at no time did all, or even most, of Trump's lawyers want him to do the interview. They would remain opposed for the duration of the investigation.

The prosecutors said they wanted the interview to be videotaped and transcribed. What precise topics, the Trump lawyers asked, did the Mueller team want to question the president about? The prosecutors listed five areas. The notes said: "want to do it efficiently…have the president prepared…maybe give you a high level list of topic areas to be covered. Get 'granular' later."

The first, and by far the most detailed, topic was the Michael Flynn case. Here are Mueller's interests, as they appeared in the defense notes:

Michael Flynn—his contacts with Ambassador K[islyak] dur-
   ing the transition about sanctions
Flynn's Communications with the VP
Flynn's interview with the FBI
Sally Yates' coming to the White House
Meeting on the 15th with Comey
Anything else with Flynn
Awareness of and reaction to investigations by the FBI, the
   House and the Senate
Reaction to the AG's recusal
Reaction to Comey's March 20 testimony—House Intel Com
Conversations with intelligence officials generally

The second topic was the fired FBI director. Again, as they appeared in the notes:

Comey—whom did the president talk to concerning Comey's
   performance?
Did the May 3 testimony lead to his termination?

The third topic was "Kisliak *[sic]*, Laboroth, Lester Holt," which was apparently a reference to the May 10, 2017, Oval Office meeting with Trump, Russian ambassador Sergey Kislyak, and Russian foreign minister Sergei Lavrov. The "Lester Holt" reference referred to the interview the president did with the NBC News anchorman the next day, May 11, 2017.

The fourth topic was "Special investigator—President's reaction to the appointment. His interaction with AG Sessions." And the fifth topic was the press release "about Don Jr.'s meeting in Trump Tower."

It was good for the Trump team to get a short list of Mueller's concerns. But there were a lot of omissions. The list said nothing, for example, about the allegation that the president ordered Don McGahn to tell the deputy attorney general to fire Mueller, even though by January 8 prosecutors had talked to McGahn at least three times. Still, though incomplete, the list was long enough to concern the Trump defense team. Dowd and Quarles, with the occasional contributions of Sekulow and Goldstein, began to discuss where things might go. The defense notes characterized the conversation:

Dowd: Would this be the last interview?

Quarles: No.

Dowd: What's the time frame from the interview to the report?

Quarles: Not weeks. Not years. Months.

Dowd: Would this be the last interview relative to obstruction?

Quarles: Not the last…still some remaining.

Dowd: Are we still in the preliminary interview stage? President is not formally under investigation? This is important to our decision regarding his testifying.

Quarles: A witness, subject, or target?

Dowd: In the context of the manual…where would it be?

Quarles: Best way to say it is, in light of the topics (Trump's active participation)…so he's someone about whom they are inquiring…looking at conduct. Would make him a subject.

Dowd: Talking about the FBI investigations before special investigator appointment…Section 1505…FBI investigation is not a proceeding. Is another statute in play?

Quarles: [No answer]

Dowd: Think about it. The advice to the president depends on it. (Espy). If we advise him not to testify, we will make sure you get the answers to all your questions. Fully transparent is our goal.

Sekulow: Any other subject? Mostly non-collusion issues…

Quarles: Not in connection with this.

Sekulow: Hillary Clinton was not videoed and transcribed.

They went on to cover a few other things. It appeared to the Trump team that Mueller was interested in the extent of Trump's awareness of the various investigations into Trump-Russia matters. The notes said that Goldstein "seemed to reiterate several times the question of when the president became aware of the FBI, House, and Senate investigations." The two sides went over a few more things—Trump's reaction to Attorney General Jeff Sessions's recusal, his reaction to Comey's testimony before Congress on March 20, and his dealings with intelligence officials. With that, the call ended with a promise to talk again.

The Client

There is no simple and accurate way to say precisely what the legal team's opinion was on whether Trump should talk to Mueller's prosecutors. Perhaps the best way to say it is that most of them, almost all of them, opposed it most, if not all, of the time.

But there was someone else involved in the matter, as well: Donald Trump himself. The president had been through a lot of litigation over the course of his career. He had been deposed a number of times. He had spent years talking in high-pressure situations as cameras rolled. He had confidence in his ability to handle an interview. So both in private and in public, he said he wanted to do it.

The president held a news conference on January 10, 2018. By that time, he knew what the lawyers had discussed with the Mueller team two days earlier. He was not terribly positive when asked if he would talk to Mueller. "There has been no collusion between the Trump campaign and Russians," Trump began. "I'll speak to attorneys. I can only say this: There was absolutely no collusion."

"But again, would you be open...."

"We'll see what happens," Trump said. "I mean, certainly I'll see what happens. But when they have no collusion and nobody's found collusion at any level, it seems unlikely that you'd even have an interview."

The next day, January 11, Trump did a long interview with the *Wall Street Journal*, whose reporters asked him repeatedly if he would testify for Mueller. He never answered but instead emphasized repeatedly—and correctly—that he had cooperated to an extraordinary degree with the investigation. "We gave them everything," he said. But he pointedly did not say anything about taking Mueller's questions.

On January 18, Ty Cobb did an interview with CBS News correspondent Major Garrett. Garrett asked, "Is it, from your vantage point right now, a virtual certainty that the president will have some Q&A with the special counsel?"

"That's my belief," Cobb answered. "The president is very eager to sit down and explain to the special counsel whatever responses are required in connection with wrapping up this investigation."

Hearing that, Dowd was surprised and unhappy. "I was unaware you were going to do this interview," Dowd wrote to Cobb, "because we had all agreed last Thursday, including the President, to stay dark and not talk about our communications with SC. Further, your comments were not accurate and undercut our communications with Quarles today. I ask you not to have any further comments on or off the record about this case."

On January 23, the *Washington Post* reported that Mueller was seeking to question Trump "in the coming weeks." The paper said Trump "has told his team of lawyers that he is not worried about being interviewed because he has done nothing wrong." The *Post* said Trump's attorneys supported the idea of sitting down with Mueller, "as long as there are clear parameters and topics."

Trump addressed the matter publicly the next day, January 24, when, as White House chief of staff John Kelly was talking to a group of reporters, he dropped in to take a few questions. The first was obvious: "Are you going to talk to Mueller?"

"I'm looking forward to it, actually," Trump said.

"You want to?"

"Yes, here's the story, just so you understand," Trump said. "There's been no collusion whatsoever. There's no obstruction whatsoever. And

I'm looking forward to it…I would love to do that, and I'd like to do it as soon as possible."

"Do you have a date set?"

"I don't know. No. I guess they're talking about two or three weeks, but I would love to do it. Again, I have to say, subject to my lawyers and all that, but I would love to do it."

Reporters asked if Trump would do the interview under oath. He noted, correctly, that Hillary Clinton did not speak to the FBI under oath but said that he would. "Oh, I would do it under oath, yes, absolutely," he said.

Later that day, a crack appeared in the legal team's position when Cobb told the *New York Times* that the president was "ready to meet with [Mueller], but he'll be guided by the advice of his personal counsel," and that arrangements were still being worked out.

After that, Dowd pulled back. "I will make the decision on whether the president talks to the special counsel," he said. "I have not made any decision yet."

But a decision had to be made, if only a decision not to decide. The story was getting hotter and hotter. As press coverage grew, the Trump team began work on a long letter to Mueller.

As that was happening, a continuing series of leaks increased the pressure on Trump to testify. Before the defense team could finish its letter to Mueller, the *New York Times*, on January 25, published a story, "Trump Ordered Mueller Fired, but Backed Off When White House Counsel Threatened to Quit." The story cited as sources "four people told of the matter." By that time, Don McGahn had already testified to Mueller's prosecutors three times (he would eventually do at least two more sessions). The story was a big flashing sign that people were talking about McGahn's testimony. The next day, Dowd shot an email to Quarles, "The President never ordered or suggested to Don McGahn to fire Robert Mueller. He asked him to discuss the alleged conflicts with DAD/AAG Rosenstein. Don declined. End of story."

Quarles response, ten minutes later: "Got it. Thanks."

Meanwhile, Trump's lawyers were finishing the letter, which would be a comprehensive response to Mueller on the question of testimony. The letter was delivered by hand on January 29. It was detailed—ten thousand words—and it addressed each of the five areas the special counsel lawyers raised in the January 8 conference call.

"After reviewing the list of topics you presented, it is abundantly clear...that all of the answers to your inquiries are contained in the exhibits and testimony that have already been voluntarily provided to you by the White House and witnesses, all of which show that there was no collusion with Russia, and that no FBI investigation was or even could have been obstructed," the lawyers wrote.

On the Flynn issue, and especially the allegation that Trump directed Comey to drop the case, the lawyers noted that Mueller's prosecutors had already interviewed the White House counsel, had already seen the extensive internal memo the counsel prepared on the case, had already seen the chief of staff's notes, had interviewed the chief of staff himself, and had notes and interviews from other members of the White House counsel's office.

"We decline to recommend to the president that he be interviewed on this subject for many reasons," the lawyers wrote. What followed was their "non-exhaustive list" of why Trump would not testify about allegations that he obstructed justice in the Flynn matter:

- First, the president was not under investigation by the FBI;
- Second, there was no obvious investigation to obstruct since the FBI had concluded on January 24, 2017, that Lt. Gen. Flynn had not lied, but was merely confused. Director Comey confirmed this in his closed-door congressional testimony on March 2, 2017
- Third, as a matter of law, even if there had been an FBI investigation there could have been no actionable obstruction of said investigation under 18 USC 1505, since an FBI

investigation is not a "proceeding" under that statute. Since there is no cognizable offense, no testimony is required;

- Fourth, both Mr. Comey and Mr. McCabe subsequently testified under oath that there was "no effort to impede" the investigation. Mr. McCabe's testimony followed Mr. Comey's testimony on May 3, 2017, just six days before his termination, that "it would be a big deal to tell the FBI to stop doing something…for a political reason. That would be a very big deal. It's not happened in my experience."
- Fifth, the investigation of Lt. Gen. Flynn proceeded unimpeded and actually resulted in a charge and a plea;
- Sixth, assuming, *arguendo*, that the president had made a comment to Mr. Comey that Mr. Comey claimed to be a direction, as the chief law enforcement official pursuant to Article II of the United States Constitution, the president had every right to express his view of the case;
- Seventh, your office already has an ample record upon which to base your findings of no obstruction. As such there is no demonstrated, specific need for the president's responses; and
- Eighth, by firing Lt. Gen. Flynn, the president actually facilitated the pursuit of justice. He removed a senior public official from office within seventeen days, in the absence of any action by the FBI and well before any action taken by your office.

In the paragraphs that followed, the lawyers went straight after Comey. The FBI director had written in his memo that Trump told him that Flynn was "a good guy and has been through a lot" and "I hope you can see your way clear to letting this go, to letting Flynn go." The letter pointed to Comey's March 20, 2017, Capitol Hill testimony, when

Republican Senator James Risch of Idaho drilled down on what Trump might have meant in that conversation.

"He did not direct you to let it go," Risch said.

"Not in his words, no," said Comey.

"He did not order you to let it go."

"Again, those words are not an order," said Comey.

"He said, 'I hope,' Risch continued. "Now, like me you probably did hundreds of cases, maybe thousands of cases charging people with criminal offenses, and, of course, you have knowledge of the thousands of cases out there where people have been charged. Do you know of any cases where a person has been charged for obstruction of justice, or for that matter, any other criminal offense, where…they said or thought they 'hoped' for an outcome?"

"I don't know well enough to answer," Comey responded. "And the reason I keep saying his words is I took it as a direction. It is the President of the United States with me, alone, saying 'I hope' this. I took it as, this is what he wants me to do. I didn't obey that, but that's the way I took it."

"You may have taken it as a direction, but that's not what he said," Risch countered. "He said 'I hope.'"

"Those are his exact words, correct," Comey said.

"You don't know of anyone that has ever been charged for hoping something, is that a fair statement?"

"I don't, as I sit here," said Comey.

The letter made a strong argument that the question of obstruction in the Flynn conversation was not so much a matter of what Trump said as what Comey heard. And it would be a miscarriage of justice, the lawyers said, for a prosecutor to accuse Trump of breaking the law based not on what he said but how the FBI director interpreted it.

The lawyers similarly argued that the president had not obstructed justice by firing Comey. First, Trump had the authority to fire the FBI director at any time for any reason. Second, both the Deputy Attorney General (Rosenstein) and the Attorney General (Sessions) "agreed, in writing, that Mr. Comey should be fired, for reasons unrelated to any investigation about Russian interference." Third, Trump said, in the Lester Holt interview, that he expected the FBI's Russia investigation would continue after the departure of Comey and might actually last longer because of the firing. "The president knew, based on the timing of the firing, that his action could actually lengthen the Russian investigation and in any event would not terminate it," the lawyers said.

The letter continued by denying the allegations surrounding the Kislyak-Lavrov Oval Office meeting; allegations Trump pressured intelligence chiefs; and allegations surrounding the July 8, 2017, Donald Trump Jr. statement to the *New York Times* about the Trump Tower meeting.

The conclusion was simple: no interview. "What all of the foregoing demonstrates is that, as to the questions that you desire to ask the president, absent any cognizable obstruction offense, and in light of the extraordinary cooperation by the president and all relevant parties, you have been provided with full responses to each of the topics you presented, obviating any need for an interview with the president."

The lawyers were also telling Trump what they were telling Mueller. "By the end of January, Jay and I had decided and told the president there wasn't going to be any testimony," said Dowd. Trump, as he usually did, said he was ready to answer any questions, but deferred to their judgment. "There was no way, as long as I was walking around, that we were going to let the president answer questions," Dowd said.

At the same time, Trump had read the January 29 letter and approved of its substance and tone. To further convince the president that submitting to an interview would be a bad idea, Dowd tried something he had not done before. "One Saturday, I took him through just a few questions, because he was reading the letter, and he really loved it," Dowd recalled. The problem was, Trump was so consumed by the other aspects of the presidency—trade, China, Russia, the economy, and everything else—that he had not focused on the details of the case until he read the letter. "So I just very casually started asking him a few questions about Flynn," Dowd continued, "and it was no surprise, by the third question, he needed his recollection refreshed, because there was no way he remembered something as insignificant as that." An interview with Mueller's prosecutors could turn those insignificant details into the basis for a false statements charge against the president, even in the absence of any underlying crime. In Trump's life, the Flynn case simply did not loom as large as it did in the press coverage. "In his daily affairs, it's just not a big deal," Dowd explained. "I could tell, there's no way he is going to remember all this stuff. That gave me confidence that our judgment was right. Plus the law was clear. It would take weeks to prepare him because he would have to put aside everything else."

It was not publicly known, but on a fairly regular basis, Dowd and Quarles met personally, usually to take a walk around the building housing Mueller's office in a Southwest Washington office complex called "Patriots Plaza." Meeting that way helped both relax and stay away from prying eyes and ears. Meanwhile, passersby had no idea the two 70-something men walking and chatting were negotiating matters of political life or death for the president of the United States. In a February talk, Dowd told Quarles that the presidential interview was not going to happen. Not at Camp David, not anywhere. "I met with Jim privately and said, 'Look, he's not going to testify," Dowd recalled. "Don't get your hopes up. It's not going to happen.'"

But that wasn't the end of it. Mueller did not want to give up. A decision was made that everyone should meet and talk it over.

Blow Up

It was what Jay Sekulow referred to as "the moment," meaning the time when Mueller's prosecutors got serious about asking—or demanding—that the president testify. The moment arrived when the two sides met at Mueller's office on March 5.

Everybody was there. The Trump team strategy was to listen to what the prosecutors had to say but to keep putting the burden back on them to prove why it was absolutely necessary to interview the president.

"It was a little different from other meetings," Dowd recalled. "I kinda got in Bob's face."

The idea was to put pressure on Mueller by stressing Trump's cooperation. "He answered the following questions," Dowd recalled. "Bob, did we give you everything you asked for? He said yes. Did any of the witnesses, like 34–35 witnesses, did anyone lie? No. Is there anybody else you want? No."

"We thought we ought to square the corners and talk to the president," Dowd recalled Mueller saying.

"What is the question that only he could answer?"

"Well, I want to know if he had corrupt intent."

"When?"

"When he fired Comey."

"Bob, you have all of the notes of contemporaneous conversations with the president in and around the time Flynn was let go and Comey was let go. You couldn't do any better.... Go look at the notes—very copious notes that have been delivered to you in real time—and you've got your answer. And before you get to corrupt intent, you've got to have corrupt intent to do what?"

"To obstruct this probe."

"Well, how can he obstruct the probe when we've made 35 witnesses available and 1,200,000 records?"

The conversation was not going well. And then it got worse.

"There came a time when Bob said, 'You know, John, we can always get a grand jury subpoena,'" Dowd recalled. A subpoena, which would inevitably lead to a titanic battle in the Supreme Court over whether Mueller had the authority to compel Trump's testimony, would be the Mueller investigation version of going nuclear.

"That was it for me," Dowd recalled. "I hit the table with my hands and I stood up and I said, 'Bring it on. Let's go. I can't wait to move to quash that damn thing. We'll take it all the way to the Supreme Court, and I want to hear you tell the district judge what the question is that you haven't answered. We're going to give the district judge copies of everything we gave you. Go ahead, pal.' I was really pissed.

"I said, 'Look, what basis do you have to do it?'" Dowd continued. "'We're not afraid of a grand jury subpoena. You want to do it, you've got yourself a war, and you're going to lose it.'"

"He said, 'John, take it easy, calm down,'" Dowd remembered. "I said, 'Look, you just threatened the President of the United States with a grand jury subpoena. Up to this time we've been operating on a god-damn handshake. It was a great fucking relationship.'" That period of trust, Dowd said, was clearly over.

Cooling down, Dowd suggested to Mueller that they go over the evidence on obstruction. "He said, 'John, I'm going to have to go back and look at all that,'" Dowd recalled Mueller saying. "I said, 'Are you telling me that you're in this meeting and you're not prepared to discuss the case about the President of the United States? Is that what you're telling me, Bob Mueller?' I didn't get an answer to that. He was purple in the face. It was such bullshit.

"I lost all respect for Mueller on March 5," Dowd said. "As a man, as a Marine, as a lawyer."

Not long later, Dowd and Sekulow went to the White House to tell Trump about the meeting. Dowd could not hide his disappointment in Mueller—and his regret at having advised the president to trust the special counsel in the investigation's early days. "Jay and I went back to the president and I told the president, I said, 'You ought to fire me,'" Dowd recalled. "'The guy's a goddamn liar. He didn't keep his word.'"

On the main issue at hand, there is no doubt the team made a strong case against Trump testifying. But they faced two problems after the March 5 meeting. The first was that Mueller would not back down; it is not unfair to say that the rest of the investigation, a full additional year, would be dominated by wrangling over the testimony question. So Dowd and the team did not settle things that day.

The other problem was the client. Although the lawyers would talk to the president, and would make the case against agreeing to appear, Trump never stopped believing that he could handle testifying. And he was particularly aware of the political consequences of not testifying. He knew he would be roasted in the media each night—what was new?—if he avoided answering questions. But Dowd remained strongly opposed, and that created friction between the two. There was also the fact that in 2017 Dowd had believed the case would wind down by the end of the year. Trump, listening to Dowd, believed that, too, and became frustrated that the case not only did not end but seemed ready to stretch out for a very long time.

Dowd resigned on March 22. Like so many who leave a job with the president, he remained in touch with him afterward, kept good relations, and is friendly with him today. But he was gone as the president's lead lawyer. He left feeling sure, then as now, that his position against Trump's testimony was correct.

"Stop here a second and just think," Dowd said. "If I had agreed to an interview, he would have been indicted for perjury. There's no way you can avoid this gotcha game. There's just no way. And it would have been the end of his presidency. They would have gotten him. And as it turns out, that's all they were about."

Rudy Giuliani and the "Public-Private" Defense

The Dowd resignation marked a formal recognition that the president had been unhappy with aspects of his legal strategy for several months. He had thought the investigation would be over by the end of 2017, but by the spring of 2018, there was no end in sight. In addition, the legal battle was being fought in memos and private arguments with Mueller's office. The lawyers weren't on TV every night defending the president. To supplement his legal strategy, Trump developed an informal public relations strategy, relying not on lawyers but on associates outside the White House who could make the case for him in the media that the legal team could not.

On a fairly regular basis, Trump would talk to those associates and direct them to make this or that point in media appearances. "Our value to the president is our ability to go on TV and drive a narrative that he wants driven," one of those associates said of that time. "Being on the outside, we can say things that people who work in the building [the White House] cannot. While we're speaking to the president, he's like, you need to go out and remind everyone that Mueller has a conflict [and] that this is a bunch of Democrat operatives and Democrat government employees who contributed to Hillary Clinton or were at her election night party. Those are valid, valid concerns for someone who is being investigated by the opposition party. His team couldn't do that because Cobb and Dowd had to supposedly work with the Mueller team to end this."

The arrangement—lawyers arguing on the inside, allies speaking on the outside—went on for months. Then Trump made the inside-outside strategy official with the arrival of Rudy Giuliani.

The former New York City mayor went back a long way, at least thirty years, with Donald Trump. They saw each other a bit back when Giuliani was in office, and Trump was one of his most famous constituents. They ran into each other from time to time after that. Giuliani always felt Trump was a political supporter and a friend—not necessarily a close personal friend, but more than just an acquaintance.

The relationship got closer over the years. "I have a tremendous debt of gratitude to Donald," Giuliani explained, "because when I went through my divorce, there was a period of time when my son was really mad at me, and [Trump] brought him back. He explained to my son how things were sort of equal in a divorce, and about four or five years ago, we got back together. There is a personal dimension to Trump that I know that actually makes me feel bad when it doesn't come across, or when he is attacked."

Trump was attacked a lot when he got into the presidential race in 2015. Giuliani did not believe he would really run, but when he did, the two men started talking regularly. Giuliani pointed out some areas where Trump clearly needed help—for example, after seeing the now-famous picture of Trump with his foreign policy team, including George

Papadopoulos, Giuliani thought, "We've got to do better with foreign policy experts." Giuliani was also put off by the extraordinary level of negative coverage of Trump.

When the Russian accusations started, Giuliani felt instinctively they were nothing. "I knew, 1,000 percent certain, that it was a big lie," he recalled. "Because I was with him. And he's a very open man. I heard his phone calls. He makes them right in front of you. If he were doing some kind of deal with the Russians of that kind of magnitude, number one, I would have known it, and number two, he would have bragged about it."

Giuliani saw Trump less during the transition and after he became president, but the two still talked once or twice a week. They talked quite a bit in August 2017 after Giuliani took a fall and seriously injured his knee. The recovery took a while, giving Giuliani time not only to talk to Trump but also to look at the Mueller investigation, by then in high gear. Giuliani—who also counted John Dowd as a friend—was carefully watching the Trump legal team.

Giuliani saw some value in the Trump cooperation strategy. For one thing, the I-already-gave-you-everything maneuver essentially laid the groundwork for Trump's refusal to sit down with Mueller's prosecutors. But Giuliani also worried about the more public side of Trump's defense. There was a flood of leaks about the case, and media commentary was heavily slanted against the president. Trump's lawyers had their hands full fighting the inside game, while Mueller went virtually unchallenged in the press. Who was playing the outside game for Trump?

"When you get to the beginning of 2018, I thought they were making a mistake in defending him," Giuliani recalled. "I thought that they were doing the usual criminal defense. Don't say anything bad about the prosecutor. Don't say *anything*, because a grand jury has to decide, and the prosecutor has all the power. But put on a very competent defense. Cooperate with him completely. I wasn't sure I agreed with that. But more than that, I could see a rationale for cooperating completely, but I couldn't understand why they weren't publicly defending him. Particularly since there would be no trial, and there would be no grand jury. This was all about impeachment and public perception. And the public perception was that he was guilty and that Mueller was a hero. And I thought if that remains, the Democrats will have an easy path to impeachment."

To Giuliani, the former prosecutor, the Mueller investigation was always about impeachment. And that meant it was about politics. There was a war for public opinion going on during the investigation, and Trump was losing it. "So I kept discussing with them, you've got to defend him every time a new allegation comes up," Giuliani continued. "We have to have five people on television explaining it's bullshit and why it is. And we've got to go after Mueller. We've got to tear him down. He's no saint. He's got an entirely Democratic staff. He treats people—we can't use the word Nazi SS, but it's pretty damn close to the Nazi SS."

At the end of March 2018, Giuliani and Trump had dinner, just the two of them, at Mar-a-Lago. Giuliani laid out the changes he would make if he joined the defense team. "I said it's going to be a different kind of defense," he told Trump. "We're going be on television every night, and it will be me and everybody else I can get, and we're going to take them down. The first thing to say is Mueller is not a cardinal. He's done a lot of bad things in this case. And he's got some people who are working for him who are animals. The public has to know that."

Giuliani also stressed that he wanted to make sure Trump never sat down with the Mueller team for an interview, particularly about obstruction of justice. "They are specialists in trapping you in perjury," he told the president. "That's what they do for a living, as you can see with Flynn. Andrew Weissmann is well known for doing that. And he has a bunch of people there who are not just Democratic lawyers—they are Democratic nuts."

Giuliani and Trump talked through early April. Adding Giuliani would put the legal team on a war footing. One event that convinced them that was necessary occurred on April 9, when the FBI raided the office and hotel room of longtime Trump lawyer Michael Cohen. Mueller, it seemed, was on a war footing, too.

The raid angered the entire defense team. "They said, this is a real double cross," Giuliani recalled. "You're asking us to tell our guy to come in and in good faith answer questions, and you go out and arrest his lawyer? Are you guys crazy?"

"That caused a real ruckus," Giuliani continued. "And I think it also caused a re-thinking within the Trump team of whether we should play more hardball. We were not conducting this investigation by the Marquess of Queensbury rules."

Trump announced Giuliani's addition to the team on April 19. That was his formal commitment to Giuliani's public-private defense strategy, with Giuliani handling the public battle. That same day, two other lawyers, the husband-and-wife team of Marty and Jane Raskin, joined the team. The Raskins, based in Florida, had a long record of success in defending white-collar criminal cases. They would handle the private side, fighting a mostly out-of-view battle with Mueller's prosecutors over the question of Trump's testimony.

On April 24, the new team had a get-acquainted meeting with Mueller and his staff. It would turn out to be the only time they met Mueller face-to-face during the duration of the investigation. After the introductions and opening talk, the meeting turned to the question of an interview. What quickly became clear was that the Mueller people believed the door was still open.

"They wanted to talk about the mechanics of the interview," recalled Jane Raskin. "How long it would be, where it would take place, what the parameters would be, would it be videoed." But the Trump team had no intention of discussing logistics for something the president had never agreed to. They took a step back and said that of course logistics could be arranged if there were to be an interview, but why do you need this? Why do you need to interview the President of the United States?"

At that point, Mueller and some of his staff said that they needed to know what the president was thinking, that they needed to know his motives when he did certain things. The defense team—all of whom, except for Sekulow, were meeting with Mueller for the first time—was taken aback. A prosecutor wasn't entitled to that sort of interview in an ordinary obstruction case, much less in a case involving the president, whose office carries with it additional privileges and considerations.

The meeting went nowhere, devolving into an argument on the question of testimony—an argument that continued long after the meeting. The Trump side never slammed the door shut to any testimony at all; there was the possibility, however slight, that Trump might answer some questions on a very limited portion of the investigation. But the defense never agreed to anything. For its part, the Mueller team escalated the urgency of its request.

Raskin and Quarles exchanged letter after letter. At one point the Trump team proposed that Mueller give them a "reverse proffer," in which the Mueller team would meet with the Trump team to go through the case and show the strength of their evidence and show why an interview was absolutely necessary.

"They would tell us nothing," recalled Raskin.

Underlying the argument was the possibility that Mueller would give up on persuading Trump to talk and resort to a subpoena against the president. Ever since Mueller himself had broached the possibility months ago, his lawyers made sure that threat was just below the surface. "It started with, 'We need to know within two weeks whether you will agree to an interview with the president,'" Raskin recalled. "Then letters back and forth. And then, 'We've been talking about this for a long time. We need an answer very shortly.' Then it escalated to, 'if we do not hear from you with an affirmative agreement to the terms we have suggested, we will have to consider other legal process.' Eventually, they literally threatened a subpoena."

The problem for Mueller was the Trump team was prepared for just that possibility. That is what "the moment" was all about: preparing to argue, certainly to the Supreme Court, that Mueller could not prove the need for presidential testimony.

It was nerve-wracking, but the Trump lawyers were also confident. They were confident because they knew Mueller had nothing to accuse the president of on the Russia part of the investigation. He had no underlying crime to charge. The fight went on and on, but when the Trump lawyers asked Mueller to put some cards on the table, to show the evidence that made a presidential interview an absolute necessity, the prosecutors always balked. For Trump, that was a good sign.

So, in the end, it did not matter what the president said publicly about wanting to testify. In private, his lawyers were fighting—and winning—the battle over testimony. "Every client wants to testify," Giuliani recalled. "And the smarter they are, the more they want to testify. And almost always, they get into a trap. I mean, Martha Stewart. Or General Flynn."

The Rest of the Story

The fights over obstruction and Trump's testimony dominated news coverage of the Mueller probe. But the Mueller team also spent much of 2018 working around the edges of the Trump-Russia affair. None of his indictments ever alleged the existence of a conspiracy or cooperation between the Trump campaign and Russia to fix the 2016 election. And the most prominent case Mueller brought, against former Trump campaign chairman Paul Manafort, had nothing—absolutely nothing—to do with the core allegation in the Trump-Russia investigation.

Mueller indicted Manafort and top deputy Rick Gates on October 30, 2017. Both had worked for years as political consultants in Ukraine, and as such had dealt with pro- and anti-Russian Ukrainians. That was entirely legal, but the problem came when Manafort was paid. He devised a variety of schemes using foreign banks to avoid paying taxes in the United States on what in the end added up to about $30 million in income. Most of the charges against Manafort related to that, and also to his failure to register as a foreign agent. The charges—for example, that he failed to file reports on his interest in foreign bank accounts and engaged in money laundering in 2011, 2012, 2013, and 2014, as well as that he failed to register as a foreign agent between 2008 and 2014— ended before Manafort became involved in the Trump campaign, and, indeed, before there even *was* a Trump campaign.

Manafort and Gates were charged with something called "Conspiracy Against the United States," a name chosen by the Mueller team. In the Justice Department's U.S. Attorney's Manual it is known as "Conspiracy to Defraud the United States." That would have been a much more descriptive title, since Manafort was accused of using a variety of schemes to hide income and avoid taxes. But "Conspiracy Against the United States" had a whiff of treason about it, and the Mueller prosecutors used that as the title.

The Mueller team seemed to want to make an example out of Manafort. That was clear on July 26, 2017, when FBI agents staged a guns-drawn raid on Manafort's home in Alexandria, Virginia, just before dawn. Manafort and his wife were asleep in their bedroom when the armed agents came through the door. (They had gotten a key from a Manafort associate.) The purpose of the raid was to execute a search warrant for documents relating to Manafort's finances. But the message from Mueller was simple: we will break you. Cooperate now.

Manafort was eventually convicted of evading taxes and failing to register as a foreign agent. He actually did those things. But for Mueller, the case was always about more than that. The special counsel wanted to pressure Manafort to spill the beans on Trump on a hoped-for charge of conspiracy or coordination between the Trump campaign and Russia.

It never worked, because there was no conspiracy or coordination between the Trump campaign and Russia. But Mueller kept the pressure up through 2017 and 2018. After all, if there had been a collusion scheme, who would have been in on it, if not Manafort? For a while, Manafort seemed to be the key to everything, and Mueller had great leverage against him. It's just that there was nothing to get.

Nevertheless, the Manafort case took up at lot of the Mueller team's time. There was the October 30 indictment. Then, on February 22, 2018,

Mueller filed additional financial charges against Manafort. The next day, February 23, a grand jury handed up another indictment. That brought on a new round of legal wrangling as Manafort's lawyers sought to have the indictment dismissed. On June 8, Mueller brought still more charges against Manafort, still without alleging conspiracy or coordination. On August 21, Manafort was found guilty of most of the original charges against him. On September 14, he pleaded guilty to some of the later charges and entered into a short-lived cooperation agreement. The case spilled into 2019, with February and March being taken up with Manafort's sentencing.

Gates was easier for Mueller to deal with. He pleaded guilty on February 23, 2018, and began a long period of cooperating with the special counsel. But he never pleaded guilty to—and was never charged with—anything alleging conspiracy or coordination with Russia.

The other big case that took Mueller's time was the investigation into the Russians who hacked into the emails of the Democratic National Committee and Clinton campaign chief John Podesta. On February 16, 2018, Mueller indicted thirteen Russian nationals and three Russian entities, including the notorious Internet Research Agency, for the election interference. "Defendants posted derogatory information about a number of candidates, and by early to mid-2016, defendants' operations including supporting the presidential campaign of then-candidate Donald J. Trump and disparaging Hillary Clinton," the indictment read. "Some defendants, posing as U.S. persons and without revealing their Russian association, communicated with unwitting individuals associated with the Trump campaign." In July, Mueller indicted twelve Russian military officers as part of the same operation.

The indictments got a lot of attention in the media. But as with all of Mueller's charges, they did not allege collusion. And the Russian defendants were in Russia, where they would never have to answer the indictment. Building on the work done by the Intelligence Community, Mueller had done a good job of documenting the Russian effort. But it meant nothing for the case against Trump.

Then there was Flynn, a case that stretched beyond the life of the Mueller investigation but never involved charges of collusion. And then Mueller appeared to have landed a blow against Trump when prosecutors in the Southern District of New York reached a plea agreement with Michael Cohen on August 21, 2018. But Cohen's big offense was evading taxes on $4.1 million in income, mostly from his taxi medallion business. He also pleaded guilty to a campaign finance violation for arranging Trump's payoff to porn star Stormy Daniels, and one count of lying to Congress. But in none of the charges did Mueller allege a collusion plot. Later, Mueller would indict and convict a close Trump associate, Roger Stone, on charges of lying to Congress. But here again, he did not allege a collusion plot.

Then there were the smaller cases. There was Richard Pinedo, a man who sold bank account numbers to the Russians attempting to meddle in the election. There was Alex van der Zwaan, a lawyer who had done some research for Rick Gates. There was Konstantin Kilimnik, a former business associate of Manafort's. There was Papadopoulos.

In the end, Mueller indicted thirty-four people and those three Russian entities, for a total of thirty-seven indictments. Seven of them were convicted or pleaded guilty. The charges against Flynn were ultimately withdrawn.

Mueller partisans often pointed to that record as proof of the extraordinary success of the Mueller investigation. But twenty-five of the indictments were against Russians who were beyond the reach of U.S. law. The remaining dozen were proof of shady financial dealing by some close Trump associates. But the Mueller investigation was about collusion, and none of the charges alleged collusion, more formally known as conspiracy or coordination, between Russia and the Trump campaign. That is what the investigation was about, and what Mueller's prosecutors failed to find.

"Holy crap, what's wrong with Bob?"

Throughout the investigation, Robert Mueller received overwhelmingly positive coverage in the press. He was the straight-shooting, just-the-facts prosecutor who knew everything and would reveal all once his investigation was over. No one suggested, or at least no one publicly suggested, that Mueller might not be the man everyone remembered when they heaped praise on him at the time of his appointment. No one suggested that the super-sharp lawyer of 2004 might have lost a step since those days. Seventy-three years old when appointed, Mueller appeared to be one of those Washington Masters of the Universe who work well past the age at which many people in the rest of the country retire. Certainly there were men his age and older working at the highest levels of the Washington legal world.

But to leap forward in the story, when Mueller testified before Congress on July 24, 2019—when his report was done and published—many who knew him in the old days were stunned by what appeared to be a dramatic slowdown in his cognitive abilities. He did not react quickly. He did not react sharply. He seemed not to follow the hearing's back-and-forth carefully. He was a different man from that of the early 2000s.

That caused those old associates to look back over the course of the investigation. When had they last seen and talked to Mueller? Might he have begun slowing down even before he took the special counsel assignment? If so, did his acuity diminish during the investigation? And if so, did that mean his top aides—those partisan Democrats over whom Mueller was supposed to be sternly riding herd—took an increasingly influential role in the investigation? People started going through their memories, trying to fit things together.

Chris Swecker spent twenty-four years in the FBI, including a couple running the bureau's Criminal Investigative Division. He left the FBI in 2006 with the highest respect for his old boss. "He was super sharp," Swecker remembered. "He reminded me of professors I had in law school where you'd be in a meeting and you might or might not get called on, but if you did get called on you damn well better be prepared. He covered everything. He was on top of everything. He was a micromanager from the start." Swecker estimated he was in perhaps two meetings a day with Mueller for more than two years.

Swecker left the FBI in 2006. In the fall of 2016, working in North Carolina, he invited Mueller to speak at a conference. Mueller flew from Washington, and Swecker met him for breakfast to brief him on the event. He noticed something he had never seen in his old boss. "I remember telling my wife after the breakfast that he's slipping," Swecker recalled. "You could tell the acuity was not there, and he was walking kind of slow, and he looked a little frail. He was a little confused about what to do after he got off. It was clear to me that his mental acuity was slipping."

Swecker emphasized that the event went well, that Mueller delivered a good speech and handled the Q&A. So Swecker was pleased when, a few months later, in May 2017, he heard that Mueller would be the special counsel. "I thought he was the best man you could possibly pick for that job," Swecker said. "When I was around him, he was apolitical. I mean, he was agnostic, and would not allow any political conversation to permeate anything we did. And I thought he was principled." Still, Swecker thought back to the conference in 2016 and wondered whether Mueller was up to it.

Friends and colleagues who had known Mueller for years were concerned about him, too. His decline was not a sudden, precipitous thing; they had witnessed a very gradual process in the years preceding his appointment as special counsel. Some thought of it when they heard that Mueller had been chosen to do the investigation; some believed he should never have accepted the job.

Mark Corallo was a Mueller fan even as he worked for the Trump defense team. After his early exit in July 2017, Corallo returned to his political communications business and awaited a call—not from his old colleagues, but from Mueller. Prosecutors wanted to question him about the events of July 8, 2017, when the president helped draft a statement in response to the *New York Times* report of the Trump Tower meeting. There was a lot of internal debate about the statement, including input from Corallo, before it was released. At some point, Mueller would want to question Corallo about it.

The interview happened on February 15, 2018, at Mueller's offices. The questioning was professionally done and unremarkable, Corallo thought. "So at the end of the interview, Mueller came in and shook my hand and put his hand around my shoulder and said, 'It's good to see you,'" Corallo recalled. "He said, 'I'm sorry you got dragged into this.' When he left the room, and they were waiting to put me in a car to leave, I said to Andrew Goldstein, 'Hey, how's he doing?' They said great. I said, 'Well, he looks a little gaunt. Is he eating? Is he tired?' They said, 'No, he's running circles around us.' This was the first time I noticed that he was not physically robust."

Nearly a year and a half later, watching Mueller testify on television, Corallo was taken aback. "When I saw him testifying, it was significantly more apparent," he recalled. "And trust me, I was not the only one. Those of us who worked with Bob at the Justice Department after 9/11 and watched his testimony—the phone calls were flying. 'Holy crap, what's wrong with Bob? Is he sick?'"

Rudy Giuliani did not join the legal team until March 2018 and had his only significant meeting with Mueller in April. Beyond that, Giuliani recalled, "I had no contact with him. None of us did until it was over." Mueller was hard to get on the phone; a more common experience was to talk with Quarles, who would say, of whatever issue was being raised, "We'll take it to Bob."

Giuliani recalled that in his one meeting with Mueller, the special counsel didn't seem familiar with a key Justice Department policy. (It was the Office of Legal Counsel opinion that a sitting president cannot be indicted, a policy that would play a critical role in the Trump case.) "There were a couple of other little facts that came up—it didn't seem like he knew about them," Giuliani remembered, "and they [Mueller's staff] would lean over and tell him."

"Bob said, 'I'll have to get back to you on that…' and it was apparent that he didn't know what we were talking about," Giuliani said.

Jane Raskin remembered that meeting, too. When the Office of Legal Counsel opinion came up, she recalled, "Bob said, 'I'll have to get back to you on that.'" It was extraordinary that Mueller was not pre-pared to talk about such an important issue. At that point, an aide stepped in to assure the Trump team that prosecutors were aware of the issue and would get back to them. They later confirmed that they planned to follow OLC policy.

"After that, we never met with Mueller and we never spoke with him on the phone," Raskin recalled. "It was all Jim Quarles and Andrew Goldstein."

Giuliani kept in touch with Dowd after Dowd left the team, and the two sometimes discussed Mueller's demeanor. "I said, 'John, I'm really surprised about how little he knows about the case,'" Giuliani recalled. The issues weren't really that complicated, and Mueller had been in it for a year. Giuliani thought Mueller was perhaps just not giving it his all. "John said, 'I had the same impression,'" Giuliani remembered. "He said, 'I think he sort of retired, he came back to do this, and now he probably regrets it.' I said okay—and that's what I would have told you the day before he testified." The day Mueller appeared on Capitol Hill, Giuliani saw something entirely different. He began to believe Mueller had suffered cognitive decline.

Later, Giuliani looked back on some of the key moments in the investigation and believed that Mueller's condition contributed to how they played out. In particular, he looked at the trust the first legal team put in Mueller. "Dowd had a lot of faith in Mueller and felt that Mueller was telling him the truth," Giuliani recalled. "I don't think he calculated the fact that Mueller was working with half a deck, and a bunch of scumbags were running the operation."

It was only reasonable for Trump team members to look back over their experiences during the investigation and wonder whether Mueller was really in charge. "What's galling to me in hindsight, knowing what we know, is that they dragged it out as long as they did," said Corallo, "which says to me that people other than Bob Mueller were running that investigation."

Jay Sekulow, who lasted the entire probe, saw that something was up. "Bob at the end was AWOL," Sekulow recalled. "That was the great con. He showed up for cameo appearances. He was the Wizard of Oz. He was back behind the big curtain, pulling some strings here and there, but when you pulled the curtain away, he wasn't even really the one pulling the strings."

CHAPTER FIVE

Impeachment 2.0: Waiting for Mueller

Seventy Democrats—The Waiting—"Stay away from that word"—"Impeach the motherfucker"

O n Capitol Hill, the drive to impeach Trump in 2017 was the work of a motley crew of Democrats with a grab bag of reasons for removing the president. Should Trump be impeached for violating the Emoluments Clause? For dividing the country? For insulting the NFL? As the year ended, Republicans found it hard to take the Democratic would-be impeachers seriously. "I still thought it was a fringe movement on their side," said Republican Representative Steve Scalise. Democrats had no compelling reason to impeach the president and, as the minority party, they had no power to make it happen.

Both of those things changed in 2018. As the year went on, Democrats began to focus the impeachment issue on Mueller. They said everyone should wait for the special counsel to finish his investigation. They projected a sense of caution and deliberation. They focused on protecting the Mueller probe from "interference" by Republicans. They believed, correctly, that Mueller's prosecutors were working to the Democrats' benefit. Just as Antonin Scalia had predicted so many years before, the special counsel's office had become the *de facto* investigative arm of

Congress as Democrats waited for Mueller to give them a bill of particulars they could turn into articles of impeachment.

Of course, they could do that only if they won control of the House in the midterm elections, coming in November 2018. Democratic leaders developed what proved to be a strikingly effective two-part, public-private strategy. The public part was to downplay impeachment. The election was not about removing the president, they said on the stump. It was about health care and jobs and issues that most concerned American voters. The private part of the strategy was to prepare for impeachment.

The private side became apparent as soon as the party picked up forty-plus seats to win control of the House, when an intense battle erupted over who would chair the House Judiciary Committee. On one side was Representative Jerrold Nadler, the veteran lawmaker from New York City who played a role in defending against the Bill Clinton impeachment in the 1990s, and who just happened to have a feud reaching back decades with the city's most flamboyant real estate developer, Donald Trump. On the other was California Representative Zoe Lofgren, who was close to Nancy Pelosi, and had also defended against the Clinton impeachment. She had even participated in the Richard Nixon impeachment as a young House staffer.

Who would win? "Within the first two weeks of transition, Jerry Nadler was saying, I want to be Judiciary chairman because I can lead impeachment," recalled Republican Representative Doug Collins, who would become the ranking minority member on the committee. "Coming out of the election, he was having to solidify his hold on the chairmanship. His argument, which we heard many times, was that he could lead impeachment."

Nadler got the job. By the end of the year, he was preparing to take over the committee and begin the work that would lead to impeachment. It was a far cry from Representative Al Green's lonely crusade in 2017. As 2018 moved on, impeachment became a real, and serious, thing.

Seventy Democrats

In January 2018, that was still in the future. In the House, the year started like the previous year ended, with Green calling for Trump's impeachment. His arguments were mostly the same, but he added a new one: Trump should be removed from office because he reportedly referred to some nations as "shithole countries."

"I refuse to accept what the president is doing," Green said on January 17. "I refuse to accept it because if you tolerate something, you will not change it. You will do little to change it. I am going to do everything that I can to change it, and it is within my power as a Member of the Congress of the United States of America to bring articles of impeachment against the president for what he has done. I have done it before, and I will do it again and again and again."

Indeed, he did. The next day, Green spoke as a "liberated Democrat" and promised new articles by the following day. He noted that just a month ago, he got fifty-eight votes for impeachment, and now "the time is ripe for additional articles." Green's new articles would "associate commentary made in the highest office in the land with the policies that are produced," an apparent reference to the "shithole countries" remark.

On January 19, Green read his new articles aloud. They were mostly old—Trump should be removed because of the travel ban, military transgender policy, and comments about Charlottesville. And then:

> On January 11, 2018, Donald John Trump held a meeting with a bipartisan group of congressional leaders that focused primarily on legislation that would provide a statutory protected status for individuals brought to the United States without documentation. At this meeting, as has been widely published, Donald John Trump made references to people from s-h-i-t-h-o-l-e (or s-h-i-t-h-o-u-s-e) countries. He also questioned why we need more Haitians or people from African countries, proclaiming that we should take them out. Donald John Trump then suggested that Norwegians were

better suited to be immigrants to this country, thereby casting contempt on citizens and noncitizens who were welcomed here by previous presidents due to natural disaster and civil unrest, thereby attempting to convert his bigoted statements into United States policy, associating the presidency and the people of the United States with bigotry, inciting hate and hostility, and sowing discord among the people of the United States on the basis of national origin.

Republican House leader Kevin McCarthy immediately moved to table the impeachment motion. A vote was taken on that motion to table. As it had been in December, the vote was on whether to put aside impeachment. In December, Green got fifty-eight votes in support of moving impeachment forward. This time, just a few weeks later, he got sixty-six.

Some of the same prominent Democrats who voted in favor of impeachment did so again—John Lewis, Maxine Waters, Jamie Raskin, and others. A few who voted for impeachment in December did not do so in January. Others who did not vote for impeachment in December did so in January. Adding up all those who voted for impeachment either in December, or January, or both, seventy Democrats were on the record supporting the impeachment of President Trump. Al Green was nowhere close to a majority, but his movement was growing.

Still, the Democrats' party leadership remained opposed. Citing the lesson of the Republicans' failed impeachment of Bill Clinton in 1998–1999, Minority Leader Nancy Pelosi rejected impeachment, as did second-in-command Steny Hoyer. Democrats who came from districts that Trump had won in 2016 worried about alienating voters before the 2018 midterms. Forcing Democrats to vote on impeachment was a "terrible plan," Representative Cheri Bustos, a Democrat from Illinois, said in an interview with former Obama aide David Axelrod. "I was very disappointed that it got to the point where we had to vote on impeaching the president at a time where we've got an investigation going on. Just let that play out, see where it leads. The truth comes out in the end."

There were obvious divisions among Democrats, and most of them opposed impeachment. Still, McCarthy took notice. Seventy votes are not nothing, especially when Democratic leaders were trying to stop the impeachment drive altogether. "Pelosi's out there saying no," McCarthy recalled. "She and Steny are saying no to it. But it's just building. So I started thinking, after that January 19 vote, I'm starting to think they're going to get the horses riled up, and they're not going to be able to rein them in."

The vote also forced McCarthy to re-think his assessment of Democratic motives. Before January 2018, he saw the impeachment rabble-rousers as ambitious politicians who were exploiting an issue to win support from the Democratic base. McCarthy, a Californian, noted that there were three Californians on the Intelligence Committee—ranking minority member Adam Schiff, Jackie Speier, and Eric Swalwell. It was conventional wisdom at the time that the elderly Democratic Senator Dianne Feinstein would not run for re-election in 2018. McCarthy interpreted the actions of Schiff, Speier, and Swalwell as three Democrats jockeying for position to replace Feinstein.

"They were all thinking back in 2017 that Feinstein wouldn't run again," McCarthy recalled. "So they really started going after it [the Trump-Russia investigation], and I think it's to get attention in the Democratic Party." (As it turned out, all of them were wrong; Feinstein ran for reelection and won.) "It did not dawn on me that these people are believing this stuff," McCarthy continued. "I thought they were playing games. And then sometime after that January 2018 vote, I thought they will really do it, if they get the majority."

Ten days after the vote on Green's articles, another group of Democrats re-introduced the Steve Cohen articles from a few months earlier. They would have impeached Trump for allegedly obstructing justice in the Russia investigation; violating the Constitution's Foreign Emoluments Clause; violating the Domestic Emoluments Clause; undermining the rule of law; and undermining the freedom of the press. No action was taken; the measure never got a vote.

Outside the Capitol, Green and his allies were taking a beating from fellow Democrats, and also from erstwhile Republican NeverTrumpers, who thought the impeachment talk was damaging the Democrats' chances of winning control of the House in November. "Any Democrat mentioning the word 'impeachment' on the campaign trail should have their campaign funds pulled by the Democratic Party," MSNBC host and former Republican congressman Joe Scarborough tweeted on February 11. "I remember 1998 too well. Republicans thought their attacks on Bill Clinton would lead to a GOP landslide. But impeachment talk backfired, Democrats outperformed all expectations and it was Newt Gingrich who got run out of town."

Al Green was not one to let criticism go unanswered, and so on February 14 he went to the floor to take on Scarborough. "I am such a candidate," he said. "I have talked about impeaching the president, and I will continue to talk about impeaching the president." Green said he would not be intimidated by TV hosts, and he would keep speaking out. "I will bring articles of impeachment to the floor of the House of Representatives again if conditions require it," he said. "I am not afraid."

Green's force of seventy pro-impeachment lawmakers was still a minority of the House's 194 Democrats. But it showed that more than one-third of the party conference was willing to go on record supporting the impeachment and removal of the president. As for the other 124 Democrats, it would not be accurate to say they opposed impeachment on principle, or that they supported Donald Trump. The reason for their position was that, as much as they might have agreed with Green in their hearts, they believed that in 2017 he was simply jumping the gun, and in 2018 he was hindering the party's emerging Trump-Russia strategy: *Wait for Mueller.*

The Waiting

Democratic Representative Emanuel Cleaver of Missouri was a longtime ally of Al Green. They both entered the House in 2005 and had been friends since then. They had co-sponsored legislation. Appeared together at events. Fought political battles alongside each other. But on April 25, Cleaver took to the floor to denounce his friend's action on impeachment.

"When there were articles of impeachment placed on the table for a vote, I voted to table it against a person I have known in Congress longer than I have known anybody else," Cleaver said. "He had brought it to the floor. I voted to table it, along with just about every Republican and a sizeable number of Democrats, and the reason was, I believed that it was important for Mr. Mueller to complete his investigation. I resent any discussion about trying to impeach the president. I am not in that group."

Cleaver's statement represented not only a personal divide with Green, but also a divide inside the Congressional Black Caucus, a key organization in early impeachment efforts. Nearly two-thirds of the CBC supported impeachment by the beginning of 2018. For many, impeachment represented a way to punish Trump not only for what he had done as president, but for what he did before running for the White House.

Cleaver, a former CBC chairman, understood that quite well. "I don't know if the people around the country understand that [Trump] has launched...an assault against African-American people starting with his refusal to accept the first African-American president, by continuing to declare that he was from Kenya," Cleaver told *The Hill* in early February 2018. "We've come to conclude that this is a part of his belief system."

Still, Cleaver held to the strategy of waiting for Mueller. In late 2018, he told the *Kansas City Star* that he was "resisting the call of impeachment" and "fight[ing] off the urge to impeach" until Mueller issued a report.

At the same time, Democrats were united in trying to stymie Republican efforts to learn more about the Trump-Russia investigation, and especially its origins. Throughout 2017, House Intelligence Committee chairman Devin Nunes investigated those origins and discovered, among other things, that the FBI had used the Steele dossier as a evidence to seek a court warrant to wiretap Carter Page. Then there was the revelation that top FBI official Peter Strzok, detailed to work on the Mueller investigation, had shared anti-Trump text messages with Lisa Page, another top bureau official with whom Strzok was having an extramarital affair. Then there were all the irregularities surrounding the Michael Flynn case.

That left Republicans wanting to know whether the Mueller probe truly had a legitimate basis or whether it was based on gossip, disinformation, and political opposition to Trump. In trying to find answers, Nunes and his GOP colleagues faced stonewalling from the FBI and the Justice Department; getting information from them took herculean effort. It did not matter that Nunes was a Republican and the Justice Department was run by a Republican; the Department hunkered down and resisted scrutiny no matter where it came from.

On June 28, the ongoing debate over Mueller flared in somewhat different form when Republicans pushed a bill that would, in their words, "insist that, by July 6, 2018, the Department of Justice fully comply with the requests, including subpoenas, of the Permanent Select Committee on Intelligence and the Committee on the Judiciary relating to potential violations of the Foreign Intelligence Surveillance Act by DOJ personnel." The Republicans wanted answers on why Carter Page had been spied upon. The FBI wiretapped Page after presenting evidence to the Foreign Intelligence Surveillance Act, or FISA, court. That evidence included parts of the Steele dossier, which were unverified—some were ridiculous on their face—and had no business in a surveillance warrant. Now Republicans were trying to find out whether the Justice Department had abused FISA in the Page case.

"We have requested information from DOJ," said Republican Representative Jim Jordan, a member of the Judiciary Committee. "They haven't given it to us. We have issued subpoenas. They haven't complied with subpoenas. We have caught them hiding information.... Enough is enough. Give us the documents we are entitled to have. Let's have the full weight of the House behind a resolution saying you have got seven days to get your act together."

It all made sense to Republicans, but Democrats saw the GOP as trying to meddle in the Mueller investigation. After all, Page was an important player in the search-for-collusion part of the probe. The opposition party in Congress is normally very inquisitive about the workings of the executive branch, but in this case, Democrats argued that Congress had no right to know what was going on in the investigation. "This resolution is premised on a demand for documents to which Congress is not entitled and which the Justice Department cannot give," Jerry Nadler said in debate that day. "We are not entitled to information that goes to the core of an ongoing criminal investigation. If they somehow bully the Department of Justice into turning over materials that go to the core of special counsel Mueller's investigation, that information could and probably would be shared with the subject of the investigation, namely, President Trump."

The resolution was "a Republican attempt to delay and derail the Mueller investigation," said Democratic Representative Hank Johnson of Georgia.

"Wake up, my colleagues, and do your jobs," said Representative Adam Schiff, who would lead impeachment the next year. "Wake up and end this duplicitous attack on the Department of Justice and the FBI and our special counsel."

"God bless the United States, and may we protect Robert Mueller," said Tennessee Democrat Steve Cohen.

As Cohen's remarks suggested, the fight over impeachment now included a fight over protecting Mueller. But protect him from what—or from whom? Leaders of both parties warned the president against firing Mueller; many Republicans believed such a move would be a political disaster for Trump. But Democrats went farther, warning Republicans not only against firing Mueller, but also about trying to learn how the Mueller investigation, and the FBI probe that preceded it, began. Normally curious overseers like Nadler were decidedly uncurious about how the whole thing started. Don't ask questions, they told Republicans; wait for Mueller.

"We'll have to see what Mr. Mueller discovers," said Nancy Pelosi.

"We should wait for the investigation to conclude," said Representative Ted Lieu.

"Let Robert Mueller do his job and let's wait for the report to come out," said Representative Cheri Bustos.

One of the reasons rank-and-file Democrats were so determined to wait for Mueller was that they believed he had something. Their own intelligence expert, the Intelligence Committee's ranking Democrat, Adam Schiff, had been telling them for more than a year that there was "damning" evidence of collusion, and that the evidence was "more than circumstantial." "I think there's plenty of evidence of collusion or conspiracy in plain sight," Schiff said on CBS on August 5, 2018. He conceded that it might not be "proof beyond a reasonable doubt of a criminal conspiracy," but he made very clear something very big was there.

But there wasn't. It would be two years before the public learned that key officials had already told the House Intelligence Committee, including Schiff, that they had seen no definitive evidence of collusion. Back in July 2017, James Clapper, President Obama's head of national intelligence, told the committee, "I never saw any direct empirical evidence that the Trump campaign or someone in it was plotting [or] conspiring with the Russians to meddle with the election." Schiff knew that the whole time, even as he strung along his colleagues and the press.

In addition, the collusion talk in the House flourished months after Mueller's investigators had confronted the reality that they could not establish that conspiracy or coordination—collusion—had occurred. Talks between the special counsel's office and the president's defense had moved on, far beyond collusion, focusing instead on alleged obstruction of justice.

But Schiff and his fellow House Democrats kept the collusion hope alive. They followed a simple, and effective, formula: appear cautious, judicious, and reluctant to act against the president. But keep stoking the fire.

"Stay away from that word"

The one thing that had the potential to change the entire dynamic of 2018 was the November election. Democrats had an excellent chance to take control of the House—history alone predicted a big pick-up for the party out of power during a president's first midterms. With a Democratic majority, impeachment would quickly turn from Al Green's pipe dream into a reality.

But how to handle the issue on the campaign trail? Should Democrats campaign on an elect-me-and-I'll-impeach-Trump platform? Or should they stay away from the issue and keep their true intentions to themselves?

The polls presented a dilemma. To select one representative survey, a poll in early September from CNN found that 78 percent of Democrats wanted the president impeached and removed from office. Just 16 percent opposed impeachment. (The rest were undecided.) A large number of independents—48 percent—also wanted Trump impeached, while only 8 percent of Republicans did.

Clearly, if Democrats were campaigning only for Democratic votes, they would run on a platform of bringing the president down. But that is not the way elections work, and senior Democrats became deeply worried that if the party seemed to be running on an impeach-Trump platform, moderate Democrats, independents, and persuadable Republicans might all be turned off.

Pelosi, who stood to serve a historic second term as Speaker if Democrats won, told everyone to shut up about impeachment. Instead, she urged a nuanced strategy in which Democratic candidates campaigned on bread-and-butter issues and also vowed to hold Trump "accountable." In an August 22 "Dear Colleague" letter to all House Democrats, Pelosi declared the party "must remain focused on our strong economic message for the people." That meant candidates should stress three things: "1) Lowering health care costs and prescription drug prices; 2) Increasing workers' pay through strong economic growth by rebuilding America; and 3) Cleaning up corruption to make Washington work for you."

Republicans had created "a cesspool of self-enrichment, secret money and ethical blindness" in Washington, Pelosi said. "While House Republicans enrich themselves and their special interest cronies, they continue to turn a blind eye to the corruption and criminality at the heart of President Trump's inner circle, and are working relentlessly to undermine special counsel Mueller and the FBI.... The special counsel's team and the prosecutors in New York are conducting thorough and professional investigations, and they must be allowed to continue free from interference. Republicans must end their complicity, join Democrats in protecting special counsel Mueller and affirm that no one is above the law.

"It is our duty as members of Congress to seek the truth, and hold the president and his administration accountable to the American people, and we will," Pelosi wrote.

Nowhere did Pelosi mention what had become known as the I-word. Her memo became the formula for Democrats on the stump: health care, prescription drugs, wages, and accountability.

The beauty of the "hold Trump accountable" formulation was that it was up to voters to decide what "accountable" meant. To that 78 percent of Democrats who already wanted Trump impeached and removed, "accountable" surely meant impeachment. To others, it might mean something short of impeachment and removal from office. That was the elegance of Pelosi's plan. Each voter could interpret the message as he or she liked.

Pelosi's position frustrated pro-impeachment Democrats. Tom Steyer, the billionaire who would later run unsuccessfully for the Democratic presidential nomination in 2020, founded a group called Need to Impeach, which lobbied party officeholders to stress impeachment in their campaigns. Steyer was frustrated by the Democrats' reliance on the word "accountable." It was a dodge for impeachment. Yes, candidates could use it, but they should not shy away from the fact that "accountable" meant "impeachment."

"Democratic base voters respond strongly to messaging urging public accountability for Donald Trump, including initiating impeachment proceedings against him," Steyer's group wrote in an August memo to candidates. "The main question is why are Democrats refusing to talk about impeachment when 70 percent or more of our base voters believe it should happen."

But Pelosi and her Democratic allies had a better sense than Steyer of where voters were. They also had a better idea than some Republican candidates and strategists. Some in the GOP were expecting Democrats to come out guns blazing for impeachment, allowing Republicans to stand in defense of Trump and the existing order. They were more prepared to do that than defend, say, their vote to repeal and replace Obamacare.

"Democrats kept impeachment in the background," recalled Representative Doug Collins. "I would agree with them when they say they campaigned in swing districts on health care. They caught many of our candidates off guard on the debacle of the health care votes in the Senate and House. A lot of our guys couldn't explain in a simple format how they voted, and unfortunately, it caught a lot of our folks off guard."

Collins made another, more subtle, point about the Democratic de-emphasis of impeachment. Democratic candidates did not have to talk about it to put it in the public's mind. It was already there, courtesy of many media outlets. The Russia investigation, Russian collusion, the president is a Russian agent—those were messages voters heard every day. They didn't need to hear Democratic candidates pounding away at the same thing. They were already getting it from most of the news networks and big media organizations.

Still, Collins's first point was vitally important in the 2018 campaign. Republicans were ill-prepared to defend their Obamacare vote, and Pelosi and her Democratic candidates were well prepared to attack it. Republicans also did a poor job explaining the benefits of the tax bill they had passed. And talking about impeachment—that is, accusing Democrats of preparing to impeach Trump if elected—appealed only to their base, which already supported Republicans.

"We did focus groups in several competitive districts just before the election where we asked, 'What do you think is going to happen?' and people said, 'They're going to impeach the president,'" said one Republican strategist who advised a number of House campaigns. "It was no surprise to any Republican that this was going to be the outcome of a Democratic House."

Perhaps the top Republican talking about impeachment was the impeachment target himself—President Trump. He traveled around the country in late summer and fall campaigning for Republicans, and he frequently veered onto the topic of impeachment.

"Maxine Waters [said] 'He will be impeached. I will impeach him,'" Trump said in a speech on July 5, in Great Falls, Montana. "Even the Democrats are saying, 'How are you saying that?' They don't want to use that word, because it gets the Republicans out to vote. They say, 'Stay away from that word.'"

On September 6, again in Montana, Trump said, "This election you aren't just voting for a candidate. You're voting for which party controls Congress. Very important thing. Very important thing. I don't even bring it up, because I view it as something that, you know, they like to use the impeach word. Impeach Trump. Maxine Waters, 'We will impeach him.' But he didn't do anything wrong. It doesn't matter, we will impeach him. We will impeach. But I say, how do you impeach somebody that's doing a great job that hasn't done anything wrong? Our economy is good. How do you do it? How do you do it? We will impeach him. But he's doing a great job. Doesn't matter. Remember that line. He's doing a great job. That doesn't matter, we'll impeach him. It's a hell of a place in Washington."

On October 9, in Council Bluffs, Iowa, Trump discussed Democratic plans to take revenge on newly confirmed Supreme Court Justice Brett Kavanaugh. "Last week, they're saying, we'll impeach him," Trump said. "Impeach him for what? For what?"

The audience booed. Then Trump continued. "Besides, I have to go first, right?" The crowd laughed. "Even though we've done nothing wrong, other than create one of the greatest economies in the history of our country. That will be interesting. You get impeached for having created the greatest economy in the history of our country. The Democrats have become too extreme. And they've become, frankly, too dangerous to govern. They've gone wacko."

A few days later, the *New York Times* picked up the Council Bluffs speech in a story, "Is Trump on a Collision Course with Impeachment?" with the subheading, "Democrats are largely ducking the topic on the campaign trail, but few people in Washington doubt that it will be on the table if they win the House." Reporter Peter Baker noted that, "The elected Democratic leadership has been reluctant to talk about it, out of worries of a public backlash or playing into Mr. Trump's hands. But it is hard to imagine Democrats not going there if they take the House, given the enormous pressure from their liberal base to at least open an impeachment inquiry."

Election night, November 6, was a disaster for Republicans. Democrats gained a net forty seats—they defeated Republicans in forty-three GOP seats while losing just three of their own in the House of Representatives—and won the majority for the first time since 2010. Pelosi faced some opposition for the speakership but ended up winning handily.

And at that moment, impeachment, under wraps through much of the campaign, came out of hiding. There were about sixty days between election night and January 3, 2019, when the new House would be sworn in. Top Democrats, especially Schiff, the new chairman of the House Intelligence Committee, and Nadler, the new chair of the Judiciary Committee, used that time to prepare investigations designed to lead to impeachment sometime in 2019.

Just hours after the Democrats' victory, Nadler unwittingly revealed part of the party's plans. He was riding the Amtrak Acela from New York to Washington and spent the entire trip talking on his phone to colleagues and advisers about what his committee would do in coming months. Nadler was sitting in one of the seats that face a table, a place where many passengers choose to work. What he did not know was that the woman sitting across the table and to the side was Mollie Hemingway, a journalist for the conservative Federalist website. Nadler's conversation was so loud that Hemingway could hear both Nadler and the person on the other end. She took notes on her laptop as Nadler spoke.

"He was having several conversations about how they had figured out that impeachment did not poll well, and how they had come up with the term 'accountability' to be the way that they would talk about impeachment," Hemingway recalled. "They would say, we just want to hold Trump accountable, we're not out to impeach him."

On the other hand, "He said on one of the calls that they were going 'all-in' on Russia, and he said it in another call, too," Hemingway said. Nadler explained that he was heading to Washington for a two-day session with staff to figure out what the game plan would be. One caller asked something to the effect of, "Why don't you start on impeachment tomorrow?" "He said we have to see what happens with Mueller, it all depends on what they find during the Mueller probe," Hemingway recalled.

But Nadler would not be leading that effort, even though the Judiciary Committee was the traditional place to begin impeachment proceedings. According to Hemingway, Nadler explained to his caller that Schiff's Intelligence Committee would take the lead on the Russia investigation because it had a head start on the subject. Nadler's panel would look into impeaching Kavanaugh. Still, the Judiciary Committee would "have a role" in the Russia probe, Nadler said.

Nadler's conversations on the train that day—just hours after Democrats declared victory—were proof that, as much as they talked about health care and prescription drugs and wages, Democrats were in fact planning all along to build a structure for impeaching the president once they took power. The Schiff-Nadler arrangement was already in place before Election Day. All it needed was a majority, which voters gave Democrats on November 6.

Some Republicans were surprised. Steve Scalise and others knew the intensity of feeling about impeachment on the Democratic side, but believed Pelosi and other party leaders would keep it isolated and controlled. "I still thought it was going to be something that a few of their members would pursue," Scalise said, "but that it would stay within a limited element of their caucus."

The Democrats first day in power showed how difficult that would be.

"Impeach the motherfucker"

As Scalise foresaw, Pelosi tried to maintain an air of caution throughout the transition period. "We have to wait and see what happens with the Mueller report," she said on January 3, 2019, the day the new Democratic House was sworn in and the day she officially became Speaker. "Let's just see what Mueller does."

The tone of restraint did not last twenty-four hours. On the night of January 3, as Democrats and their supporting groups celebrated across Washington, one of the new Democratic members of the House, Representative Rashida Tlaib of Michigan, attended an event sponsored by the left-wing activist group MoveOn. Tlaib was already receiving a lot of attention as the first Palestinian-American woman elected to Congress. She would become, along with Representatives Alexandria Ocasio-Cortez, Ayanna Pressley, and Ilhan Omar, a member of "The Squad"—a group of young, mediagenic freshmen, all far to the left, and all unhesitant to challenge the authority of not just the president but their party's leadership as well.

As the MoveOn event wound down, Tlaib began to tell what sounded, in the beginning, like a warm and touching story about her son. Celebrating her victory, she said the boy looked up at her and said, "Mama, you won—bullies don't win." Tlaib then related her response: "I said, 'Baby, they don't, because we're gonna go in there and we're gonna impeach the motherfucker!'"

No one had to ask who the motherfucker was. Just as they had often been embarrassed by Al Green, Pelosi and other Democratic leaders were embarrassed that a high-profile freshman would speak so frankly in public. But hours before Tlaib spoke, on the first day of Democratic control of the House, another Democrat, Representative Brad Sherman, filed a resolution of impeachment, renewing the cycle begun by Al Green. But this time, in 2019, with Democrats in power, everyone knew things would be different.

Republicans could see what was coming. Of course, they could not envision the precise form impeachment would take, but they could see it on the horizon. Listening to Tlaib, Representative Chris Stewart had two reactions. "One was that the language was so foul it could only be driven by hate," Stewart recalled. "And the other was, it's good to know what these new members are here for."

CHAPTER SIX

The Report

The Indictments Tell a Story—Seventy-One Questions—
"The infamous March 5 meeting"—Volume One—
Volume Two—"We won, they lost"

September 17, 2018, was a key date in the Mueller investigation, although no one in the public knew it at the time. On that day, Mueller formally surrendered in the Great Testimony War. The special counsel's prosecutors had threatened, huffed, and puffed, but in the end they chose not to subpoena the president. Instead, they accepted Trump's offer to answer written questions. September 17 was the day they submitted those questions to the president. The testimony fight was officially over. Trump won.

The months leading up to the agreement were filled with various "bombshell" media reports about supposedly critical developments in the case. There was the report that Michael Cohen was prepared to testify that Trump knew about the infamous Trump Tower meeting ahead of time; that came to nothing. There was the report that Rod Rosenstein had suggested wearing a wire to the Oval Office to record Trump as part of an effort to invoke the 25th Amendment to remove the president from office; that was true, but the wire was never worn. There was the Manafort trial; the subject of collusion never came up.

Whatever their accuracy, the reports amounted mostly to a continuing level of noise surrounding the investigation. The real action was the duel between the Mueller and Trump teams over the president's testimony.

The Indictments Tell a Story

The key moments in the testimony fight had been the Trump team's letter to Mueller on January 29, 2018; the March 5, 2018, meeting that included John Dowd slamming the table, rising to his feet, and declaring that there would be "war" if Mueller attempted to subpoena the president; and the leak, on April 30, 2018, of an old list of questions, created several months earlier, that the Mueller team wanted to ask Trump. By the summer of 2018, the debate was essentially over. There were more discussions about topics, but the two sides never got seriously close to reaching an agreement on testimony. It just dragged on.

Here is what hobbled Mueller from beginning to end: he could not find collusion. When prosecutors said they wanted to interview Trump, they could not point to a crime that formed a reason so compelling that they would be able to meet the standard for interviewing the President of the United States. When the subject turned to obstruction, their inability to find collusion put them in the position of alleging that Trump impeded an investigation into something that did not happen. The problem underlying it all was the failure to find collusion.

What was striking was that Mueller's weakness was there for all to see, and yet his ongoing failure did not receive much attention in the press. Mueller indicted seven Americans, and in none of those cases did he allege that they took part in a conspiracy or coordination with Russia to fix the 2016 election. It was apparent from the prosecutor's very first cases:

1. Paul Manafort and Richard Gates, who were indicted on October 30, 2017, on charges of tax evasion, bank fraud, and failure to register as a foreign agent, among other things. Prosecutors detailed Manafort's

extravagant spending, like a $15,000 ostrich coat, but left out any accusation that Manafort or Gates played any role in any conspiracy or coordination between the Trump campaign and Russia.

2. George Papadopoulos, who pleaded guilty, also on October 30, 2017, to making false statements to the FBI. The indictment did not allege that Papadopoulos played any role in any conspiracy or coordination between the Trump campaign and Russia.

3. Michael Flynn, who pleaded guilty, on December 1, 2017, to making false statements to the FBI about his phone calls with the Russian ambassador during the transition. Flynn was deeply involved in shaping the Trump campaign's foreign policy positions. If there were a conspiracy between the campaign and Russia, it is hard to believe Flynn would not have been involved or would not have known about it. In addition, he was required to testify at length as a condition of his plea agreement. But Mueller, with all Flynn's information, did not allege that there was any conspiracy or coordination between the Trump campaign and Russia.

By the end of 2017, Mueller had indicted three key figures in the Trump campaign—Manafort, Gates, and Flynn—and one bit player, Papadopoulos. None of the charges involved a conspiracy or coordination between the Trump campaign and Russia, the discovery of which was, after all, Mueller's main assignment.

Mueller brought no more charges until February 2018. On February 16, he indicted the thirteen Russian nationals and three Russian entities, as well as small fry Richard Pinedo for unwittingly providing bank numbers to the Russians. On February 20, he indicted lawyer Alex van der Zwaan on charges of lying about his work with Richard Gates. On February 22, he filed more charges against Manafort. None of these indictments or charges involved allegations of conspiracy or coordination.

Mueller did not charge anyone else until June 2018, when he brought still more charges against Manafort and also charged Manafort associate Konstantin Kilimnik. Still there were no conspiracy allegations. On July 13, Mueller indicted thirteen Russian military officers, but made no allegation of a conspiracy with any Americans. In August, Michael Cohen pleaded guilty to tax evasion, bank fraud, and other charges brought by Justice Department prosecutors in the Southern District of New York. (Mueller had handed off the case to the New York office, a sure sign that the Cohen investigation did not involve issues inside Mueller's area of concentration.) Cohen also separately pleaded guilty to a Mueller charge of lying to Congress about the timing of the abandoned Trump Tower Moscow project. Yet again, Mueller did not allege conspiracy or coordination between the Trump campaign and Russia.

In some cases, Mueller's prosecutors issued what were known as "speaking indictments," that is, indictments that told a story, that contained more than the minimum information necessary to level charges against a defendant. And yet in all those indictments, Mueller not only did not allege that this or that Trump figure was part of a conspiracy or coordination—he never alleged that any conspiracy or coordination took place at all. The situation could not have been clearer: Mueller had not found collusion.

Trump lawyers tried privately to explain that to reporters and commentators in the media. Look, they said, if Mueller had found a conspiracy with Russia, wouldn't he have included it in the indictments? Manafort, Flynn, Gates, Papadopoulos, Cohen, somebody? If they were not in on a collusion scheme, who was?

The argument got nowhere. In the media debate, the discussion of collusion raged with greater and greater heat, even as Mueller's failures mounted. The talk was particularly intense on the cable networks CNN and MSNBC, which were deeply invested in coverage of the Trump-Russia investigation. Two representative examples of the coverage were MSNBC's *All In with Chris Hayes* and CNN's *Anderson Cooper 360*, on May 1, 2018, the day the *New York Times* reported that old list of possible questions for Trump.

"Tonight on All In," Hayes said as the program began, "The clearest window yet into the Russia probe and signs that Mueller already has evidence of collusion.

"We've already seen a ton of evidence of collusion, and Mueller's questions indicate it's all very much a focus of his investigation," Hayes added. "Mueller's questions on collusion show that it's likely Mueller has already identified crimes involving collusion."

Hayes and the show's guests noted that Trump had repeatedly denied collusion and had, in fact, made "no collusion" something of a mantra. Do not believe it, one guest said; Trump was just trying to "work the refs." Over the course of the program, the word "collusion" was uttered thirty-six times.

On CNN, legal analyst Jeffrey Toobin, also working off the *Times* report, declared flatly, "This is an investigation about collusion." Toobin continued: "The fact that the president keeps saying over and over again, there was no collusion, there was no collusion, that has not been established and in fact there is lots of evidence that collusion did take place, starting with the infamous meeting in Trump Tower where Donald Trump Jr. sought to get dirt on Hillary Clinton from the Russian government. That is collusion right there, and that's just the beginning."

"They are looking at questions of collusion, whether the White House, the president wants to admit it," added CNN White House reporter Jim Acosta. Over the course of the program, the word "collusion" appeared thirty-one times.

The problem was that the commentary was outdated. Mueller had essentially finished looking for collusion more than six months before these broadcasts. But Trump's lawyers' protests, their requests that journalists simply look at the charges Mueller had brought, fell on deaf ears. There was always something new and spectacular to come that would prove beyond any doubt that Donald Trump was guilty of collusion.

Seventy-One Questions

Even as the media commentary went down the collusion rabbit hole, behind the scenes Mueller's failure to find collusion was shaping the argument over the president's possible testimony. Trump's lawyers specifically fashioned a defense that sought to exploit the weaknesses in Mueller's position.

In the simplest terms, the Trump team argued the law on obstruction and the facts on Russia. On obstruction, they argued that Trump, as president, had the authority under Article II of the Constitution to fire Comey. He had done nothing that could reasonably be construed as criminally obstructing the Russia investigation and had, in fact, cooperated with the special counsel to an extraordinary degree. On the Russia investigation itself, they argued that there were simply no facts to support the theory that the Trump campaign and Russia conspired or coordinated to fix the 2016 election. In addition, they put forward the overarching argument that without any evidence of an underlying crime, Mueller never got close to meeting the standard required for a presidential interview as set out in *Espy*.

If one had to briefly characterize the Trump team's argument to Mueller, it would be: you got nothing.

Trump's lawyers knew what was on that old list of questions the special counsel wanted Trump to answer—the defense team had actually compiled them, based on a meeting with Mueller's prosecutors back in December 2017. (Who leaked them? Someone on the extended Trump team, either in the core group of lawyers or the lawyers with whom Trump had a joint defense agreement.) There were fifty-two questions in all, thirty-seven on issues involving obstruction and fifteen on issues involving collusion, and some were extremely broad and general.

Trump's lawyers did not believe the list merited serious consideration. "We asked, 'What crime are you investigating?'" Jane Raskin recalled. "You're asking the President of the United States to come in and give you an interview on these so-called Russia topics. But before you ask for that, you ought to be at a point in your investigation where you're close enough to making a prosecution or declination decision—regarding our client or somebody else—that you need his testimony to complete your work. That's the whole point of *Espy*. It's not enough that you would really like to sit down and talk to the President of the United States about these random issues, contacts with Russia. You've had how much time? Over a year to look at this stuff? You haven't gone anywhere—why do you need him?"

Raskin got no response. "It was just crickets," she recalled.

By mid-2018, the Russia questions were along the lines of "squaring the corners" in anticipation of a final report, to use Mueller's term. The defense team noticed that prosecutors made fewer and fewer inquiries related to Russia. "In retrospect, they were done with Russia," Raskin recalled. "They were done with Russia long before we came in. They knew there was nothing there. And they never said anything to us that indicated otherwise."

A new topic would arise occasionally to rekindle interest in Russia—Michael Cohen's testimony that the never-begun Trump Tower Moscow project remained a live possibility longer than he had previously said, or allegations about Roger Stone and WikiLeaks. But those topics also came to nothing, and Mueller's focus went back to where it had been since the end of 2017: obstruction of justice.

The reason prosecutors gave for requiring Trump's testimony focused entirely on obstruction—Mueller said he needed to know what Trump was thinking about the Flynn case, about Comey, the Lester Holt interview, and more. Prosecutors said they needed to know Trump's state of mind in order to know whether he acted with the intention of impeding the investigation.

In response, the Trump team argued that the White House had given Mueller everything he needed to know about Trump's actions and motives, including the testimony of more than thirty witnesses—many of whom observed Trump close-up—plus 1.2 million documents. In addition, unlike the subjects of most ordinary obstruction investigations, Trump had done countless media interviews and made public statements in which he discussed why he did what he did. That, the Trump team said, was more than enough for Mueller to understand the president's motives.

The interview argument continued, both in private and in public. Giuliani played his role as Trump's public advocate—on one day in

August 2018, he and Sekulow actually guest-hosted all three hours of Sean Hannity's radio show—while the other lawyers kept the pressure on Mueller in letters and phone conversations. There were two main areas of conflict. One was the issue of whether Trump would submit to an in-person interview or just answer questions in writing. The other was whether Trump would be questioned on obstruction as well as Russia-related issues.

The key to the defense team's position was their view of Trump's authority as president. The obstruction allegations were invalid, they argued, because they involved Trump using powers granted to him by Article II of the Constitution. Trump's lawyers believed it would set a dangerous precedent if they allowed prosecutors to interview a president to probe his motives for clearly constitutional exercises of his authority. On the other hand, the Russia allegations concerned events that happened before Trump became president. Trump would be willing to answer questions on those. On that subject—collusion—the president's defenders knew Mueller had nothing; they had read all the indictments. So they argued that while Trump could theoretically answer questions about events that occurred before he became president, Mueller, because he could not even allege that collusion took place, did not have sufficient reason under the *Espy* case to force the president to sit down for an interview. That was especially true, they said, because the president had given the Mueller prosecutors unprecedented cooperation. He even allowed his White House counsel to be interviewed for dozens of hours.

In sum, the Trump position was: No interview, written questions only. And no questions about obstruction, only about Russia.

"The Mueller team was not making much headway with us on the obstruction investigation," Jane Raskin recalled. "We had signaled that we were not inclined to bring the president in to answer questions about his state of mind. We viewed it as an unconstitutional intrusion. They had not set forth any theory, let alone any legally viable theory, of obstruction that we thought would justify bringing our client in to answer questions under the *Espy* standard."

On Russia questions, the lawyers wondered why Mueller wanted to sit down with the president, given that he had no crime to pursue. It was just a perjury trap, they concluded.

"Testimony is out of the question, will not happen," said Jay Sekulow. "And I could tell, although they threatened and pushed, they did not have the authority to do it. And they were legally on very shaky ground, because of all the cooperation."

Nevertheless, the Trump team did not want to appear completely unbending. After all, Mueller still might issue a grand jury subpoena that Trump would have to fight in court. If that happened, the lawyers would want to be able to tell a judge (or the justices of the Supreme Court) that they had tried to be accommodating to Mueller. So they offered to answer written questions on Russia-related matters from before Trump's presidency.

After weeks of arguing turned into months of arguing, Mueller finally gave up. On August 30, the special counsel's office sent the Trump team a letter agreeing to the president's offer to answer questions, in writing, related to alleged Russian collusion with the Trump campaign. On September 17, the questions arrived. In general, they weren't substantially different from the questions that had been on the table for nearly a year—they were an attempt to discover whether Trump had any personal knowledge of events that Mueller could not establish as a conspiracy or coordination between the Trump campaign and Russia.

In all, Mueller asked seventy-one questions divided into five subject headings. The first section was twenty-one questions on the June 9, 2016, Trump Tower meeting. The second was seventeen questions on Russian hacking. The third was ten questions on the Trump Tower Moscow project. The fourth was eleven questions on contacts with Russians during the campaign. And the fifth was twelve questions on contacts with Russians during the transition.

The questions were complex and detailed. For example, here are the first five queries about the Trump Tower meeting:

> a. When did you first learn that Donald Trump, Jr., Paul Manafort, or Jared Kushner was considering participating in a meeting in June 2016 concerning potentially negative information about Hillary Clinton? Describe who you learned the information from and the substance of the discussion.
>
> b. Attached to this document as Exhibit A is a series of emails from June 2016 between, among others, Donald Trump, Jr. and Rob Goldstone. In addition to the emails reflected in Exhibit A, Donald Trump, Jr. had other communications with Rob Goldstone and Emin Agalarov between June 3, 2016 and June 9, 2016.
>
> > i. Did Mr. Trump, Jr. or anyone else tell you about or show you any of these communications? If yes, describe who discussed the communications with you, when, and the substance of the discussion(s).
> >
> > ii. When did you first see or lean about all or any part of the emails reflected in Exhibit A?
> >
> > iii. When did you first learn that the proposed meeting involved or was described as being part of Russia and its government's support for your candidacy?
> >
> > iv. Did you suggest to or direct anyone not to discuss or release publicly all or any portion of the emails reflected in Exhibit A? If yes, describe who you communicated with, when, the substance of the communication(s), and why you took that action.

Imagine that Trump had sat for an interview with Mueller's prosecutors. The questions would have taxed the memory of someone who had spent weeks doing nothing but preparing for them. For Trump, distracted by all the other concerns of the presidency, it would have been a grueling and dangerous exercise, especially since Mueller's prosecutors had already shown themselves to have a hair trigger when it came to charging interview subjects with making false statements. Trump returned his written answers on November 20, 2018. Here is his answer to the questions above:

> I have no recollection of learning at the time that Donald Trump, Jr., Paul Manafort, or Jared Kushner was considering participating in a meeting in June 2016 concerning potentially negative information about Hillary Clinton. Nor do I recall learning during the campaign that the June 9, 2016 meeting had taken place, that the referenced emails existed, or that Donald J. Trump, Jr., had other communications with Emin Agalarov or Robert Goldstone between June 3, 2016 and June 9, 2016.

Mueller was of course unsatisfied with that and most of Trump's other answers. There was talk that Mueller would try to leverage his unhappiness into another attempt to get Trump to agree to an interview. On December 3, Mueller wrote to the Trump team. He noted that in the written answers the president said he "does not recall or remember" or that he had no "independent recollection" on more than thirty occasions. Trump's responses, Mueller said, "demonstrate the inadequacy of the written format, as we have had no opportunity to ask follow-up questions that would ensure complete answers and potentially refresh your client's recollection or clarify the extent or nature of his lack of recollection."

Mueller again asked Trump for an interview, and on December 12, the Trump team again said no. Mueller weighed whether to subpoena the president. "But at that point," Mueller wrote later, "our investigation had made significant progress and had produced substantial evidence for our report." That appeared to be a tacit admission of what the Trump team had been saying all along, that with the president's cooperation, Mueller had the material he needed to conclude the investigation.

Mueller also realized that to pursue Trump's testimony would involve "constitutional litigation," which would take an enormous amount of time. Finally, in December 2018, he gave up for good.

"The infamous March 5 meeting"

As 2018 closed and 2019 began, the Trump team felt that Mueller was finished. His prosecutors contacted Trump's team less frequently; they seemed more interested in tying up loose ends than in in (the parallelism was messed up) opening new areas of investigation; and they appeared to be in "wind-down mode," writing a report.

But what kind of report would it be? Or should there even be any report at all? One of the reasons Congress let the old independent counsel statute expire was that lawmakers were not happy with its requirement that the independent counsel write a report for Congress. That requirement led to an era of big, accusatory reports that sometimes did not allege any violations of law. The new special counsel regulations did not require an investigator like Mueller to report to Congress, requiring instead that he write a report for the attorney general giving his decisions on whether to charge the people under investigation. A report under those rules might be quite brief. A short, summary report seemed just what the all-business, no-nonsense Bob Mueller would do.

But it was not what the group of prosecutors President Trump called the "thirteen angry Democrats" would do. It was likely they would want a reprise of those lengthy reports from the independent counsel years. Such a report might be hundreds of pages long and imply wrongdoing in all sorts of areas where none was charged.

There were differences of opinion inside the Trump team as to what path Mueller would take. Some thought he would throw the rules out the window and write a big document like the Clinton-era Starr report, which ran to 453 pages. Others thought he would be more modest. "I thought Mueller would do a very summary report that said there was no collusion, but as for obstruction, the president did this and the president did that, we looked into all of these things, and while these are not norms or best practices, we can't say they rise to the level of obstruction," defense team member Michael Bowe remembered. "Instead, we got this tome, which I don't believe for a moment he actually wrote or understood."

Making the report public proved to be an extraordinarily difficult and controversial process. In early March 2019, the Mueller team informed the Justice Department that it was done, and a meeting was set for March 5 at the Department's Washington headquarters where Mueller would brief the Department of Justice leadership on what was in the document. It proved to be difficult for all involved.

"The infamous March 5 meeting," is how one Justice Department source described the gathering. On that day, Mueller and two top aides, James Quarles and Aaron Zebley, met with Attorney General William Barr, Deputy Attorney General Rod Rosenstein, and two other top officials closely involved in the Mueller matter, Edward O'Callaghan and Brian Rabbitt. The Mueller team's description of its findings on collusion was simple. "We're very comfortable saying there was no collusion, no conspiracy," Zebley told the group, according to notes taken by one of the Justice Department officials present.

The difficulty came when Quarles discussed obstruction. First there was Mueller's decision *not* to decide about whether Trump obstructed justice. "We are going to conclude that it is not appropriate for us to make a final determination as to whether there was a crime [obstruction]," Quarles said, according to the official's notes. "We're going to report the facts and analysis and leave it there." Barr and his aides were baffled. Mueller's job was to identify whether a crime had been committed, and if so, who did it. How could he just punt on that key question?

Even more confusing was what became known as the "but for" issue—that is, was Mueller saying he would have charged Trump with obstruction but for the Justice Department's Office of Legal Counsel (OLC) opinion that a sitting president could not be indicted? If so, the report was tantamount to accusing the president of committing a crime.

"We did not reach a final judgment that any specific conduct equaled a crime," Quarles said. And then he answered "no" to the "but for" question—three separate times.

"We are not going to say we would indict but for the OLC opinion," Quarles said, according to the notes.

On another occasion, he said, "We are not going to say but for the OLC opinion, this would be a prosecutable offense."

And on yet another occasion, Quarles said, "We are trying to state the evidence dispassionately, to not leave the impression we would indict but for the OLC opinion."

The "but for" question would bedevil both sides in the coming months. It was the cause of enormous confusion as everyone, including Mueller himself at times, struggled to fully understand what prosecutors had done.

The special counsel's office turned the report over to the Justice Department on Friday, March 22. Beyond the question of understanding precisely what Mueller was saying, there was a more pressing problem: How should the Department make the report public? It contained grand jury and other secret material, and would take weeks to do all the redacting necessary for public release. But the public, at least the part of the public that really cared, was in an uproar. There was no way Barr could sit on the report for two or three weeks. There would be cries of cover-up, a million conspiracy theories, and a general political frenzy. So after forty-eight hours of intense reading and study, Barr decided to write a brief summary of what Mueller found on the two topics that had consumed the public debate—collusion and obstruction.

On Sunday, March 24, Barr sent a four-page letter to the chairmen and ranking members of the House and Senate Judiciary Committees. "Although my review is ongoing, I believe that it is in the public interest to describe the report and to summarize the principal conclusions reached by the Special Counsel and the results of his investigation," Barr wrote.

Barr continued: "The Special Counsel's investigation did not find that the Trump campaign or anyone associated with it conspired or coordinated with Russia in its efforts to influence the 2016 U.S. presidential election." He quoted the passage in which Mueller wrote that, "[T]he investigation did not establish that members of the Trump campaign conspired or coordinated with the Russian government in its election interference activities."

On obstruction, Barr wrote that Mueller "did not draw a conclusion—one way or the other—as to whether the examined conduct constituted obstruction." Instead, Mueller examined a number of incidents, and his report "sets out evidence on both sides of the question and leaves unresolved what the special counsel views as 'difficult issues' of law and fact concerning whether the president's actions and intent could be viewed as obstruction." Barr also included Mueller's note that "while this report does not conclude that the president committed a crime, it also does not exonerate him."

That was an entirely accurate and fair representation of what Mueller concluded, both on collusion and obstruction. But Barr added one more note on the obstruction side. Since Mueller had decided not to decide, Barr wrote, it was up to him, as attorney general, to "determine whether the conduct described in the report constitutes a crime." Barr, along with Deputy Attorney General Rod Rosenstein, decided that the evidence Mueller compiled "is not sufficient to establish that the president committed an obstruction-of-justice offense." That judgment, Barr wrote, was not based on the Justice Department opinion that a sitting president cannot be indicted. Rather, it was Barr's and Rosenstein's best assessment of the evidence at hand.

To say that Barr's letter set off an uproar would be a gross understatement. His terse description of Mueller's findings on collusion dashed the dreams of many Democrats, Resistance activists, and some Never-Trump Republicans. They had heard about and believed in collusion for more than two years, and Mueller's conclusion was a devastating blow.

On obstruction, Mueller's non-conclusion let everyone create his or her own narrative. And Barr's decision to take it upon himself to declare that the president did not commit obstruction led to accusations he was carrying the president's water.

Among those who protested was Mueller himself. "The summary letter the Department sent to Congress and released to the public late in the afternoon of March 24 did not fully capture the context, nature, and substance of this office's work and conclusions," Mueller wrote in a letter to Barr not long after the summary was released. "There is now public confusion about critical aspects of the results of our investigation. This threatens to undermine a central purpose for which the Department appointed the special counsel: to assure full public confidence in the outcome of the investigation."

The arguing continued without resolution for nearly four weeks while the Justice Department worked to black out grand jury material and other secret content from the Mueller report. The report was released to the public on April 18, 2019.

Volume One

The report was organized into two volumes, beginning with 199 pages on collusion and the Russia meddling operation, and closing with 182 pages on obstruction. There were a few dozen additional pages of appendices in which Mueller included the complete text of his written questions and the president's answers.

The first volume was a dissertation on what Mueller did not find. The casual reader could discover that by searching the text for the word "establish," as in what the investigation was able to establish and what it was not able to establish.

The fundamental finding of Volume One was, "The investigation did not establish that members of the Trump campaign conspired or coordinated with the Russian government in its election interference activities." (That was the sentence Barr quoted in his summary.) No matter the qualifications and explanations Mueller might add, the basic fact was that he could not establish that a conspiracy or coordination took place. Nor did he establish that what was popularly called "collusion" took place. (Mueller addressed the use of the word "collusion," which had no legal definition, as shorthand for "conspiracy" or "coordination." Mueller wrote that, "even as defined in legal dictionaries, collusion is largely synonymous with conspiracy as that crime is set forth in the general federal conspiracy statute." Mueller did not use "collusion" to describe what he was searching for, but he let the public know that he considered it to be essentially the same as his search for "conspiracy" or "coordination.")

Democrats and other Trump adversaries pointed out that the critical sentence—the "investigation did not establish" sentence—actually began this way: *"Although the investigation established that the Russian government perceived it would benefit from a Trump presidency and worked to secure that outcome, and that the campaign expected it would benefit electorally from information stolen and released through Russian efforts,* the investigation did not establish that members of the Trump campaign conspired or coordinated with the Russian government in its election interference activities."

Democrats argued that Mueller was saying that in fact, Trump had kind of colluded, even if Mueller could not prove to a legal standard that there was a conspiracy. Mueller encouraged that impression when he added, "A statement that the investigation did not establish particular facts does not mean there was no evidence of those facts." The hopeful reading by some Democrats was that there was evidence of conspiracy; it was just that Mueller decided, for whatever reason, that he would not take it to court.

The flaw in that conclusion became apparent when one looked at the individual components of the collusion allegation. Exhibit A for collusion was always the Trump Tower meeting. Mueller pursued it on the theory that it might have been a campaign finance violation. The theory was that the information that publicist Rob Goldstone teased Donald

Trump Jr. with—information that did not, in fact, exist—was a "thing of value" under the campaign finance laws and might have represented an illegal contribution, albeit it one that never happened, from Goldstone to the Trump campaign.

"The office considered whether to charge Trump campaign officials with crimes in connection with the June 9 meeting," Mueller wrote. "The office concluded that, in light of the government's substantial burden of proof on issues of intent ('knowing' and 'willful') and the difficulty of establishing the value of the offered information, criminal charges would not meet the Justice Manual standard that 'the admissible evidence will probably be sufficient to obtain and sustain a conviction.'"

"Accordingly, taking into account the high burden to establish a culpable mental state in a campaign-finance prosecution and the difficulty in establishing the required valuation, the office decided not to pursue criminal campaign-finance charges against Trump Jr. or other campaign officials culminating in the June 9 meeting."

The short version of all that was that Mueller failed to show that Donald Trump Jr., or anyone else in the Trump campaign, had engaged in any conspiracy or had the motive to engage in any conspiracy. Exhibit A of collusion fell completely apart.

Then there were the other elements of the collusion allegation. Carter Page was once thought to have been a key suspect in collusion— remember that the Steele dossier said Paul Manafort used Page in a "well-developed conspiracy" between Trump and Russia. The dossier also said powerful Russians offered a huge amount of money, potentially billions of dollars, to influence Trump to end U.S. sanctions against Russia. But Mueller concluded: "The investigation did not establish that Page coordinated with the Russian government in its efforts to interfere with the 2016 presidential election."

Or Manafort, another collusion suspect: Mueller could not find any evidence that polling data Manafort had given Konstantin Kilimnik was used in any sort of scheme with Russians to interfere in the election. Beyond that, Mueller concluded that, "The investigation did not establish that Manafort otherwise coordinated with the Russian government on its election-interference activities." Mueller could have taken out the word "otherwise" and the sentence would have more accurately reflected his findings.

Then there was George Papadopoulos. Mueller forced Papadopoulos to plead guilty to lying to the FBI about the timing of his contacts with some mysterious and possibly Russia-related figures who may or may not have targeted Papadopoulos for unknown reasons, but Mueller did not claim, either in the charges against Papadopoulos or the final report, that Papadopoulos was part of a conspiracy or coordination between the Trump campaign and Russia.

Then there was the 2016 Republican convention matter, in which the Trump campaign allegedly "gutted" the GOP platform on Ukraine in order to please Vladimir Putin. Mueller found nothing to support that allegation. "The investigation did not establish that one campaign official's efforts to dilute a portion of the Republican Party platform on providing assistance to Ukraine were undertaken at the behest of candidate Trump or Russia." Not only was there no wrongdoing, Mueller actually described the matter incorrectly. The alleged dilution, which was not a dilution at all, was not of a portion of the party platform but rather of one delegate's proposed amendment to the party platform. It was even less than Mueller described.

Then there were a few seemingly random contacts between Trump figures and Russians during the campaign. "The office investigated several...events that have been publicly reported to involve potential Russia-related contacts," Mueller wrote. "For example, the investigation established that interactions between Russian ambassador Kislyak and Trump campaign officials both at the candidate's April 2016 foreign policy speech in Washington, D.C., and during the week of the Republican National Convention were brief, public, and non-substantive.... The investigation also did not establish that a meeting between Kislyak and [Senator Jeff] Sessions in September 2016 at Sessions's Senate office included any more than a passing mention of the presidential campaign."

Nor did Mueller find any other contact between Trump people and Russians that constituted collusion, either before the election or during the transition. "The investigation did not establish that the campaign coordinated or conspired with the Russian government in its election-interference activities," the report said. Democrats clung to Mueller's notion that "A statement that the investigation did not establish particular facts does not mean there was no evidence of those facts," but the fact was, Mueller's prosecutors could not establish collusion, and in the report, they finally admitted it.

Volume Two

The second volume of Mueller's report was devoted to obstruction. It elaborated on what Mueller and Quarles told Justice Department officials at the March 5 meeting—that Mueller did not draw a conclusion on whether the president obstructed justice. The report used the phrase "traditional prosecutorial judgment" five times to explain what the report was *not* providing. "A traditional prosecution or declination decision entails a binary determination to initiate or decline a prosecution," the report said, "but we determined not to make a traditional prosecutorial judgment."

Why not? In the very next sentence, Mueller explained, "The Office of Legal Counsel (OLC) has issued an opinion finding that 'the indictment or criminal prosecution of a sitting president would impermissibly undermine the capacity of the executive branch to perform its constitutionally assigned functions.'" In short, it appeared Mueller was saying he chose not to charge Trump only because of the OLC decision.

That was precisely the opposite of what Quarles, in Mueller's presence, had told Barr and the other DOJ officials on March 5, when he said, "We are not going to say we would indict but for the OLC opinion." A fair reader of the report might well conclude that Mueller was saying he *would* have concluded that Trump obstructed justice but for the OLC opinion.

Even more serious, in the eyes of the Trump team, was the report's statement that prosecutors would have exonerated the president if they could, but the evidence did not allow it:

> If we had confidence after a thorough investigation of the facts that the president clearly did not commit obstruction of justice, we would so state. Based on the facts and the applicable legal standards, however, we are unable to reach that judgment. The evidence we obtained about the president's actions and intent presents difficult issues that prevent us from conclusively determining that no criminal conduct occurred. Accordingly, while this report does not conclude that the president committed a crime, it also does not exonerate him.

With that, Mueller appeared to replace the normal standard of American justice—innocent until proven guilty—with a newly created standard of "not exonerated," which allowed prosecutors to cast a cloud of possible guilt over a president while not actually accusing him of wrongdoing.

It was a mind-blowing moment for some Justice Department veterans. Since when did prosecutors hand out certificates of exoneration to people they investigate? (Answer: they don't.) Since when has "not exonerated" been an accepted legal outcome—as in, "How does the jury find the defendant? We find him not exonerated." (Answer: never.)

The report detailed ten instances in which Mueller strongly suggested that Trump obstructed justice. The first was Trump's statements to Comey concerning the Michael Flynn investigation. The second was Trump's efforts to get Comey to say that he, Trump, was not the target of the Russia investigation. The third was Trump's firing of Comey. The fourth was Trump's alleged attempt to fire Mueller. The fifth was Trump's alleged further efforts to curtail the investigation. The sixth was Trump's attempt to prevent public release of the Trump Tower meeting emails. The seventh was Trump's alleged attempt to have Sessions un-recuse himself and re-take control of the investigation. The eighth was Trump's alleged attempt to have McGahn publicly deny that Trump wanted to fire Mueller. The ninth was Trump's actions toward Manafort. And the tenth was Trump's actions toward Michael Cohen.

Some were easily dismissed. Some were more serious and required a closer look.

Among the easily dismissed was Trump's attempt to prevent public release of the Trump Tower meeting emails. In that instance, the president was trying to keep information out of the press, which is not a crime. It was surprising that Mueller included it in a list of alleged acts of obstruction. Also easily dismissed were Trump's efforts to get Comey to say that he, Trump, was not the target of the Russia investigation. Comey had privately told Trump on three occasions that he was not a target. Comey had told lawmakers the same thing. Asking him to say the same thing publicly was not an obstructive act. Another easily dismissed allegation was Trump's firing of Comey. As Trump's lawyers often argued, the president had the authority to do it, and he said explicitly at the time that he did not believe it would curtail the Russia investigation.

If these allegations were easily dismissed, others were also not terribly serious. On Trump's actions toward Michael Cohen—allegedly trying to get Cohen to lie to Congress—Mueller himself admitted that "the evidence available to us does not establish that the president directed or aided Cohen's false testimony." On Trump's statements toward Comey concerning the Flynn investigation, Mueller faced the discrepancy between what the president said and what Comey inferred, making a definitive account nearly impossible. On Trump's actions toward Manafort, Mueller lacked evidence that Trump encouraged Manafort not to cooperate with the special counsel.

Those are six of the ten examples. Three of the remaining four warranted more serious attention, because they concerned Trump's alleged efforts to fire Mueller.

The report said Trump's behavior changed dramatically beginning on June 14, 2017, when the *Washington Post* reported that Mueller—in office less than a month—was investigating Trump personally for obstruction of justice. It was then, Mueller suggested, that Trump began to obstruct the investigation by telling White House counsel Don McGahn to call Deputy Attorney General Rod Rosenstein and tell him to fire Mueller. This is the special counsel's brief summary of what happened:

> The Acting Attorney General appointed a Special Counsel on May 17, 2017, prompting the President to state that it was the end of his presidency and that Attorney General Sessions had failed to protect him and should resign. Sessions submitted his resignation, which the President ultimately did not accept. The President told senior advisors that the Special Counsel had conflicts of interest, but they responded that those claims were "ridiculous" and posed no obstacle to the Special Counsel's service. Department of Justice ethics officials similarly cleared the Special Counsel's service. On June 14, 2017, the press reported that the President was being personally investigated for obstruction of justice and the President responded with a series of tweets criticizing the Special Counsel's investigation. That weekend, the President called McGahn and directed him to have the Special Counsel removed because of asserted conflicts of interest. McGahn did not carry out the instruction for fear of being seen as triggering another Saturday Night Massacre and instead prepared to resign. McGahn ultimately did not quit and the President did not follow up with McGahn on his request to have the Special Counsel removed.

Mueller recounted Trump's "I'm fucked" moment and his insistence that Mueller had conflicts of interest. He discussed Trump considering the possibility of firing Mueller even before the June 14 *Post* story. Three days after the story appeared, on June 17, according to the report, Trump "called McGahn and directed him to have the special counsel removed"—the central act of alleged obstruction in the Mueller report.

Trump called McGahn twice that day. During both calls, Mueller said Trump "directed [McGahn] to have the special counsel removed." Mueller's evidence for what was said—and thus for the obstruction allegation—came entirely from McGahn. "On the first call," Mueller wrote, "McGahn remembered that the president said something like "You gotta do this. You gotta call Rod."

Those words—"the president said something like"—did not inspire confidence in the accuracy of the quotes that followed. Plus, "You gotta do this. You gotta call Rod" were the only quotes, or semi-quotes, that Mueller cited from the first call. The report said McGahn told the president he would see what he could do, but in fact McGahn "did not intend to act on the request."

Later, Trump called again to follow up. In that call, according to the Mueller report, "McGahn recalled that the president was more direct, saying something like, 'Call Rod, tell Rod that Mueller has conflicts and can't be the special counsel.'" That was another semi-quote—"saying something like." But Mueller also said McGahn "recalled the president telling him 'Mueller has to go' and 'Call me back when you do it.'" Mueller said McGahn "left the president with the impression that McGahn would call Rosenstein," but had no intention of doing so and was only trying to get Trump off the phone.

McGahn did not call Rosenstein. Instead, he called his personal lawyer, and later his chief of staff, and told them he had decided to resign. McGahn did not tell the chief of staff what Trump wanted because, according to Mueller, he wanted to keep her out of it.

Later that same day, McGahn called then-White House Chief of Staff Reince Priebus, and then-White House adviser Steve Bannon, to tell them he intended to resign. Again, McGahn did not tell either Priebus or Bannon what Trump wanted, although Priebus remembered that McGahn told him the president asked him to "do crazy shit."

There was not a third phone call from Trump; the president did not follow up on whatever he told McGahn. McGahn did not resign. Rosenstein was not called. Mueller did not resign. The investigation continued unimpeded.

In late November 2017, McGahn began an extensive series of interviews with Mueller's prosecutors. In late January 2018, the *New York Times*, citing "four people told of the matter," published a story with the headline, "Trump Ordered Mueller Fired, but Backed Off When White House Counsel Threatened to Quit."

On February 5, 2018, according to Mueller, Trump told the White House staff secretary Rob Porter that he, Trump, believed McGahn had leaked to the media. Trump wanted Porter to tell McGahn "to create a record to make clear that the president never directed McGahn to fire the special counsel." The president, apparently focusing on the word "fired" because it was in the *Times* headline, wanted McGahn "to write a letter to the file 'for our records.'" Porter took the president's message to McGahn, who "shrugged off" the request, according to the report. "McGahn told Porter that the president had been insistent on firing the special counsel," the report said, citing an interview with Porter.

On February 6, Trump called McGahn to a meeting in the Oval Office with John Kelly, who by then had replaced Priebus as chief of staff. McGahn had a detailed memory of that meeting. McGahn recalled the president said, "I never said to fire Mueller. I never said 'fire.' This story doesn't look good. You need to correct this. You're the White House counsel."

McGahn said that he told the president that the *Times*' account of the firing order was accurate. "The president asked McGahn, 'Did I say the word 'fire'?" the report said. "McGahn responded, 'What you said is, 'Call Rod, tell Rod that Mueller has conflicts and can't be the special counsel.'"

"I never said that," Trump responded, again according to McGahn's account. "The president said he merely wanted McGahn to raise the conflicts issue with Rosenstein and leave it to him to decide what to do," the report said. "McGahn told the president he did not understand the conversation that way and instead had heard, 'Call Rod. There are conflicts. Mueller has to go,'" according to the report, again citing McGahn's account. Trump asked McGahn to "do a correction," according to McGahn, and McGahn refused.

Kelly, who was also in the meeting, was barely mentioned. But the report did say that Kelly recalled McGahn telling him that he really "did have that conversation" about firing Mueller. Later, Mueller reported, "the president's personal counsel called McGahn's counsel and relayed that the president was 'fine' with McGahn."

That was pretty much the entirety of the fire-Mueller obstruction allegation.

In each case in which he alleged obstruction, Mueller analyzed the evidence in light of the "three basic elements [that] are common to most of the relevant obstruction statutes." They were: "(1) an obstructive act; (2) a nexus between the obstructive act and an official proceeding; and (3) a corrupt intent."

Mueller argued that if Trump had fired him, it could have been an obstructive act, because even if the result was only the appointment of a new prosecutor, the investigation might have suffered some delay. In addition, a firing—had it happened—might possibly "chill the actions" of any replacement special counsel. But the firing, of course, did not happen.

Mueller also argued that Trump's request for McGahn to create a record denying that Trump had ordered him to fire Mueller could have been obstructive if it "had the natural tendency to constrain McGahn from testifying truthfully." But by that time McGahn had already told his story to Mueller's prosecutors, with Trump's consent.

Mueller expressed faith in McGahn's account because McGahn had a "clear recollection" of the matter and was "a credible witness with no motive to lie or exaggerate." What bits and pieces of evidence Mueller could glean from other sources were consistent with McGahn's account, Mueller said.

As far as a nexus to an official proceeding was concerned, Mueller said Trump "knew his conduct was under investigation" by a prosecutor who could present evidence to a grand jury. Therefore, there was a connection.

As far as corrupt intent was concerned, Mueller said there was "substantial evidence" that Trump tried to remove Mueller because he was investigating Trump's conduct. On the other hand, Mueller noted that as late as the end of January 2018, when the *Times* story was published, "there is some evidence that...[Trump] believed he had never told McGahn to have Rosenstein remove the special counsel."

"The president told Priebus and Porter that he had not sought to terminate the special counsel," the report said, "and in the Oval Office meeting with McGahn, the president said, 'I never tried to fire Mueller. I never said fire.'" That evidence could indicate that the president was not attempting to persuade McGahn to change his story but was instead offering his own—but different—recollection of the substance of his June 2017 conversations with McGahn and McGahn's reaction to them.

Mueller knocked down that explanation in the next paragraph, however, saying the evidence showed Trump really was trying to fire Mueller and that Trump's position "runs counter to the evidence."

Mueller's recounting of the McGahn story was long and complex because it was the centerpiece of his allegation that Trump obstructed justice. But Trump had significant defenses. One, the firing never happened. Two, the investigation was not obstructed. Three, Trump could have been venting in the phone calls (something he did every day), and perhaps there was some misunderstanding between the president and McGahn. It is not unusual for Donald Trump to say one thing and a person around him to hear another. Given that Mueller relied so heavily on McGahn's account, such a misunderstanding, if it occurred, could have become the centerpiece of the allegation. And four, there was no underlying crime of conspiracy or coordination, the purported point of the investigation, which made any allegation of "obstruction" almost a *non sequitur*. The fire-Mueller allegation, the strongest of the list in the Mueller report, had significant weaknesses.

Finally, there was the allegation that Trump tried to bring Jeff Sessions, the then-attorney general who had recused himself from the Russia investigation, into the effort to get rid of Mueller. The report said Trump enlisted outside supporter Corey Lewandowski, a former head of the Trump 2016 campaign, to "ask Attorney General Jeff Sessions to reassert control of the investigation and limit its scope."

According to the report, on June 19, 2017—two days after the phone calls with McGahn—the president met one-on-one in the Oval Office with Lewandowski. In that meeting, according to Mueller, Trump "dictated a message to be delivered to Attorney General Sessions that would have had the effect of limiting the Russia investigation to future election interference only." Lewandowski took dictation, Mueller said, writing "as fast as possible to make sure he captured the content correctly."

Trump wanted Lewandowski to give the message to Sessions, who would then deliver it as a public statement. This is what Trump told Lewandowski to tell Sessions to say, according to Lewandowski's notes reproduced in the report:

> I know that I recused myself from certain things having to do with specific areas. But our POTUS...is being treated very unfairly. He shouldn't have a Special Prosecutor/Counsel b/c he hasn't done anything wrong. I was on the campaign w/him for nine months, there were no Russians involved with him. I know it for a fact b/c I was there. He didn't do anything wrong except he ran the greatest campaign in American history. Now a group of people want to subvert the Constitution of the United States. I am going to meet with the Special Prosecutor to explain this is very unfair and let the Special Prosecutor move forward with investigating election meddling for future elections so that nothing can happen in future elections.

Mueller reported that Lewandowski arranged a meeting with Sessions to deliver the message, but Sessions canceled "due to a last minute conflict." A month passed, and Trump said nothing more about the matter to Lewandowski. During that time, Lewandowski decided to ask Rick Dearborn, a White House official who used to work for Sessions, to deliver the message.

On July 29, 2017, Trump and Lewandowski met again, and Trump asked about the status of his now month-old request. "Lewandowski told the president that the message would be delivered soon," according to the report. A short time later, Lewandowski ran into Dearborn and actually gave him the message for Sessions. Dearborn later told Mueller that "being asked to serve as a messenger to Sessions made him uncomfortable," according to the report. He decided not to give the message to Sessions and later told Lewandowski he had "handled" the situation. As he had with the fire-Mueller situation, Trump apparently let the matter go.

The message was not delivered. The investigation was not obstructed.

Beyond that, there was the question of what Trump's dictated message actually meant. Trump wanted Sessions to say that he would "let the special prosecutor move forward with investigating election meddling for future elections so that nothing can happen in future elections." Mueller said that was intended to "limit [Mueller's] jurisdiction to future election interference." Mueller continued: "The president's directives indicate that Sessions was being instructed to tell the special counsel to end the existing investigation into the president and his campaign, with the special counsel being permitted to 'move forward with investigating election meddling for future elections.'"

It was all a bit confusing. For one thing, how does one investigate "future election interference"? And was Trump telling Lewandowski to tell Sessions to tell Mueller "to end the existing investigation into the president and his campaign"? Trump's words could just as easily be interpreted as an intention to allow the Russia portion of the investigation to continue, which could have the effect of preventing future interference. One could infer that Trump also meant that he would forbid Mueller from continuing to investigate alleged obstruction of justice, but that did not happen. Trump brought it up once. He waited a month and brought it up again. Then he dropped it.

The entire Lewandowski episode was murky. It was simply not clear what the president meant when he dictated the message he wanted Lewandowski to give to Sessions about Mueller. And in both the McGahn and Lewandowski instances, Trump expressed a desire, gave a vague instruction, and then let the matter drop when nothing was done. In terms of, say, Watergate, it was as if Richard Nixon ordered his White House counsel to tell the attorney general to fire the special prosecutor, but the counsel did not do it, the prosecutor was never fired, and Nixon let the matter drop. There was no Saturday Night Massacre. And that made for a difficult obstruction of justice case.

"We won, they lost"

The Justice Department allowed the Trump defense team to read the report a few days before its April 18 release. Giuliani and Sekulow and Jane and Marty Raskin went to a secure room in Department headquarters and spent two days studying the report and making notes. They were not allowed to have any computers, phones, or any other devices, and could not make copies or photos or take away anything other than their hand-written notes.

They initially tried to divide up the work—I'll read Volume One, and you'll read Volume Two—but pretty soon everyone was just plowing through it. Their first impression was along the lines of what they had told Mueller and his deputies so many times in the last year: you've got nothing.

"I remember we stopped at one point and said they had nothing, and they knew they had nothing two months after this investigation started," Sekulow recalled. "And they kept going, to try to get somebody to perjure themselves."

"We were very happy that they brought up nothing new," Giuliani recalled. "They didn't have the smoking gun. They didn't have anything that hadn't already…been debated, discussed, was on television."

"Pick your words—exoneration, vindication, whatever—but we thought it was as close as you could come to a total victory as we had ever expected or hoped," said Jane Raskin.

"I said to Jane and Marty," Sekulow recalled, "so what all this really says, when you go through all 400 pages is: We won, they lost."

Some parts they found appalling. For instance, they instantly caught Mueller's unique "not exonerated" standard. "The first thing I underlined, and I said to Jay that we're going to shove this down their throat," said Giuliani, "is that he [Trump] had to prove his innocence. Where the hell did that come from? Who invented that? I can't conclude with certainty that he didn't obstruct justice? It's the craziest interpretation of American jurisprudence that I've ever heard."

"They had that cockamamie conclusion of theirs," Sekulow added, "that is total irresponsibility on the part of Mueller and his entire team. First of all, prosecutors do not exonerate. They either make a case or they do not. He [Mueller] put a standard in there that is not the standard in the Justice Department Manual. So, for all of their 'We're doing it by the book,' they were full of crap. I still get angry at that one."

Jane Raskin focused on a related passage, in which Mueller argued that it would be unfair for a prosecutor to present accusations against a president, who, because of the OLC opinion, could not defend himself in court, the way other Americans charged with crimes do. And then, Raskin said, "Mueller did essentially that, presenting untested evidence and inconclusive observations about the president's conduct without making a prosecution or declination decision."

All the irritation, though, was overshadowed by satisfaction that Mueller simply did not have the case against Trump. They had indeed won.

In the weeks preceding the report's release, the defense team had prepared a rebuttal report, an answer to the allegations they expected Mueller to make. It was about ninety percent finished when the report was released, meaning the team could fill in a few things and have it ready to go quickly. They never did. Reading the report, they all agreed no rebuttal was necessary. That work was put aside for good.

CHAPTER SEVEN

Impeachment 3.0: A Mueller Fiasco

"It's too early to talk about impeachment"—
The Mueller Show—"He wasn't in charge"

By the time the Mueller report was released, some Democrats in Congress had spent more than a year telling their colleagues—and themselves—that they should wait for Mueller before going forward with impeaching the president. Sure, Al Green kept tilting at windmills, but the smart money said the special counsel's report would give Democrats the evidence they needed to begin the real work of removing Trump. So better to wait for Mueller. While they waited, lawmakers on the House Judiciary and Intelligence committees prepared for the moment when the report came out.

And then it was in everyone's hands. It was clear to all, or it should have been, that the Mueller report was not the document that would rally the country around the cause of impeachment. It might not even rally enough House Democrats to vote for impeachment—and that was with a head start of the seventy who already had.

Yet Democrats kept on with their plan. They were a bit like the classic *Roadrunner* cartoon in which Wile E. Coyote, going at full speed, runs off the edge of a cliff and, through sheer momentum, keeps going, through the air, until he realizes there is no longer anything under him and plunges to earth.

In the Trump-Mueller impeachment, Democrats kept going even though firm ground—the hoped-for Mueller case against Trump—had disappeared beneath them.

"It's too early to talk about impeachment"

Al Green seemed on his way to creating a tradition of opening each new session of Congress with a call for impeachment. On January 3, 2019, he was back, only this time he was a member of the majority party. With Brad Sherman, Green introduced a new set of articles based on Trump's firing of James Comey. A few days later, on January 9, Green took to the floor to declare, "Impeachment is not dead."

In early February and again in early March, Green declared that he did not care what was in the Mueller report, or whether it helped or hurt his side. "Still I rise, as I did some 659 days ago...when I first stood on the floor of the House of Representatives and called for the impeachment of the president," Green said. "I rise now, understanding that we have to fend off those who have said: You have to wait for the Mueller report. You have to wait." Mueller, Green explained, was looking for violations of law. But impeachment was about "misdeeds," as Congress defined them. "There will be a vote on impeachment, regardless of what the Mueller commission says," Green told the House.

As 2019 progressed, he would be proven right, many times over. There would indeed be a very big vote on impeachment.

Some Republicans could see it coming. It wasn't very hard. A significant number of Democrats were already on the record favoring impeachment, the party had just won power, and a broad majority of the Democratic base strongly supported impeachment. Why *wouldn't* House Democrats devote 2019 to removing the president?

In January, Republican Representative Devin Nunes, whom the election demoted from chairman to ranking minority member on the

Intelligence Committee, called a meeting of Republican committee members. "I brought everybody in and said, 'Look, we are now officially the impeachment committee,'" Nunes recalled. "'If you haven't been paying attention to the Russia hoax, you better get totally up to speed on it, because this is going to be the only thing we are going to work on.'"

It was true, even though leading Democrats were still saying they opposed impeachment. The first three months of the year saw a quick series of events on Capitol Hill, all seeming to point toward impeachment without actually requiring anyone (other than Green and his allies) to formally support impeachment:

On January 4, House Intelligence Committee chairman Adam Schiff said he would give the Mueller team transcripts of interviews the House Intelligence Committee conducted as part of its Trump-Russia investigation.

On January 10, Michael Cohen—apparently desperate for congressional help in seeking a reduced sentence in his New York tax evasion case—announced that he would testify before the House Oversight Committee on February 7. (He ended up testifying on February 27 instead.)

On January 11, the *New York Times* published a leaked story saying that shortly after the president fired James Comey in 2017, the bureau opened a counter-intelligence investigation specifically targeting the president to determine "whether he had been working on behalf of Russia against American interests."

On January 15, the Senate held confirmation hearings for William Barr to be attorney general. After facing many questions about Mueller and the Trump-Russia investigation, he was confirmed on February 14 by a fifty-four to forty-five vote.

On January 25, FBI agents working for Mueller arrested Roger Stone on charges of lying to Congress. The arrest came in the form of a pre-dawn, paramilitary-style raid on Stone's home in Fort Lauderdale, Florida. Agents with assault weapons and bulletproof vests came to Stone's front door, while other heavily armed agents arrived by boat via a canal next to Stone's backyard. Stone, sleepy, unarmed, and wearing a t-shirt, cooperated with the arrest.

On February 12, House Judiciary Committee chairman Nadler announced the hiring of two "special oversight counsels," that is, lawyers who were expected to play key roles in an impeachment investigation. The two were Norm Eisen, a former Obama White House ethics official who was fanatically anti-Trump, and Barry Berke, a former prosecutor and defense lawyer from New York.

Also in February, Schiff hired Daniel Goldman, a former federal prosecutor in the Southern District of New York and a former MSNBC analyst, as a special counsel to lead an impeachment investigation of Trump.

On February 28, Michael Cohen testified privately to Schiff's Intelligence Committee. He testified again on March 6.

On March 4, Nadler sent out document requests to eighty-one people and organizations, targeting a broad range of Trump topics, from the Russia affair to the president's business dealings.

On March 14, Schiff sent a letter to Trump lawyers demanding documents about their role in a statement Cohen had made to the House two years earlier.

It was obvious to everyone, or should have been, that the Democrats were gearing up to impeach the president. There were some details to be worked out, some jurisdictional issues for new Speaker Nancy Pelosi to decide—Schiff or Nadler? —but the party's direction was clear.

The action began in earnest on March 24, when Barr released his summary of the special counsel's principal findings. Republicans claimed vindication, and Democrats were angry, believing Barr must have misled the nation by downplaying findings of wrongdoing. Schiff went on ABC to claim that there was "significant evidence of collusion." Nadler went on Fox News to say, "We know there was collusion." Still, Nadler added, "It's way too early to talk about impeachment or not."

At that point, no one in Congress had seen the report, so they were arguing in the dark. On March 28, Majority Leader Steny Hoyer and

Minority Whip Steve Scalise argued on the floor of the House about the unseen report.

"Everybody was waiting on the Mueller report," Scalise said. "Many were hanging their hat, saying it is going to show all these things.... And now the Mueller report comes out, and it is clear those claims are baseless. There was no collusion."

"The Mueller report is not out," Hoyer said.

"There was no collusion," Scalise responded.

"The Mueller report is not out," Hoyer repeated. "The only report that is out is the Barr four-page letter report.... I would think the gentleman ought to be very reserved, very frankly, in terms of making conclusions based upon a four-page letter before we have seen the Mueller report, before we have seen the actions of the Southern District of New York, and before we have seen the results of the oversight hearings that are continuing."

Still, Hoyer was careful to appear cautious about impeachment. When Scalise said that Democrats "have spent the last two years trying to impeach this president," Hoyer replied, "I know that [Scalise] knows the overwhelming majority of Democrats voted 'no' [on impeachment]. I know that he must have heard Speaker Pelosi say that we are not pursuing impeachment and that we want to focus on the needs of the American people." Even as key chairmen pushed steadily toward impeachment, the leadership line, as expressed by Hoyer, was: no impeachment.

Three weeks later, on April 18, the full report (with some redactions) was released. Hoyer was even more negative. "Based on what we have seen to date, going forward on impeachment is not worthwhile at this point," he told CNN. "Very frankly, there is an election in 18 months and the American people will make a judgment."

Schiff and Nadler also got the leadership's let's-appear-cautious memo. Schiff told CNN that a decision to move forward on impeachment was "above my pay grade." Nadler said the report "outlines disturbing evidence that President Trump engaged in obstruction of justice and other misconduct." But impeachment was just "one possibility," Nadler added, cautioning that it was "too early to reach those conclusions."

The next day, April 19, Nadler subpoenaed the Justice Department for a complete, unredacted copy of the report. On April 22, Nadler subpoenaed Don McGahn, the now-former White House counsel who had testified so extensively to Mueller's prosecutors. A few weeks later, on May 20, the new White House counsel, Pat Cipollone, told Nadler that the White House had directed McGahn not to obey the subpoena. "The Department of Justice has advised me that Mr. McGahn is absolutely immune from compelled congressional testimony with respect to matters occurring during his service as a senior adviser to the president," Cipollone wrote.

Nadler also subpoenaed close presidential aide Hope Hicks and Annie Donaldson, McGahn's chief of staff who had written extensive notes of White House activities during 2017 and 2018. The White House responded that any documents they might possess were White House property and would not be turned over. It was not clear whether either Hicks or Donaldson would testify.

Nadler was obviously trying to conduct a pre-impeachment investigation. But he ran into difficulty after difficulty. Even before the release of the Mueller report, on March 29, Attorney General Barr offered to testify about the report before Nadler's committee on May 2. Barr specifically promised to explain his much-criticized summary of the report's principal conclusions.

It seemed a good offer. Nadler would get to put a big witness in the chair. But Nadler pressed his luck. He demanded that Barr answer questions, not from lawmakers, but from the "special oversight counsels"—Norm Eisen and Barry Berke—brought in for the pre-impeachment probe. The idea was that the lawyers, given a large block of time, could conduct a more penetrating cross-examination of Barr than would happen if Democrat and Republican members alternated five- or ten-minute periods of questioning.

Barr did not take well to the idea. He was not under investigation. It was the normal practice of the House to have elected lawmakers question the attorney general. Republicans took Barr's defense. "The chairman insisted staff ask questions of the attorney general," ranking Republican Doug Collins said. "Over the 206-year history of this committee, staff have never questioned witnesses in such a hearing. Never."

May 2 approached. Barr stuck to his guns. Nadler said he would not allow "a witness to try to dictate...what our procedures for questioning him are." When Barr still did not budge, Nadler accused him of cowardice. "He is terrified of having to face a skilled attorney," Nadler told reporters.

When the day came, Barr did not appear. Democrats were ready; the message of the day was that Barr had chickened out of the scheduled testimony. Representative Steve Cohen came to the dais with a bucket of Kentucky Fried Chicken, and, even though it was 9:00 a.m., chomped into a crispy breast as photographers crowded around. Cohen also brought a small plastic chicken, which he placed at the witness table so the photographers could get a picture of the chicken right behind the nameplate reading "THE HONORABLE WILLIAM P. BARR."

The hearing room was a "circus," Doug Collins, who was sitting next to Nadler on the dais, remembered. "The obsession of the Democrats over this issue had spilled out in full display. This was not about real investigations—it was about hurting an administration and getting on TV. I used the incident many times in the months afterward to highlight the Democrats' insincerity."

McGahn, Donaldson, Barr—Chairman Nadler was not able to get anyone to testify before his committee, even though several of them had testified extensively to Mueller. That was, by the way, another benefit of the original Trump defense cooperation strategy. When Mueller wanted Trump to testify personally, the Trump side argued that the president had already cooperated so much, and that there were so many cooperative witnesses and such an extensive record, that Trump's testimony wasn't necessary. Now, when Nadler wanted White House aides to testify, the White House said those aides had already testified at great length to the investigation that really mattered—the federal criminal investigation. A House oversight committee, they said, just didn't have the same claim to the testimony.

Meanwhile, as Nadler struggled, Schiff kept moving forward with his own pre-impeachment strategy, issuing subpoenas for Michael Flynn and Richard Gates. There was never a chance either man would testify, but Schiff was staying in the game. The Flynn and Gates subpoenas were the first to people who had actually been charged in the Mueller investigation.

Nadler won a small victory on June 19, when Hicks, who had left the White House, testified in closed session. The interview lasted eight hours, and even before it ended, Democrats complained that Hicks would not answer any of their questions. She certainly came lawyered up, with two private attorneys, two from the White House counsel's office, and one from the Justice Department. As the Trump defense team had done with Mueller, White House lawyers directed Hicks not to answer questions relating to Trump's time as president. Perhaps worst of all, Hicks appeared behind closed doors, with no cameras present, meaning there would be no dramatic video of her refusing to answer the committee's questions.

Hicks agreed to answer questions that concerned the period before she became a White House adviser. But after that, nothing. Nadler was in a peevish mood as the White House lawyers reminded him time after time that Hicks had an "absolute immunity" from questions about Trump's time in the White House. "I'm not going to debate it," Nadler snapped. "It's nonsense."

Nadler tried to zero in on June 19, 2017, the day which, according to Mueller, Trump assigned Corey Lewandowski to deliver a message to Attorney General Jeff Sessions. Nadler pointed to Volume Two of the Mueller report—for which Hicks cooperated extensively, spending three days answering prosecutors' questions in December 2017 and March

2018—as the basis for his questions. But Hicks, under the direction of White House lawyers, would not answer.

"Your contention is that as a result of absolutely immunity she cannot state anything about her knowledge of anything during the period of time in which she was employed in the White House?" Nadler asked White House lawyer Mike Pupura.

"For the purpose of this hearing, yes," Pupura answered.

Nadler's frustration grew. On three occasions, he referred to Hicks as "Ms. Lewandowski."

"My name is Ms. Hicks," Hicks said after the third time.

"I'm sorry, Ms. Hicks," Nadler said. "I'm preoccupied."

And so it went. Democrats repeatedly referred to this or that episode in the Mueller report, which included the testimony of Hicks. But Hicks would add nothing to Mueller's account. The situation was clearly driving Democrats crazy. The only reason Nadler and his colleagues knew to ask about particular moments was because they were described in the Mueller report as a result of the Trump-ordered cooperation. But the White House's cooperation did not extend to congressional oversight hearings. Nadler was stymied.

Trump himself teased Nadler and Democrats for what appeared to be an ill-considered effort to re-create the Mueller investigation. "The Dems are very unhappy with the Mueller report, so after almost 3 years, they want a redo, or do-over," the president tweeted as Hicks testified. "This is extreme presidential harassment."

What could Democrats do? Nadler was reduced to trying to produce an impeachment show without any stars. One measure of his difficulties came on June 10, when Nadler, with no good witnesses willing to speak to him, invited former White House counsel and Watergate felon John Dean to testify before the committee. Finally, the chairman had a witness who would show up. Dean began by telling lawmakers that the last time he appeared before them was July 11, 1974—forty-five years earlier. Of course, he had no knowledge beyond media reports of any of the matters currently under investigation. He spent his testimony delivering the type of analysis he normally gave on CNN.

The Nadler strategy was simply not working. "We beat them at every punch," recalled Collins. "Every time they turned around, nothing was sticking. Their witness list was terrible—John Dean! We were hearing backchannel from rank-and-file Democrats, especially some freshmen, that they were going to Pelosi and saying, you've got to pull this."

It was time to try for the biggest star of all, Robert Mueller himself.

The Mueller Movie

Many Democrats increasingly believed that a Trump-Russia impeachment would never take off unless it could be effectively presented on television. Watergate captured the public's attention when dramatic hearings were televised. The Mueller report, on the other hand, was a dry, 400-plus page legal document that might appeal to the hard-core Trump resistance, or to scandal aficionados, but would never speak to the broad public.

So the question: how to make the Mueller report exciting? How to turn it into a drama that everyone would want to know about? By having dramatic, Watergate-style hearings. And the most dramatic figure in the entire affair, save President Trump himself, was Mueller. Put Mueller in a Capitol Hill hearing room jammed with lawmakers and journalists, cameras rolling, and a Trump-Russia impeachment proceeding would become something the nation would want to watch.

"Not everybody is reading the book, but people will watch the movie," a House Judiciary Committee official told *Politico*'s Playbook.

Nearly every Democrat, it appeared, believed in the movie strategy. Even Speaker Pelosi, who had been publicly opposed to impeachment for months, began to say that nothing was "off the table" when it came to impeachment. "But we do want to make such a compelling case," Pelosi said in late May, "such an ironclad case, that even the Republican Senate, which at the time seems not to be an objective jury, will be convinced of the path we have to take as a country." The way to make that compelling case was the Mueller movie.

So in late April, just days after the report's release, Nadler's staff began talks with the Justice Department aimed at calling Mueller to testify. The problem was that Mueller did not want to testify. Even though he had gone beyond what many thought were Department requirements in writing a lengthy report, he did not want to add even more to the record by answering the House's questions. He also saw the matter as closed and had no desire to turn his work into a movie.

The talks went on as May began. Attorney General Barr said he had "no objection" to Mueller testifying. Nadler's staff got in touch with the Mueller office directly but could not secure Mueller's agreement to testify. Capitol Hill sources began talking about the possibility of a hearing on May 15, but nothing was set. May 15 came and went.

On May 29, Mueller held a surprise news conference at the Justice Department. It was the first time he had spoken publicly during the entire investigation. Given the amount of attention paid to him every moment, the number of times his name was spoken in the media every day, the appearance of the actual, walking, talking Robert Mueller took on an almost oracular quality. There he was, speaking at last.

Mueller announced that, with the investigation finished, he was resigning from the Department to return to private life. He repeated the baffling "not exonerated" standard from the report: "If we had had confidence that the president clearly did not commit a crime," he said, "we would have said so." He again linked his decision not to decide on obstruction to the OLC opinion, one more time contradicting what Quarles had told the Justice Department at the time of the report's release.

Then Mueller addressed the debate about his proposed testimony. "I hope and expect this to be the only time that I will speak to you in this manner," he said. "I am making that decision myself. No one has told me whether I can or should testify or speak further about this matter.... The report is my testimony. I would not provide information beyond that which is already public in any appearance before Congress."

What did that mean? It meant Mueller was not really saying no, but not really saying yes, either. To some Democrats, desperate to have him appear, that was nearly as good as an outright yes. So they kept pressing, and when Mueller did not immediately agree, they brought up the possibility of subpoenaing him to testify.

It was not discussed publicly at the time, but there was something else going on behind the scenes. There were serious concerns in some quarters about whether Mueller would be up to testifying. The Trump team had believed for a year that the once-sharp Mueller had slowed down to the point that he was not really in charge of the investigation. The lawyers noticed that Mueller always stayed out of sight, and on the few occasions they saw him, he seemed unfamiliar with some of the basic facts of the investigation. They saw his top aides cover for him and deny that there was a problem. But they suspected there really was a problem.

Those worries were compounded at the "infamous March 5 meeting," the session in which Mueller and two deputies previewed the report for Barr and top Justice Department aides. Some in the meeting had heard rumors that Mueller had been in cognitive decline even before becoming special counsel, and should not have taken the job.

The meeting did nothing to allay those concerns. According to *Washington Post* reporters Philip Rucker and Carol Leonnig, who provided a detailed account of the meeting in their book, *A Very Stable Genius*, "Mueller kicked off the meeting by pulling out a piece of paper with some notes. The attorney general and his aides believed they noticed something worrisome. Mueller's hands shook as he held the paper. His voice was shaky, too. This was not the Bob Mueller everyone knew." The Justice Department officials, who knew about the rumors going in, were concerned about Mueller's health. "They were taken aback," Rucker and Leonnig wrote. "As Barr would later ask his colleagues, 'Did he seem off to you?' Later, close friends would say they noticed Mueller had changed dramatically, but a member of Mueller's team would insist he had no medical problems."

Now Democrats wanted Mueller to testify separately to the House Judiciary and Intelligence committees in two widely televised, high-pressure hearings. Mueller's staff wanted to avoid putting him in that position, even though they insisted nothing was wrong with him. They hoped the Justice Department would solve the problem by forbidding Mueller to testify. But Barr had already said he had "no problem" with Mueller going to Capitol Hill.

On June 25, Nadler and Schiff issued subpoenas to Mueller for his testimony. At that point, Mueller really had no choice. He agreed to appear on July 17.

Barr offered Mueller a way out. On a trip to South Carolina on July 8, Barr was asked about the Mueller situation and answered that he was "disappointed to see him subpoenaed." Barr then sent a very intentional message to Mueller and his team: it would be okay to cancel. "It seems to me the only reason for doing that [to have Mueller testify] is to create some kind of public spectacle," Barr said. "If he decides he doesn't want to be subjected to that, the DOJ will certainly back that."

But the hearing, rescheduled for July 24, proceeded. At the last minute, the special counsel's office asked that a close Mueller aide, Aaron Zebley, sit at the witness table with Mueller. All sides agreed, although it was understood that Zebley would not testify. In any event, he would serve as support for Mueller should the hearing become difficult.

Mueller was scheduled to appear before the Judiciary Committee in the morning to discuss Volume II of the report, dealing with allegations of obstruction of justice. That afternoon, he would appear with the Intelligence Committee and discuss Volume I, on the Russian conspiracy and coordination investigation.

Things went badly from the start. Mueller had a difficult time hearing and grasping questions. On more than thirty occasions, he asked to have a question repeated. He gave short, yes-or-no answers and never developed an extended thought. He did not seem to be conversant with some issues. He contradicted himself and his report.

Nadler walked Mueller through a series of questions on Trump's refusal to submit to an interview with the special counsel's office. During the investigation, both the Trump team and the special counsel agreed that Trump would take written questions, but only on the Russia side of the investigation, and not on obstruction of justice. Nadler was trying to get Mueller to say that Trump refused to answer even a single question on obstruction—that was, in fact, true—but Mueller could not recall if that were the case.

"The president still refused to sit for an interview by you or your team?" asked Nadler.

"True, true," said Mueller.

"And did you also ask him to provide written answers to questions on the ten possible episodes of obstruction of justice crimes involving him?"

"Yes."

"Did he provide any answers to a single question about whether he engaged in obstruction of justice crimes?"

At that point, Mueller was expected to say, "No, he did not." Instead, Mueller said, "I would have to check on that. I'm not certain."

Mueller made a serious error when Democratic Representative Ted Lieu tried to get him to say that he would have indicted Trump had it not been for the Justice Department's Office of Legal Counsel opinion that a sitting president cannot be indicted. That, of course, had been the subject of much confusion after the Mueller team said three times during their March 5 meeting with Barr that they specifically *would not* claim that Mueller would have indicted Trump but for the OLC opinion. Then the report suggested the opposite. And then came Mueller's exchange with Lieu.

"I believe any reasonable person looking at these facts could conclude that all three elements of the crime of obstruction of justice have been met," Lieu said. "And I'd like to ask you the reason, again, that you did not indict Donald Trump is because of the OLC opinion stating that you cannot indict a sitting president, correct?"

"That is correct," said Mueller.

Later, in the second hearing, Mueller clarified his answer. "That is not the correct way to say it," he told lawmakers. "We did not reach a determination as to whether the president committed a crime."

Mueller made contradictory statements on whether his investigation was hampered by President Trump or his allies. "It's fair to say, then, that there were limits on what evidence was available to your investigation of both Russia election interference and obstruction of justice," Democratic Representative Val Demings said.

"That's usually the case," Mueller said.

"And that lies by Trump campaign officials and administration officials impeded your investigation?"

"I would generally agree with that," Mueller answered.

But in another exchange, Doug Collins asked Mueller, "At any time in the investigation, was your investigation curtailed or stopped or hindered?"

"No," said Mueller.

Mueller also engaged in a long back-and-forth with Collins over whether the words "collusion" and "conspiracy" were "essentially synonymous." The Mueller report said they were, but Mueller could not seem to get his arms around the question. First, he said they were not, contradicting his report, then he said they were, and then he seemed to just not know. "I – I – I – I leave it with the report," he said.

The talk at the break between the Judiciary Committee and Intelligence Committee hearings was all about Mueller's performance. Some commentators generously called it "clipped" and suggested it was simply Mueller's just-the-facts style. But others saw something more serious at work.

"This is delicate to say," tweeted former Obama aide David Axelrod, "but Mueller, whom I deeply respect, has not publicly testified before Congress in at least six years. And he does not appear as sharp as he was then."

Fox News' Chris Wallace was less delicate. "I think it's been a disaster for the Democrats," he said, "and I think it's been a disaster for the reputation of Robert Mueller."

The afternoon session with the Intelligence Committee was no better. The problems Mueller had in the morning session were just as evident. Republicans were unhappy that Mueller seemed to know little or nothing about the questions they had raised about the origins of the Trump-Russia investigation—the Steele dossier, the FBI's confidential informants, the Carter Page surveillance warrant. But the big picture had been set in the morning. By the end of the day, Mueller's appearance was widely viewed, as Wallace had said, as a disaster.

"He wasn't in charge"

Afterward, Republicans reacted with a mix of concern for Mueller and satisfaction that Democrats were not able to create the movie they wanted.

"Are you watching this?" asked Devin Nunes in a private conversation during a break in the hearings. "Is there something that is more descriptive than 'train wreck'? It sheds a lot of light on what happened the last two years. He wasn't in charge."

"What stood out in my mind was not only was it sad to watch Mueller," recalled Republican Representative Brad Wenstrup of Ohio. "What sticks in my head is looking over and seeing Daniel Goldman, the hired gun attorney, almost tearing up. You could just see the glaze in their eyes, literally, his and Adam Schiff's. There was nothing there. They were getting nothing out of this. It was a complete backfire."

"It was horrendous," recalled Kevin McCarthy. "It almost got to the point, I remember we talked to the members as they came back, it almost got to the point where members said we ought to stop asking him questions. It was like going after an old uncle who's not there any more."

As for the Democrats, McCarthy could almost—almost—feel their pain. "The thing I've always thought," he said, "was that every time you have these big hearings, and you're in the majority, and you think you're really going to get somebody—Benghazi and all that—it always turns out to be less. The anticipation and the expectations are too high. But with Mueller, oh man, that was bad."

The obvious hope for Republicans was that the impeachment talk was now officially dead. How could it go forward? The Mueller report could not establish conspiracy or coordination, and now Democrats had failed in their attempt to use Mueller's testimony to juice up public support.

But impeachment was not dead. It never was.

Here's something few people took much note of: on July 17, exactly one week before Mueller testified, when all of official Washington and big-time media was Mueller, Mueller, Mueller, Al Green took to the House floor to offer yet another article of impeachment. Green was spurred to action by recent Trump tweets directed at the so-called "Squad" of Democratic Representatives Ilhan Omar, Rashida Tlaib, Alexandria Ocasio-Cortez, and Ayanna Pressley, suggesting they go back to where they came from. Green's impeachment article was brief, focused mostly on Trump's alleged racism, which Green said had "sown seeds of discord among the people of the United States."

As with Green's previous impeachment efforts, McCarthy moved that the matter be tabled. A vote was held. In a similar situation in December 2017, fifty-eight Democrats voted to move Green's impeachment articles forward. A month later, sixty-six Democrats voted to move the articles forward. And this time, on July 17, 2019, a total of ninety-five Democrats voted to move impeachment forward.

Ninety-five votes. It wasn't a majority of Democrats in the House, but it was about 40 percent of them. And the point of Green's resolution was not that it was a serious case for impeachment. The point was that it showed the extent of Democratic support for a non-serious case for impeachment.

What the Green vote proved was that the number of Democrats willing to impeach Trump for *any* reason was increasing. It was no longer under Nancy Pelosi's control. Pro-impeachment Democrats were a growing movement in search of a new leader and a new direction. As it turned out, both were soon on the way.

CHAPTER EIGHT

Impeachment 4.0: "Here We Go Again"

"In effect"—A Whistleblower?—An Audacious Plan—
"The serious misconduct at issue involves the President of
the United States"—A Two-Track Impeachment—
Pelosi's Big Move

I t would be an exaggeration to say that Trump's defenders disbanded
after the Mueller testimony. But they did relax and let their guard
down. They had been fighting the Trump-Russia battle full-time for
more than two years. Mueller's testimony, coming on the heels of the
findings in the Mueller report, appeared to be the end. Trump had won.
It was time for a rest.

Jay Sekulow and his wife headed to the mountains of North Carolina. Jane and Marty Raskin headed out west for some down time and
then went back to their law practice. Others turned to other business.
"We all kind of dispersed," Jane Raskin recalled.

Republican members of Congress relaxed, too. The House's last day
of business before the August 2019 recess was July 26, two days after
Mueller's testimony. The break would last until September 9. GOP lawmakers who had defended Trump throughout the Russia affair headed
home hoping the Russia fever had broken.

That did not mean anyone expected Adam Schiff, or Jerry Nadler,
or the ninety-five Democrats who voted to move impeachment forward
to give up their efforts to remove Trump from office. But Republicans

believed the Democratic cause had been badly set back. Mueller was a dud. It would take Democrats time to recover. Now was a moment to rest.

They were wrong.

"In effect"

Contrary to GOP expectations, Mueller's appearance actually *increased* Democratic support for impeachment in the House. A *Washington Post* count at the end of July found 114 Democrats who said they supported "at least opening an impeachment inquiry into whether Trump committed 'high crimes and misdemeanors.'" And they weren't just backbenchers. On July 31, Representative Eliot Engel, chairman of the House Foreign Affairs Committee, called for impeachment. "Mr. Mueller's testimony provided ample evidence that the president committed obstruction of justice," Engel said in a press release, "and I believe the House must pursue a formal impeachment inquiry."

Tom Steyer, the Democratic billionaire who had a few weeks earlier announced his presidential candidacy, put Mueller's one-word answers into a commercial to air on CNN and MSNBC during the July 31, 2019, Democratic debate in Detroit. The ad featured questions at the Mueller hearing from Nadler, Schiff, and others. Steyer's group, Need to Impeach, spent what was reported to be "mid-six figures" to air the ad.

"Robert Mueller was panned last week for being short in his testimony before Congress, giving little ammo to Democrats who wanted to capitalize politically from his appearance," *Politico* Playbook reported. "But Democratic ad-maker Mark Putnam has cut the first paid ad from the hearings, funded by Tom Steyer's Need to Impeach, a spot that's going to grab many eyeballs in the coming days." The idea was to create public pressure on Democrats in Congress to support impeachment, no matter the reviews of Mueller's performance.

To the lawmakers most closely involved in Trump-Russia matters, the impeachment inquiry was already under way. On July 26, Nadler held a press conference to announce the "next steps in our work to hold President Trump accountable." He said Mueller's testimony "removed all doubt" that the president had obstructed justice. He said the Judiciary Committee would work through the August recess to hear from more witnesses, including issuing subpoenas if necessary. And he announced that the committee had filed papers seeking the grand jury material underlying the Mueller report. It would be "critically important for our ability to examine witnesses," Nadler said.

Nadler appeared with other Democrats—Mary Gay Scanlon, Eric Swalwell (also a candidate for the Democratic presidential nomination), Madeleine Dean, Steve Cohen (the Chicken Man from the Barr no-show hearing), Sheila Jackson Lee, Veronica Escobar, Jamie Raskin, and Joe Neguse—many of whom had already called for impeachment. Several of them repeated those calls from the microphone, and then Nadler himself left little doubt that the Judiciary Committee was working toward impeachment. Given that Speaker Nancy Pelosi was still on record opposing impeachment, Nadler could not come out and directly say: we are working toward impeaching the president. But he could tiptoe up to that point—he invented a new euphemism for impeachment, "full Article I authority"—and then step back as his colleagues made the case for him.

"There's got to be a point, Mr. Chairman, where you break from the Speaker and you announce publicly your support for impeachment," a reporter said.

"As I said and as is clear in the court filings, we are exercising our full Article I authority," Nadler said. "We are continuing our investigation of the president's malfeasance. And we will do what we feel—and we will consider what we have to consider, including whether we should recommend articles of impeachment to the House."

"But what's holding you back from publicly voicing your support for impeachment here?"

"Well, if I can jump in," said Mary Gay Scanlon, "impeachment isn't a binary thing that you either are or you aren't. What we've been saying and what we've been doing is starting a process where we are engaging in an investigation to see if we should recommend articles of impeachment."

Others at the podium were more direct. "I would say we are in an impeachment investigation," said Jamie Raskin. Swalwell added, "I support what Mr. Raskin just said, which is this is an impeachment investigation."

Then reporters said to Nadler: "Mr. Chairman, you're saying there's no difference between what you're doing now and impeachment inquiry, correct?"

"In effect," Nadler answered. "Well, I suppose there is one difference which you could draw, if you said that an impeachment inquiry is when you're considering only impeachment. That's not what we're doing. We're investigating all of this, and we are going to see what remedies we could recommend, including the possibility of articles of impeachment. We're not limited to that, but that's very much the possibility as a result of what we're doing."

At that moment, the news conference became news. Media reports focused on Nadler's use of the phrase "in effect" to claim that he had finally announced an impeachment investigation. And indeed there was no doubt Nadler was, in fact, conducting an impeachment investigation. But what the news conference showed most clearly was that some influential Democrats, on the Friday after Mueller's Wednesday testimony, were ready to move forward with impeachment but believed it was still not safe to say so openly.

Remember back to Nadler's Amtrak phone conversations, the day after the 2018 midterms, overheard by Mollie Hemingway. As Hemingway described it, Nadler told the unknown person on the other end of the line that while Democrats would be "all-in" on Russia, they "had figured out that impeachment did not poll well, and…they had come up with the term 'accountability' to be the way that they would talk about impeachment." Nadler said three times during the news conference that he would hold President Trump accountable.

Schiff was also being cautious. The morning after the Mueller hearing, he noted that even if House Democrats succeeded in impeaching Trump, the effort to remove him would fail in the Republican Senate. "Can we make the case to the country, and does the country benefit going through an impeachment, if it's going to be unsuccessful?" Schiff asked. "And we know in the Senate at least it would be unsuccessful. So I'm not there yet, but I'm keeping an open mind, and I may get there."

Schiff's words led to a spate of "Is-Schiff-backing-away-from-impeachment?" stories. Three days later, Schiff appeared on NBC's *Meet the Press* and took the cautious line again. "Where we are now is most accurately described as a preliminary to a judicial proceeding, and that judicial proceeding is a potential impeachment," he said.

August passed with Congress out of Washington. There were fewer interviews and (a little) less press coverage. Even impeachment seemed to take a brief break at summer's end. What appeared to be coming was that Democrats would return to the Capitol in September and start hitting Trump-Russia again.

The Trump defense team, still savoring victory, was watching. They were not surprised that Schiff and Nadler did not give up; they expected them to try to salvage something from the Mueller report. But they were not worried. They had already dealt with the Terminator in the form of the Mueller investigation. Next to that, Congress did not seem terribly intimidating.

"Both Schiff and Nadler, they did not stop," a Trump defender said. "We knew that. From our perspective, jousting with Nadler and Schiff was child's play. We had been dealing with a federal prosecutor who had real power—who could take away people's liberty. As much as we thought the Mueller investigation was going nowhere, it was serious. It was a team of very powerful people trying to take people down. Not to be trifled with."

But Nadler and Schiff, and even Congress in general? "I don't mean to belittle it, but we can deal with Congress," the defender said.

Here was the flaw in that thinking, which every Republican member of Congress who had defended Trump also shared: it assumed that Democrats would keep going back to the same old Russia well. After all, they had been doing it for more than two years. Why wouldn't they continue? It stunned Trump's defenders to learn that Schiff had something else up his sleeve.

A Whistleblower?

Mueller testified on July 24. The day after, doing presidential business that appeared to be entirely unrelated to the Mueller probe, Trump had a phone call with Volodymyr Zelensky, the president of Ukraine. In the call, Trump congratulated Zelensky on winning the presidency. "It's a fantastic achievement," he said. Zelensky flattered Trump by suggesting that Trump had been a model for his campaign. "We wanted to drain the swamp here in our country," Zelensky said. "You are a great teacher for us and in that."

Trump complained that European countries were not doing enough to help Ukraine but said the United States "has been very, very good to Ukraine." Zelensky, obsequious throughout the call, told Trump that he was "absolutely right," and that "even though logically, the European Union should be our biggest partner but technically the United States is a much bigger partner." "I'm very grateful to you for that," he said.

"I would also like to thank you for your great support in the area of defense," Zelensky said. "We are ready to continue to cooperate for the next steps, specifically we are almost ready to buy more Javelins from the United States for defense purposes." That was a reference to Trump's decision to sell the Javelin anti-tank missile to Ukraine to defend itself against Russian aggression, something the Obama administration had refused to do.

"I would like you to do us a favor, though, because our country has been through a lot and Ukraine knows a lot about it," Trump said. "I would like you to find out what happened with this whole situation with

Ukraine, they say CrowdStrike…I guess you have one of your wealthy people…The server, they say Ukraine has it. There are a lot of things that went on, the whole situation. I think you're surrounding yourself with some of the same people. I would like to have the Attorney General call you or your people, and I would like you to get to the bottom of it."

It was hard to make out precisely, but Trump was referring to rumors he had heard that the Democratic National Committee server that was hacked by Russians during the 2016 election had somehow found its way to Ukraine. The reference to "CrowdStrike" was to the tech company that the DNC employed. When the FBI began to investigate the hacking, the DNC refused the bureau access to its servers and instead had Crowd-Strike supply investigators with what CrowdStrike called "an exact byte-for-byte copy" of the hard drives involved. The DNC's refusal to allow the FBI full access led to persistent speculation that it had something to hide. But law enforcement and the Intelligence Community both determined that Russians had, in fact, hacked the DNC.

Nevertheless, Trump asked Zelensky to look into it. "As you saw yesterday, that whole nonsense ended with a very poor performance by a man named Robert Mueller," Trump told Zelensky—the "whole non-sense" being the Trump-Russia investigation. Trump said Mueller's testimony was "an incompetent performance, but they say a lot of it started with Ukraine. Whatever you can do, it's very important that you do it, if that's possible," Trump said.

"Yes, it is very important for me," Zelensky said, adding that he was "open for any future cooperation."

Trump then brought up Ukraine's troubled history with corruption, and with prosecutors investigating that corruption. "I heard you had a prosecutor who was very good and he was shut down and that's really unfair," Trump said. "A lot of people are talking about that, the way they shut your very good prosecutor down and you had some very bad people involved." Trump then told Zelensky that Rudy Giuliani, a member of his legal team, was looking into it. "Mr. Giuliani is a highly respected man. He was the mayor of New York City, and I would like him to call you," Trump said. "I will ask him to call you along with the Attorney General. Rudy very much knows what's happening and he is a very capable guy. If you could speak to him that would be great."

Trump added that Marie Yovanovitch, the U.S. ambassador to Ukraine whom Trump had recalled in May, was "bad news…and the people she was dealing with in the Ukraine were bad news." In addition, Trump brought up former Vice President Joe Biden, then leading the race for the Democratic presidential nomination in 2020. "There's a lot of talk about Biden's son, that Biden stopped the prosecution," Trump said, "and a lot of people want to find out about that, so whatever you can do with the Attorney General would be great. Biden went around bragging that he stopped the prosecution, so if you can look into it…It sounds horrible to me."

Zelensky said that now that he had an absolute majority in Parliament, he would bring in a new prosecutor who "will look into the situation." Zelensky also told Trump that he agreed with Trump's assessment of Yovanovitch. "It was great that you were the first one who told me that she was a bad ambassador, because I agree with you 100 percent," Zelensky said. "Her attitude towards me was far from the best, as she admired the previous president and she was on his side. She would not accept me as a new president well enough."

"Well, she's going to go through some things," Trump said, adding that he would have Giuliani, and also Attorney General Barr, call Zelensky. After some pleasantries, the call ended.

As was normally done, the Trump-Zelensky call was monitored, on the American side, by a number of national security officials, most of them in the White House's National Security Council. They took notes and afterward compiled the rough transcript quoted in the exchanges above. The ellipses in a few places were in the original and indicated that the staff either missed or left out some portion of the conversation.

Trump's concerns, as expressed on the call, were a mix of the reasonable and the far-fetched. First, they showed the lasting effects of the Trump-Russia pursuit on the president's psyche and worldview. It had caused him so much grief that, now that it was (apparently) over, he was determined to get to the bottom of how it began. There were, as he implied, several instances of prominent Ukrainians, some government officials, who made efforts to influence the 2016 U.S. presidential election on behalf of Hillary Clinton. There was evidence that some of them attacked Paul Manafort as a way to stop Trump. There was evidence that some of them worked with Trump's opponents in the United States. None of it approached the scale, or centralized governmental direction, of the Russian election interference effort. But it happened nonetheless, and it was not surprising for Trump to inquire about it.

On the issue of CrowdStrike, Trump's questions seemed to have no basis in fact. No investigator had suggested that the DNC server was in Ukraine or that Ukraine was somehow involved in the DNC hack. Whatever information the president had was bad information.

On the issue of prosecutors and Joe Biden's son, there was reason for concern. At a time when then-Vice President Biden was the Obama administration's point man on Ukraine, a corrupt Ukrainian energy company, Burisma, placed Biden's son Hunter on its board of directors at a salary of at least $50,000 a month. Burisma's obvious purpose was to influence Ukrainian relations with the United States. At the same time, the Obama administration sought to remove Ukraine's prosecutor general, Viktor Shokin, the man nominally investigating Burisma, on grounds that he was not actually attacking corruption. Joe Biden traveled to Ukraine in 2016 to demand that Shokin be fired. Biden threatened to cut off $1 billion in U.S. loan guarantees to Ukraine if Shokin was not axed immediately.

"I looked at them and said, 'I'm leaving in six hours. If the prosecutor is not fired, you're not getting the money,'" Biden said, recounting the incident in 2018. "Well, son of a bitch. He got fired."

On the call with Zelensky, Trump did not bring up the general issue of Ukrainian corruption, which was a chronic problem in U.S.-Ukraine relations. But the Burisma-Hunter Biden matter was certainly one element of Ukraine's culture of corruption.

Also, at the time, Trump had placed a hold on the delivery of U.S. aid to Ukraine. He did not bring the subject up with Zelensky, did not suggest that the delivery of U.S. aid depended on anything, and there is no evidence that Zelensky knew about the hold at the time of the call.

Of the several people listening to the call, one of them, Lieutenant Colonel Alexander Vindman, the National Security Council's expert on Ukraine, believed Trump's behavior was improper. Vindman, a Ukrainian-born naturalized American, later testified that he "did not think it was proper" for Trump to "demand that a foreign government investigate a U.S. citizen." Vindman said he was worried that "if Ukraine pursued an investigation into the Bidens and Burisma, it would likely be interpreted as a partisan play, which would undoubtedly result in Ukraine losing the bipartisan support it had thus far maintained." That, Vindman argued, would "undermine U.S. national security."

Vindman related his concerns to his identical twin brother, Lieutenant Colonel Yevgeny Vindman, who was a lawyer and ethics official on the National Security Council. Together, the two brothers discussed the issue with the NSC's counsel, John Eisenberg. Alexander Vindman was the only person listening to the call who was concerned that something improper had happened. Vindman's direct superior, Tim Morrison, testified that he, Morrison, did not believe anything he heard on the call was improper. But Morrison nevertheless told Eisenberg he worried that the contents of the call might leak and feared how that might "play out in Washington's polarized environment." A leak "could affect the bipartisan support our Ukrainian partners currently experience in Congress," Morrison later testified, and it could "affect the Ukrainian perceptions of the U.S.-Ukraine relationship."

In reaction, Eisenberg moved the call record to a highly classified server. But by that time, word of the call had already spread far beyond the White House.

The next day, July 26, a CIA officer wrote a memo in which he said he had a conversation "with a White House official" about the

Trump-Zelensky call. The CIA officer, who told his superiors he wished to remain anonymous, wrote that the White House official who had "listened to the entirety of the phone call"—and who also remained anonymous—was "visibly shaken by what had transpired." The fact that the officer described the White House official's appearance suggests the conversation was face-to-face, but at another point in the memo the officer described their conversation as a "call." It is not clear how the two men spoke. Some Republicans came to believe the CIA officer had actually been in the White House complex on the day of the Trump-Zelensky call, but they were never able to confirm that.

"The official described the call as 'crazy,' 'frightening' and 'completely lacking in substance related to national security,'" the CIA officer's memo said. "The official asserted that the president used the call to persuade Ukrainian authorities to investigate his political rivals, chiefly former Vice President Biden and his son, Hunter. The official stated that there was already a conversation underway with White House lawyers about how to handle the discussion because, in the official's view, the president had clearly committed a criminal act by urging a foreign power to investigate a U.S. person for the purposes of advancing his own re-election bid in 2020."

The CIA officer who wrote the memo would later become known as "the whistleblower." The identity of the White House official who told him about the call was never revealed. But House Republican investigators came to believe strongly that it was Alexander Vindman. Later testimony revealed that Vindman discussed the call with his brother, with Eisenberg, with another NSC lawyer, Michael Ellis, with Morrison, and with a State Department official who dealt with Ukraine named George Kent. According to the testimony, Vindman also talked to one other person outside the White House, but Intelligence Committee Chairman Schiff, who was in charge of the investigation, forbade anyone from asking Vindman who that outside person was. The obvious conclusion Republicans drew was that Vindman talked to the person at the CIA who became the whistleblower—in other words, that Vindman set the entire whistleblower process in motion. But that was never definitively proven, or disproven, because of Schiff's blackout on information about one of Vindman's contacts.

All of that was happening behind the scenes at the end of July. On July 26, for example, the day the whistleblower spoke to the White House official and wrote the memo, the news was filled with Jerry Nadler's declaration that the House Judiciary Committee was "in effect" conducting an impeachment investigation based on the Mueller report. No one knew it, but at that moment one impeachment drive was ending while another was beginning.

An Audacious Plan

At some point around the end of July and the beginning of August, the whistleblower got in touch with Schiff's Democratic majority staff at the Intelligence Committee. It has never been clearly established how it worked, but at the very minimum the whistleblower described his complaint to staff—it's not clear in what level of detail—who then talked to Schiff. It is not clear whether Schiff himself ever communicated with the whistleblower. In any event, by early August, Schiff knew about a whistleblower who had a charge to level against President Trump.

Schiff kept it a closely held secret. Senior Republicans on the committee, who should have been apprised of committee business, were not told what Schiff and the Democratic staff had learned. Republicans were kept in the dark for all of August—while the whistleblower shaped and polished his complaint—and did not learn what was going on, even in the vaguest terms, until the second week in September. Schiff and his colleagues were working away while Republicans remained unawares.

As for the whistleblower himself, how should he proceed? He retained a law firm and settled on an audacious idea: he would lodge a formal whistleblower complaint, making use of whistleblower laws passed by

Congress to protect witnesses who allege wrongdoing in the various federal agencies, against the President of the United States.

It was audacious because there was no scenario in which the president, as head of the executive branch, was covered by any whistleblower law. The whistleblower laws were designed for an employee at, say, the Occupational Safety and Health Administration, who had evidence that his or her supervisor was, say, misusing a government credit card, and who needed protection from retaliation by the supervisor in order to bring the misconduct to light. Whistleblower complaints covered all sorts of alleged wrongdoing, but no whistleblower law included making a complaint against the president.

Given that, how could the whistleblower—he would become widely known as that even though the whistleblower laws did not apply to his complaint—actually press his case? Should he go to Congress directly? To the press? To the CIA leadership?

Going to Congress was a reasonable option. After all, the complaint was a political matter, and if anyone would have the authority to oversee the president, it would be Congress. (Although in this particular case, Congress might have little to say, since the president has extensive constitutional authority to conduct foreign policy.) Going straight to the press would be more difficult, since the whistleblower would be open to accusations that he revealed classified information.

The law governing the process was known as the Intelligence Community Whistleblower Protection Act. It required whistleblowers in the Intelligence Community to first go, not to Congress, but to the Intelligence Community Inspector General, or ICIG. The Inspector General would then have fourteen days to evaluate the whistleblower's complaint, and if he determined that it "appears credible" and constituted an "urgent concern," he would pass it on to the Director of National Intelligence, who would then have seven days to pass it to the intelligence committees in Congress. The law defined an "urgent concern" as:

A serious or flagrant problem, abuse, violation of law or
Executive Order, or deficiency relating to the funding, administration, or operation of an intelligence activity within the
responsibility and authority of the Director of National Intelligence involving classified information, but does not include
differences of opinions concerning public policy matters.

The whistleblower's complaint—that Trump had tried to persuade
the president of Ukraine to investigate a political rival—simply did not
fit into the structure established by the Intelligence Community Whistleblower Protection Act. One could argue whether Trump's action was "a
serious or flagrant problem," but there was no doubt that it did not relate
"to the funding, administration, or operation of an intelligence activity
within the responsibility and authority of the Director of National Intelligence involving classified information." The President of the United
States is not under the authority of the Director of National Intelligence.
And there were other ways to deal with alleged presidential wrongdoing,
including an extensive system of congressional oversight and, at least in
Trump's case, a robustly adversarial press. But the Intelligence Community Whistleblower Protection Act did not apply to the president.

Nevertheless, that is the route the whistleblower, acting on the advice
of Schiff's staff, decided to take. On August 12, the whistleblower filed
a complaint—carefully drafted by his lawyers—with the Intelligence
Community Inspector General, Michael Atkinson. The whistleblower
said that "in the course of my official duties," he had "received information from multiple U.S. government officials" that President Trump was
"using the power of his office to solicit interference from a foreign country in the 2020 U.S. election." The whistleblower said he had received
that information "over the past four months," and that he had received
it from "more than half a dozen U.S. officials," and that he had received
it "in the course of official interagency business." The whistleblower
admitted that he was "not a direct witness" to the Trump-Zelensky call.

"I am deeply concerned that the actions described below constitute 'a serious or flagrant problem, abuse, or violation of law or Executive Order' that 'does not include differences of opinions concerning policy matters,'" the whistleblower wrote. The quoted phrases were taken straight from the Intelligence Community Whistleblower Protection Act in an effort to argue that the complaint was covered by the law. But it was a highly selective quotation that left out the part of the law requiring that a complaint involve "an intelligence activity within the responsibility and authority of the Director of National Intelligence." The complaint did not meet that standard of the law, so the lawyers ignored it and moved on to a discussion of the July 25 Trump-Zelensky call.

The whistleblower said that "multiple White House officials with direct knowledge of the call" described the contents of the Trump-Zelensky conversation to him. It was never clear what "multiple" meant; all the whistleblower's information about the content of the call appeared to come from Alexander Vindman, who was the only person listening to the call who expressed objections to what Trump had said. The whistleblower's description appeared to come straight from the White House rough transcript of the call, which Alexander Vindman had helped prepare. The complaint then repeated the allegation that Trump had sought foreign interference in the 2020 campaign and that his actions "pose risks to U.S. national security and undermine the U.S. government's efforts to deter and counter foreign interference in U.S. elections."

"The White House officials who told me this information were deeply disturbed by what had transpired in the phone call," the whistleblower said. "They told me that there was already a 'discussion ongoing' with White House lawyers about how to treat the call because of the likelihood, in the officials' retelling, that they had witnessed the president abuse his office for personal gain."

The rest of the complaint covered other matters the whistleblower said he learned from sources, but which also seemed to come from news accounts. The whistleblower's claim that he had been receiving reports "over the past four months"—in other words, since well before the

Trump-Zelensky call—appeared to be an effort to beef up the complaint to make it about more than just the Trump-Zelensky call. But it was in fact nearly all about the Trump-Zelensky call.

The whistleblower might not even have been able to make his complaint had not the Intelligence Community Inspector General changed the procedures governing the filing of complaints. Until the time the whistleblower raised his concerns, the ICIG required that a complainant have "first-hand information" of alleged wrongdoing. Indeed, when the whistleblower approached the office about filing a complaint, he was given a standard document that said:

> In order to find an urgent concern "credible," the ICIG must be in possession of reliable, first-hand information. The ICIG cannot transmit information via the ICWPA [Intelligence Community Whistleblower Protection Act] based on an employee's second-hand knowledge of wrongdoing. This includes information received from another person, such as when a fellow employee informs you that he/she witnessed some type of wrongdoing.... If you think wrongdoing took place, but can provide nothing more than secondhand or unsubstantiated assertions, ICIG will not be able to process the complaint or information for submission as an ICWA.

The requirement was clear: a complainant must have first-hand knowledge. The whistleblower had none concerning the Trump-Zelensky call. And yet the complaint was allowed to go forward anyway. Why? As Inspector General Atkinson later told it, at the moment the whistleblower filed his complaint, the office's Center for Protected Disclosures just happened to be reviewing the forms provided to whistleblowers. As part of that review, and as a result of press inquiries about the whistleblower, the Inspector General came to realize that "certain language in those forms and, more specifically, the informational materials accompanying the forms, could be read—incorrectly—as suggesting that whistleblowers must possess first-hand information in order to file an urgent concern complaint."

So the form was changed in a way that retroactively made it appear that the whistleblower had met all the requirements of the complaint process.

Once the complaint was filed, Atkinson had fourteen days to determine whether it appeared credible and met the definition of an "urgent concern." Atkinson spent that time conducting a "preliminary review" into the matter, but he appears not to have done anything that could be called a serious investigation. He did not, for example, seek to learn what was said in the Trump-Zelensky phone call, which was the heart of the complaint. Nevertheless, on August 26, exactly fourteen days after receiving the complaint, Atkinson sent a letter to the Acting Director of National Intelligence, Joseph Maguire, stating that the whistleblower's complaint qualified as an "urgent concern" according to the law.

Atkinson's reasoning was somewhat complex. He explained that Trump's discussion with Zelensky about a possible investigation of Hunter Biden's business dealings in Ukraine might be a violation of American campaign finance laws. Atkinson wrote that Trump might have solicited a thing of value—information—for his 2020 re-election campaign and thus solicited an illegal foreign campaign contribution. "U.S. laws and regulations prohibit a foreign national, directly or indirectly, from making a contribution or donation of money or other thing of value, or to make an express or implied promise to make a contribution or donation, in connection with a federal, state, or local election," Atkinson wrote. "Similarly, U.S. laws and regulations prohibit a person from soliciting, accepting, or receiving such a contribution or donation from a foreign national, directly or indirectly, in connection with a federal, state, or local election."

Atkinson's analysis was similar to Mueller's analysis of the June 9, 2016, Trump Tower meeting, in that Mueller's prosecutors considered whether the information promised to Donald Trump Jr. might have been an illegal campaign contribution. But Mueller could not figure out, first, whether Trump Jr. knew enough about the law to know such a contribution was prohibited. Second, Mueller had no way to place an actual dollar value on the promised information, if it had any value at all. (The law required that prosecutors prove the information was worth at least $2,000 for a misdemeanor charge and at least $25,000 for a felony charge.) And third, Mueller admitted that "no judicial decision has treated the voluntary provision of uncompensated opposition research or similar information as a thing of value that could amount to a contribution under campaign finance law."

So Mueller gave up. Michael Atkinson did not. Based on his interpretation of the campaign finance laws, he informed Maguire that the whistleblower matter was indeed an "urgent concern." At that point, the law gave Maguire just seven days to send the case to Congress. But Maguire did not send the complaint to Congress immediately. He felt that the case raised "totally unprecedented" concerns, as he later told Congress. Since it involved the president's communications, Maguire initially worried that the complaint might raise executive privilege issues, so he checked with the White House. And then he went to the Justice Department's Office of Legal Counsel for an opinion on whether officials there agreed that the complaint qualified as an "urgent concern" under the law.

If the Justice Department advised Maguire that the complaint was indeed an "urgent concern," Maguire would then send it on to Congress. If not, he would not. "Opinions from the Department of Justice Office of Legal Counsel are binding on all of us in the executive branch," Maguire told Congress. So off the question went to the Office of Legal Counsel.

The answer that came back on September 3 was a resounding repudiation of Atkinson's position. No, the whistleblower complaint was not an "urgent concern," the Office ruled, because the whistleblower law covered nothing about the Trump-Zelensky situation. The Office went word-by-word through the relevant law and applied it to the whistleblower situation. "The complaint does not arise in connection with the operation of any U.S. government intelligence activity," the opinion said, "and the alleged misconduct does not involve any member of the intelligence community. Rather, the complaint arises out of a confidential diplomatic communication between the president and a foreign leader that the intelligence community complainant received secondhand."

The Trump-Zelensky call was not a whistleblower matter, the opinion concluded, because it did not concern a matter "under the authority" of the Director of National Intelligence. The law covers matters under the authority of the DNI, "but it does not include allegations of wrongdoing arising outside of any intelligence activity or outside the intelligence community itself," the Office concluded.

Not covered in the OLC opinion was the additional fact that the President of the United States is simply not subject to any whistleblower laws. "Inspectors general do not oversee the Executive Office of the President," Michael Horowitz, the Justice Department's inspector general, said later. "There is not an inspector general for the Executive Office of the President."

With the OLC guidance in hand, Maguire declined to send the whistleblower complaint to the Hill intelligence committees. But things were moving ahead without it.

"The serious misconduct at issue involves the President of the United States"

Adam Schiff had known about the whistleblower since before the complaint was filed on August 12. But it is not clear exactly what Schiff knew and when he knew it. After Atkinson's letter to Maguire on August 26 declaring that the whistleblower matter was an "urgent concern," and after the Justice Department informed Maguire on September 3 that no, it was not an "urgent concern," and thus there was no requirement to notify Congress, it was not clear where the matter would go next.

On September 9, Atkinson took matters into his own hands and notified Congress himself. In a letter to Schiff and ranking Republican

Devin Nunes, Atkinson said the Inspector General's office had received "a disclosure from an individual regarding an alleged 'urgent concern.'" Atkinson said that his own 14-day review of the matter determined that the complaint was "credible." Atkinson wrote that he sent the matter to Maguire's office on August 26, and then: "It is my understanding that the Acting DNI has determined that he is not required to transmit my determination of a credible urgent concern or any of the complainant's information to the congressional intelligence committees because the allegations do not meet the definition of an 'urgent concern' under the statute."

Atkinson did not mention that it was the Justice Department that had determined that the matter did not constitute an "urgent concern." He said he was trying to persuade Maguire to send the whistleblower complaint to Congress and would keep lawmakers informed of his efforts. He did not include the whistleblower complaint or characterize it in any way other than using the legal term "urgent concern." He did not say it was about the president or any other person. But he told Congress: there's an urgent matter the Director of National Intelligence is not telling you about, even though I want him to. Don't blame me.

Atkinson's letter was the first hint to Republican lawmakers that something was up. But they had no idea *what* was up.

The next day, September 10, Schiff wrote to Maguire demanding that he immediately turn over the whistleblower complaint to the Intelligence Committee. It doesn't matter whether it's an "urgent concern" or not, Schiff said; the DNI should hand over the complaint now. Schiff also strongly hinted—the source of his knowledge unknown—that the matter involved the White House. "We do not know whether this decision to withhold the disclosure was made only by you, or whether it involved interference by other parties, including the White House," Schiff wrote. "The committee's recent experience has heightened concern of improper White House efforts to influence your office and the Intelligence Community."

If Maguire did not immediately produce the whistleblower complaint, Schiff threatened to "resort to compulsory process"—a subpoena—to get it. "The committee will also require your appearance before the committee to testify publicly about this matter," Schiff said.

Schiff got his response on September 13, in a letter not from Maguire but Maguire's lawyer, the Director of National Intelligence general counsel Jason Klitenic. Klitenic again made the point that the whistleblower complaint "did not concern allegations of conduct by a member of the Intelligence Community," nor did it "involve an intelligence activity under the DNI's supervision." As for Schiff's demand that the DNI turn it over anyway, no matter the circumstances, Klitenic wrote, "those are not the words of the statute." The law simply did not require the Director to turn over any complaint to Congress. It applied only to a member of the Intelligence Community who had an "urgent concern" to report, which the whistleblower did not have. Klitenic's message to Schiff could be summarized in one word: no.

That is when Schiff went nuclear, and when Republicans learned a little bit about what was going on. That same day, September 13, Schiff unilaterally issued a subpoena to Maguire for the "complete and unaltered" whistleblower complaint. Schiff accused Maguire of breaking the law, saying he had "neither the legal authority nor the discretion to overrule" the Inspector General. Schiff further argued that the Director of National Intelligence did not have any "discretion to review, appeal, reverse, or countermand in any way the [Inspector General's] independent determination." Nor did Maguire have, according to Schiff, any right to consult the Justice Department for a legal opinion on the matter.

And then the nuclear part: "The committee can only conclude, based on this remarkable confluence of factors, that the serious misconduct at issue involves the President of the United States and/or other senior White House or administration officials." At the same time he sent the response to Maguire, Schiff issued a long press release describing the impasse with Maguire and highlighting his accusation that the whistleblower complaint involved the president. That assured that the issue would get some news coverage and raise the mystery of what might be going on. Schiff did not say how he knew, or suspected, that the president was named in the still-secret whistleblower complaint.

September 13 was a Friday. On Sunday, Schiff appeared on CBS's *Face the Nation* and gave viewers the impression that he knew a good bit about the complaint. "I can't go into the contents, but I can tell you that at least according to the Director of National Intelligence, this involves an issue of privileged communications," Schiff said. "Now, that means it's a pretty narrow group of people that it could apply to that are both above the DNI in authority and also involve privileged communications. So I think it's fair to assume this involves either the president, or people around him, or both."

At that point, Republicans did not know what was up, but they knew that Schiff knew what was up.

On Tuesday, September 17, Atkinson wrote another letter to Schiff. He and Acting Director Maguire could not resolve their differences about whether the whistleblower complaint constituted an "urgent concern" and therefore whether it should be passed on to Congress. "I have now determined that the Acting DNI and I are at an impasse," Atkinson wrote. He could neither give the complaint to Congress nor instruct the whistleblower to do it himself, Atkinson said. There was no immediate solution.

At 6:30 that evening, the Intelligence Committee was scheduled to meet in the SCIF, or Sensitive Compartmented Information Facility, a secure room underneath the Capitol. The committee was briefed on routine matters from a member of the Intelligence Community. The members discussed a motion to push for release of a series of 2018 interviews that were part of the Trump-Russia investigation. At the end Schiff concluded the meeting's business and immediately added, "Let me just make a few comments about the whistleblower situation. We learned...."

At that point, Devin Nunes interrupted to note that there were still staff in the room and a stenographer present who should be dismissed before the members discussed any confidential matters.

"Yes, the committee is adjourned," Schiff quickly said. The staff left, and the talk turned to the whistleblower. Schiff acknowledged that there was a whistleblower complaint with the Intelligence Community and that the committee was seeking to get it. He remarked that everyone had probably seen his press release from Friday night. He was vague about what the complaint might involve. But he immediately raised Republican suspicions.

"At that point we had no idea what the hell was going on," said Nunes. There is no transcript of Schiff's remarks—Nunes noted wistfully that was because he, Nunes, said the stenographer should leave the room. And even though Schiff was vague, he gave Republicans the impression he knew more than he was saying. "It was totally bizarre, because he knew way too many details," Nunes recalled.

Most Republicans assumed the whistleblower complaint was some sort of effort to keep alive the Russia investigation. They guessed it was no big deal; after all, there had been many false alarms in the past. But there was something about Schiff's manner that caught their attention.

"He was so, I don't want to say giddy—he was so *anticipating* that we all noticed it," recalled Representative Chris Stewart. "We knew that something was up. Schiff didn't poker face this thing at all."

"I was like, 'Oh God, what now?'" recalled Brad Wenstrup. "I kind of blew it off because I had just heard two and a half years of the-Russians-are-coming. And so I didn't pay much attention to it."

Part of Wenstrup could not believe that Schiff would still be going on about Russia. "I thought after Mueller, can we just get on with business?" Wenstrup recalled. "But I had no idea that they would continue a full-fledged attack, because if I were Adam Schiff, after what he did for two years, I would be so embarrassed about being wrong." But Wenstrup overestimated the chairman; Schiff was not at all embarrassed about having been wrong.

The next day, September 18, the *Washington Post* reported, for the first time, some key details about the whistleblower complaint, including that it involved President Trump. The complaint concerned Trump's "communications with a foreign leader," the paper reported, citing "two former U.S. officials familiar with the matter." The paper said Trump's conversation "included a 'promise' that was regarded as so troubling that it prompted an official in the U.S. intelligence community to file a formal whistleblower complaint with the inspector general for the intelligence community." The *Post* also said it was "unclear whether the whistle-blower witnessed Trump's communications with the foreign leader or learned of it through other means."

The story was getting out. Schiff would tell his Republican colleagues virtually nothing, but somebody out there was talking.

A Two-Track Impeachment

Republicans weren't crazy to assume that the whistleblower was somehow linked to the Trump-Russia investigation, because at the same time Schiff was teeing up the whistleblower complaint, Nadler was continuing to push for impeachment on the basis of the Mueller report. For a period of time in September, there was a sort of two-track impeachment effort going on—Nadler on the now-traditional Russia issue, and Schiff on some hot and new but still unknown accusation.

On August 15, 2019, just three days after the whistleblower filed his complaint, Nadler subpoenaed former Trump campaign head Corey Lewandowski and former White House aide Rick Dearborn to testify at a September 17 hearing. Lewandowski said he would be happy to appear. "They didn't have to subpoena me," he told Fox News Radio. "They could have just said, 'Corey, will you show up?' I'm happy to come. Because I want to explain that there was no collusion, there was no obstruction. These guys are such phonies."

On August 26, the same day the Intelligence Community Inspector General declared the whistleblower account an "urgent concern," Nadler subpoenaed former White House staff secretary Rob Porter. Nadler also went to court to press his subpoena against former White House counsel Don McGahn.

On September 12, the Judiciary Committee approved new procedures that would make a formal impeachment inquiry easier to conduct. The committee gave Nadler the authority to designate whether a hearing was part of an impeachment inquiry; it allowed counsel to question witnesses for extended periods of time; and it allowed the committee to receive evidence in closed session. That same day, the *Washington Post* reported that a group of committee Democrats had "begun privately mapping a list of possible charges against President Trump, sketching out the contours of potential articles of impeachment even as House leaders publicly resist taking such action." The paper said the committee had zeroed in on five examples of possible obstruction in the Mueller report, which they would explore in coming hearings, beginning with the Lewandowski hearing on September 17.

On Friday, September 13, the day Schiff issued his press release and pointed toward possible White House involvement in the whistleblower complaint, news coverage was still divided between the emerging story—the whistleblower—and the old one, Russia. "We have breaking news right now," CNN's Chris Cuomo announced that night. "The House Intel chair has just issued a subpoena, and he's also making a very serious accusation against the Acting Director of National Intelligence. This is big, and it's happening right now. Also—why all this confusion about what's happening with the investigation of this president in Congress? Impeachment or not, does it matter or not? We have the one person who would know."

Cuomo went on to interview that knowledgeable guest—Nadler—who was still trying to describe what he was doing as an impeachment investigation without actually calling it an impeachment investigation. Nadler seemed unaware and uncomfortable when he was asked about the whistleblower. That was Schiff's territory.

On September 16, the president directed Rob Porter and Rick Dearborn not to appear at Nadler's hearing, but allowed Lewandowski to testify about limited matters. The next day, September 17, Lewandowski testified before Nadler's committee, and whatever still existed of the old Russia track of impeachment collapsed entirely.

Nadler apparently thought Lewandowski would elaborate on his extensive testimony to Mueller, and also on his testimony to earlier investigations by the House and Senate. Instead, Lewandowski jerked Democrats around—and around and around. He delayed. He asked for specific citations when anyone referred to the Mueller report. He repeated, over and over, his instructions from the Trump White House not to discuss his conversations with the president: "The White House has directed that I not disclose the substance of any discussion with the president or his advisers to protect executive branch confidentiality."

Nadler was visibly frustrated from the start. "'When you refuse to answer these questions, you are obstructing the work of our committee," Nadler said. "You are also proving our point for the American people to see: The president is intent on obstructing our legitimate oversight. You are aiding him in that obstruction."

What Nadler was seeing first-hand was the back side of the Trump strategy for dealing with the Russia investigation. The front side was to cooperate with the law enforcement investigation, that is, Mueller. The back side was to *not* cooperate with congressional impeachment efforts— by citing earlier cooperation with Mueller.

Lewandowski, who never worked in the White House, made clear he would address the specific contents of the Mueller report, for which he had cooperated at great length. Indeed, whenever he was asked to confirm this or that passage in the report, he did.

But Nadler and Democrats wanted more. They did not get it. Instead, they got a witness playing around with them, making everything difficult and staying carefully within the bounds of his testimony to Mueller's prosecutors. In response, Nadler appeared exasperated. The consensus after the hearing was that the chairman was not skilled enough to run an investigation as big, complex, and critically important as the impeachment of the president.

For the Trump team, Lewandowski's appearance was the final nail in the Trump-Russia coffin. "When Mueller testified, and then when they tried to resurrect it with Corey's testimony, it was very clear that this was going nowhere," Jay Sekulow recalled. "Bob was a terrible witness. And when Corey went up and they just couldn't handle him, it was dead."

The same could be said for Nadler's leading role in impeaching Donald Trump.

Pelosi's Big Move

Nadler's failure occurred right at the moment that Schiff's whistleblower gambit was gaining momentum. And perhaps because of the obvious failure of the Russia investigation, intense media coverage, discussion, and speculation moved seamlessly from Russia to the still-unknown, and thus much sexier, topic of the whistleblower.

Schiff's subpoena had directed Acting DNI Maguire to appear before the Intelligence Committee on September 19. Maguire did not show up but agreed to appear the next week. But on September 19, members of the Intelligence Community did meet with Inspector General Atkinson in the SCIF. It was not a terribly enlightening meeting; for one thing, Republicans were still unaware of what the whistleblower had alleged. "We don't know what the complaint is," Representative Chris Stewart said in a phone conversation that evening. "The IG does seem concerned about the contents of the actual complaint, and his seriousness gives me a little concern."

Some Democrats were equally uninformed about the whistleblower's complaint, but they, too, wondered if it might be linked to Russia. "Some of the meeting was Democrats saying, 'Does this have anything to do with previous things that we have investigated?'" Stewart said. Atkinson would not answer.

Most of the meeting revolved around lawmakers asking questions and arguing about the definition of the word "urgent." Why did the IG label the whistleblower matter "urgent," which set off all sorts of legal mechanisms? Atkinson would not answer. At the end, Stewart asked Atkinson what would come next. Atkinson said he did not know.

On the evening of September 19, the *Washington Post* published more about the whistleblower complaint, specifically that it concerned Ukraine. The next day, September 20, the *Wall Street Journal* published the most detailed description yet of the whistleblower call. "President Trump in a July phone call repeatedly pressured the president of Ukraine to investigate Joe Biden's son, according to people familiar with the matter," the *Journal* reported, "urging Volodymyr Zelensky about eight times to work with Rudy Giuliani on a probe that could hamper Mr. Trump's potential 2020 opponent."

The leaks were accelerating. Repeated over and over on television, they helped build the sense that the president had done something wrong, although no one quite knew what it was. On September 21, Trump denied any impropriety. Everything said on the call was "totally appropriate," he told reporters. Later, he tweeted, "Nothing was said that was in any way wrong." He and Zelensky had had a "beautiful conversation," Trump said. He added that, "I don't know the identity of the whistleblower. I just hear it's a partisan person."

On Sunday, September 22, Schiff went on CNN to hint that the whistleblower case was so important that it might change his previous opposition to impeachment. Yes, there was still no chance of convincing a Republican Senate to remove Trump from office. In the past, Schiff had said that itself was enough to discourage the House from impeaching. But now Schiff said, "I want to make sure, before we go down this road, that we can persuade the public that this was the right thing to do. And part of persuading the public that impeachment is the right thing to do is making sure that the country understands that this was a last resort."

"I have spoken with a number of my colleagues over the last week, and this seems different in kind," Schiff said, referring to the whistleblower matter. "And we may very well have crossed the Rubicon here."

That same Sunday, Pelosi sent a letter to Democratic members—something rare for a speaker to do on a weekend. She noted that on Thursday, Acting DNI Maguire was scheduled to testify before the

Intelligence Committee. She called on Republicans to go along with Democrats in demanding that Maguire turn over the whistleblower complaint. And then, a threat: "If the administration persists in blocking this whistleblower from disclosing to Congress a serious possible breach of constitutional duties by the president, they will be entering a grave new chapter of lawlessness which will take us into a whole new stage of investigation." Pelosi's message was unmistakable: she was now open to impeachment. Now, the energy that had powered a Russia-based impeachment for more than two years shifted, almost overnight, to impeachment based on, officially at least, an unknown issue, from an unknown accuser.

Pressure grew on Trump to release the National Security Council's rough transcript of the Zelensky call. Joe Biden joined those calling for release. Such records are usually kept in the highest confidence, but Trump, earlier in his administration, had already suffered the leak of transcripts of his discussions with the president of Mexico and the prime minister of Australia. Now, Trump faced the question of whether to leak on himself and release the transcript.

Administration sources began to quietly suggest that if the transcript were released, it would support Trump's side of the story and knock down some of the more fevered speculation about the call. Those sources suggested the transcript would show definitively that Trump did nothing illegal. The president's adversaries, determined to use the issue to demand his impeachment, might still argue that he acted inappropriately, they said, but release of the president's precise words would make it more difficult for critics to claim that Trump did something flat-out wrong.

Publicly, Trump continued to argue that there was nothing at all wrong with the call. "The conversation I had was largely congratulatory, was largely corruption, all of the corruption taking place, was largely the fact that we don't want our people, like Vice President Biden and his son, [adding] to the corruption already in the Ukraine," Trump said. "And Ukraine—Ukraine's got a lot of problems."

Trump decided to release the transcript. The administration set a time to do it—10:00 a.m. on Wednesday, September 25. But Pelosi made a more momentous decision. She would not wait to see the transcript, nor would she wait to see the whistleblower complaint. On Tuesday, September 24, she made the announcement that her more zealously anti-Trump critics inside the Democratic Party always thought she was too timid to make: the House would begin an impeachment inquiry.

Maguire's refusal to hand over the whistleblower complaint was "a violation of law," Pelosi said. She also noted that the press had reported that Trump "call[ed] upon a foreign power to intervene in his election." That, Pelosi said, was "a breach of his constitutional responsibilities." And now, she continued, "the president has admitted to asking the president of Ukraine to take actions which would benefit him politically."

Trump's actions were a "betrayal of his oath of office, betrayal of our national security, and betrayal of the integrity of our elections," Pelosi said. "Therefore today, I'm announcing the House of Representatives is moving forward with an official impeachment inquiry. I'm directing our six committees to proceed with their investigations under that umbrella of impeachment inquiry. The president must be held accountable. No one is above the law."

There were serious questions about the legitimacy of what Pelosi had done. Before her unilateral action, presidential impeachments had involved a vote by the entire House authorizing the inquiry. Pelosi had not taken any vote; she acted on her own say-so. But the headline was, after eleven months of cautious statements, the Speaker of the House had formally, publicly acknowledged what she and her party had been preparing for since election day 2018—moving to impeach the president.

In the larger picture, Pelosi's strategy marked a historic turn in the effort to get Trump. Faced with the new Ukraine evidence, Pelosi could have called for a special counsel to investigate. The Nixon impeachment effort relied on a special counsel to gather evidence against the president. The Clinton impeachment relied on an independent counsel to investigate and report to Congress.

But the Democrats had already once placed their faith in a special counsel, Robert Mueller, and he had failed to give them the case they wanted against Trump. Plus, he took two years to do it. Democrats did not want a replay of the Mueller experience. (Some Democrats claimed that they could not seek a special counsel because Attorney General Bill Barr would surely refuse to appoint one, but the fact is, they never tried.)

In any event, the clock was ticking. It was September 2019. The next year would be a presidential election year, and Trump might possibly win re-election while a special counsel investigation plodded along.

Given all that, Pelosi decided to abandon the special counsel precedent. House Democrats would do this one themselves. They would control the entire process—the questioning of witnesses, the handling of evidence, the drafting of charges. This time, they would get the results they wanted.

CHAPTER NINE

The Secret Chamber

A Stumbling Start—Adam Schiff's Theory of the Case—
A Rush of Witnesses—"Process matters"—
Lieutenant Colonel Vindman

As the drive to impeach Trump accelerated, Republican Representative Chris Stewart began keeping a journal. Even though he was a member of the Intelligence Committee, the Republican congressman from Utah's Second District knew virtually nothing about what was going on. So in an effort to be able to remember the moment as events progressed, Stewart began writing down his thoughts every few days.

"I think things are going to unfold in such a way that I need to keep track of it," Stewart wrote on Friday night, September 27. Pelosi had announced impeachment on Tuesday. "Last week we started to hear rumblings from the majority about some kind of whistleblower complaint that was supposed to be forwarded to Congress but hadn't been. The DNI was holding it." It was a little confusing, Stewart wrote. The focus of the complaint was outside the Director of National Intelligence's jurisdiction and also protected by executive privilege, and thus did not appear to fit the law's definition of "urgent." The DNI—"poor guy, so glad I don't have that job"—went to the Office of Legal Counsel for an opinion.

"Non-partisan professional lawyers, who said it was not urgent…and couldn't be passed on," Stewart continued. "So he didn't. Bomb goes off! Boom!!!"

Stewart was not at all surprised that the main themes of the complaint were leaked. "So things blow up on Tuesday when we got in," he wrote. "No one had seen anything. Not a word of the transcript of the phone call, not a word of the complaint, nothing. But Pelosi announced they were going to open an impeachment investigation. Boom! More bombs go off. Of course, she doesn't actually vote to open an investigation. Supposed to do that. But she won't."

A Stumbling Start

When Pelosi announced the impeachment inquiry, she told fellow House Democrats the party should "strike while the iron is hot." Indeed, Democrats had succeeded in heating the iron to an extraordinary temperature. Even though no one had seen the Trump-Zelensky transcript, and no one had seen the whistleblower complaint, some press coverage of Pelosi's announcement suggested the public already knew all it needed to know.

"At this point, the facts are pretty much in the open and agreed to," wrote Politico's Playbook. CNN's Chris Cillizza wrote that, "Donald Trump already admitted everything you need to know about the Ukraine drama." Opinions like that, repeated often in media discussions, set the stage for Pelosi to announce an impeachment inquiry before the transcript or complaint were even released.

When the transcript was made public, on September 25, it gave both sides ammunition. Democrats argued it proved Trump demanded a *quid pro quo*—a Ukraine investigation of the Bidens in return for resumed U.S. aid, or a White House visit for Zelensky—while Republicans argued that it showed just the opposite, that Trump had not in fact demanded any *quid pro quo*. Both sides pored over the transcript—and it was just a rough transcript—with the intensity of scholars studying a religious text. The transcript would become the basic document for both prosecution and defense.

And it did, in fact, benefit both sides. For Democrats, it showed that Trump really did bring up CrowdStrike, the 2016 election, and the Bidens. For Republicans, it showed that Trump did not condition Ukraine's receipt of U.S. aid on anything; indeed, at the time of the call, Zelensky did not even know that aid was being held up at all.

The day after the transcript was released, September 26, acting DNI Maguire testified before Chairman Schiff and the House Intelligence Committee. Because the president had made the transcript public, Maguire said, he could finally give the whistleblower complaint to the committee. It was released the same day. Maguire was questioned for hours about why he did not quickly pass the complaint on to Congress, about why he checked with the White House about privilege issues and with the Justice Department on whether the complaint fit within the confines of the Intelligence Community Whistleblower Protection Act. Democrats rejected his answers, but everybody knew that going in.

The Maguire testimony was mostly unproductive, but the hearing was still memorable because in his opening remarks, Schiff made one of the biggest mistakes he would make in the entire impeachment battle. Describing the Trump-Zelensky conversation as something that "reads like a classic organized crime shakedown," he went on to characterize what the president told Zelensky:

> We've been very good to your country, very good. No other country has done as much as we have, but you know what, I don't see much reciprocity here. I hear what you want. I have a favor I want from you, though. And I'm going to say this only seven times, so you better listen good. I want you to make up dirt on my political opponent, understand, lots of it, on this and on that. I'm going to put you in touch with people, not just any people, I'm going to put you in touch with the Attorney General of the United States, my attorney general, Bill

Barr, he's got the whole weight of the American law enforcement behind him. And I'm going to put you in touch with
Rudy. You're going to love him, trust me. You know what I'm
asking, and so I'm only going to say this a few more times. In
a few more ways. And by the way, don't call me again. I'll call
you when you've done what I asked.

Schiff did not present it as a direct quotation; he said it was "the
essence" and "in sum and character" what Trump said to Zelensky.
What it was, in fact, was Schiff's caricature of Trump's actual words.
Many listeners missed his explanation and instead heard Schiff's invented
conversation between Trump and Zelensky as if it were an actual quote.
It was not the sort of sober investigative analysis that one might expect
in an impeachment inquiry, and Schiff's performance seemed not only
misleading but evidence that he had made up his mind before the investigation began.

"Schiff's opening statement was just obscene," Chris Stewart wrote
in his journal. "He makes up a conversation supposedly between the
president and Ukraine which sounds like a script from a cheap comic
book. Lies and innuendo. He was called out on it and said, well, I meant
it as a parody. Geez, that's great. The fun begins."

After the Maguire hearing, Schiff began planning for witness testimony in the new impeachment inquiry. Democrats created an unprecedented structure for the investigation, in which witnesses would be
questioned by a group of lawmakers from the Intelligence Committee,
the Oversight Committee, and the Foreign Affairs Committee. Schiff
hoped the testimony would lay the foundation for public hearings that
would sell the case for impeachment to Americans across the country.

One of the first witnesses was to be the whistleblower. After all, the
still-anonymous complainant, known to be a CIA officer, had started
the whole investigation, and Schiff said it was critical to hear his story.
Democrats began work on an arrangement by which the whistleblower
could testify and remain anonymous. Perhaps he would testify via video,

with his appearance concealed and his voice altered. However it was done, Schiff said it was vitally important that the American people hear the whistleblower's story and that he be able to speak without pressure from Republicans or the White House.

"Have you reached an agreement yet with the whistleblower and his or her attorneys about coming before the committee and providing the information firsthand?" ABC's George Stephanopoulos asked Schiff on September 29.

"Yes, we have," said Schiff. "The whistleblower will be allowed to come in, and come in without a minder from the Justice Department or from the White House to tell the whistleblower what they can and cannot say. We'll get the unfiltered testimony of that whistleblower." Schiff said the witness would be protected not only from public exposure, but from any possible threats by Trump supporters as well.

"So when do you expect to hear from the whistleblower?"

"Very soon," Schiff said, vowing to "ride shotgun" to make sure the administration did not do anything to delay the testimony.

News accounts were filled with anticipation of whistleblower testimony. The allegations were often characterized as "explosive." Surely his testimony would be explosive, too.

All that changed on October 2, just three days after Schiff appeared on ABC, when the *New York Times* published a story with the headline, "Schiff Got Early Account of Accusations as Whistleblower's Concerns Grew." The paper reported that Schiff learned the "outlines" of the whistleblower complaint days before it was filed. The early tip from the whistleblower "explains how Mr. Schiff knew to press for the complaint when the Trump administration initially blocked lawmakers from seeing it," the paper reported.

The *Times* said a "CIA officer" originally approached a "House Intelligence Committee aide" seeking advice on what to do with his complaint. The aide suggested the CIA officer get a lawyer and file an anonymous whistleblower complaint with the Intelligence Community Inspector General. The paper said the committee aide told Schiff about the CIA officer's story but "did not share the whistleblower's identity with Mr. Schiff."

Republicans jumped on the revelation. Schiff was now a witness in his own investigation, they said. If it was essential to learn how the matter began—and GOP lawmakers believed it was—then Schiff himself should answer questions about the role he and his staff played in the whistleblower complaint.

Republican calls for Schiff testimony became even louder after Michael Atkinson, the Inspector General, testified on October 4. The testimony was outside of the structure Schiff had established for the impeachment inquiry. It was only before the Intelligence Committee, meaning no members of other committees could take part. The session was to be held in secret, with no members allowed to publicly discuss what was said.

According to three sources who knew what was said in the hearing, Republicans focused on an August 26 letter, written by Atkinson, in which he said that the whistleblower showed "some indicia of an arguable political bias…in favor of a rival political candidate." Later news reports suggested that bias consisted entirely of the fact that the whistleblower was a registered Democrat. That wasn't much for Republicans to seize upon; simple party registration was surely not evidence of overwhelming bias.

But under questioning, Atkinson revealed more about those "indicia." The whistleblower's possible bias was not that he was a registered Democrat. It was that he had a significant tie to one of the Democratic presidential candidates then vying to challenge President Trump in the 2020 election.

"The IG said [the whistleblower] worked or had some type of professional relationship with one of the Democratic candidates," one knowledgeable source said.

"The IG said the whistleblower had a professional relationship with one of the 2020 candidates," said another source.

"What [Atkinson] said was that the whistleblower self-disclosed that he was a registered Democrat and that he had a prior working relationship with a current 2020 Democratic presidential candidate," said a third source.

All three sources said Atkinson did not identify the Democratic candidate with whom the whistleblower had a connection. Later reporting suggested it was former Vice President Joe Biden, who of course figured prominently in the whistleblower's complaint.

In his August letter, Atkinson said that even though there was evidence of possible bias on the whistleblower's part, "such evidence did not change my determination that the complaint relating to the urgent concern 'appears credible,' particularly given the other information the ICIG obtained during its preliminary review."

With Atkinson sitting in front of them on October 4, Republicans sought to drill down into what that meant. How closely did he examine the whistleblower's past, his connections, and his motivation? Beyond the revelation of the "professional relationship," it remains unclear what Atkinson said. Schiff decreed that the Atkinson transcript remain secret. Even when he released transcripts of other impeachment inquiry interviews, the Atkinson transcript remained under wraps.

After the *Times* revelation about his own role in the whistleblower's work, and after Atkinson's testimony about the whistleblower's political ties, Schiff's enthusiasm for whistleblower testimony virtually disappeared. It was no longer necessary to hear from the whistleblower, the chairman claimed, because investigators had other evidence with which to prove his allegations. What had once been critically important—hearing from the whistleblower personally—became something Schiff and his fellow Democrats no longer cared about at all. Republicans, and the public, could forget about learning how the complaint that led to a presidential impeachment actually began.

Adam Schiff's Theory of the Case

The formal interviews on the Ukraine investigation began on October 3 with Kurt Volker, the former U.S. special envoy to Ukraine, who had close connections to some of the major figures in the Ukraine affair. Things did not go well for Democrats.

Schiff's plan was to press Volker to testify that the president's decision to put a hold on U.S. aid to Ukraine created pressure on Ukrainian officials to investigate Joe Biden's son Hunter. Problems arose early when Volker denied that that was the case, noting that Ukrainian leaders did not even know the aid was being withheld. They believed they had a good relationship with President Trump and the United States, and did not feel obligated to announce, let alone conduct, an investigation of the Bidens. In short, Volker implied that the Ukrainians felt no *quid pro quo* was attached to Trump's July 25 phone call.

"Ambassador, you're making this much more complicated than it has to be," Schiff said, after Volker declined to accept Schiff's characterization of events.

The Ukrainians did not want to be pulled into a U.S. political campaign, Schiff asserted, especially in the context of "vital military support…being withheld from Ukraine during this period."

"That was not part of the context at the time," Volker said. "At least to my knowledge, they [Ukrainian leaders] were not aware of that." Volker testified that as far as he knew, the Ukrainians first learned about the military hold when an article in *Politico*, "Trump holds up Ukraine military aid meant to confront Russia," appeared on August 29. That was well after the July 25 Trump-Zelensky call.

Schiff then began a long argument with Volker about whether Trump exerted pressure on Ukraine during the call. Would Volker agree that "no President of the United States should ever ask a foreign leader to help intervene in a U.S. election?"

"I agree with that," said Volker.

"And that would be particularly egregious if it was done in the context of withholding foreign assistance?" Schiff continued.

Volker balked. "We're getting now into, you know, a conflation of these things that I didn't think was actually there."

Schiff wanted Volker to agree that "if it's inappropriate for a president to seek foreign help in a U.S. election, it would be doubly so if a president was doing that at a time when the United States was withholding military support from the country."

But Volker would not agree. "I can't really speak to that," he said. "My understanding of the security assistance issue is…"

"Why can't you speak to that, ambassador?" Schiff snapped. "You're a career diplomat. You can understand the enormous leverage that a president would have while withholding military support from an ally at war with Russia. You can understand just how significant that would be, correct?"

"I can understand that that would be significant," Volker said.

"And when that suspension of aid became known to that country, to Ukraine, it would be all the more weighty to consider what the president had asked of them, wouldn't it?"

"So again, congressman, I don't believe…" Volker began.

"It's a pretty straightforward question," Schiff said.

"But I don't believe the Ukrainians were aware that the assistance was being held up…"

"They became aware of it," Schiff said.

"They became aware later, but I don't believe they were aware at the time, so there was no leverage implied," Volker said.

Schiff changed his argument slightly, speculating that the Ukrainians would have felt pressure whenever they learned about the withheld aid. "At the point they [the Ukrainians] learned that, wouldn't that have given them added urgency to meet the president's request on the Bidens?" Schiff asked.

"I don't know the answer to that," Volker said.

Schiff pressed Volker to agree one more time. By then, Volker had finally lost his patience. He tried to explain that, in his experience, the Ukrainians did not seem to be feeling pressure from Trump and the United States. As a matter of fact, they were receiving good signals from the United States about an improving relationship.

"Congressman, this is why I'm trying to say the context is different, because at the time [the Ukrainians] learned that, if we assume it's August 29th, they had just had a visit from the national security advisor, John Bolton. That's a high-level meeting already. He was recommending and working on scheduling the visit of President Zelensky to Washington. We were also working on a bilateral meeting to take place in Warsaw on the margins of a commemoration on the beginning of World War II. And in that context, I think the Ukrainians felt like things are going the right direction, and they had not done anything on—they had not done anything on an investigation, they had not done anything on a statement, and things were ramping up in terms of their engagement with the administration. So I think they were actually feeling pretty good then."

Schiff gave up in frustration. Volker would simply not accept his narrative of events. "Ambassador, I find it remarkable," Schiff said, "as a career diplomat that you have difficulty acknowledging that when Ukraine learned that their aid had been suspended for unknown reasons, that this wouldn't add additional urgency to a request by the President of the United States. I find that remarkable."

Later, Republican Representative Scott Perry questioned Volker, returning to the colloquy with Schiff. Perry asked Volker whether he, Volker, had close relations with Ukrainian officials and whether, if those officials felt something were amiss, they would tell Volker.

"The folks that you dealt with in Ukraine at the very highest level, I don't know, but I'm going to ask, do you feel like they had a fair amount of trust in you?"

"Absolutely," said Volker.

"So they would confide things in you if they had a question?"

"They would confide things," Volker answered. "They would ask questions. They would ask for help. We had a very candid relationship..."

"In your conversation with Representative Schiff, he kind of implied and wanted you to intimate that there was an agreement based on that conversation that: If you do the investigation, then you can have a meet-ing [with Trump] and maybe we'll consider this military aid. If that were the case from the call, do you feel, because they had some trust in you, that they would have come to you and said, 'Hey, how do we handle this? Is this what the President of the United States is asking?' Would they confide—would they ask you that?"

"Yes," said Volker. "They would have asked me exactly that, you know. How do we handle this?"

But the Ukrainians never did. Volker's testimony was a poor start for Schiff's interviews, because he did not confirm Schiff's theory of the case. "Volker was such a bad witness for the Democrats," said a senior Republican aide. "For us, Volker changed everything. He was the definitive fact witness on everything Schiff needed to prove his case. He was the number one person on the U.S. side of things who had a relationship with the Ukrainians. He was the number one person the Ukrainians trusted."

When the aide said Volker "changed everything," he did not mean that Volker stopped Democrats in their tracks. That obviously did not happen. Instead, Volker's value to Republicans was in telling them that there was a case to be made in Trump's defense that did not rely on Schiff's preconceived narrative. Volker gave the GOP energy and ammunition.

There was another reason Volker's testimony was critical, and it had to do with the inner workings of the House of Representatives, largely unseen by the public. Volker appeared for what was known as a transcribed interview. While it was held behind closed doors, there was no penalty for members to later publicly reveal what was said. If the interview had been conducted as a formal deposition, House secrecy rules would have applied and there would have been significant penalties for lawmakers who violated them. But for Volker, the level of secrecy was low.

That allowed Republican members to leave the hearing and talk to the press about what had been said. A few days after the Volker testimony,

Republican Representative Lee Zeldin of New York, frustrated by some journalists' lack of curiosity about Volker's appearance, took to the microphones in the hallway to lecture the press:

> Maybe you should ask: What was said inside of Volker's deposition, during his transcribed interview, with regard to Adam Schiff's fairy tale *quid pro quo* charge that aid from the United States to Ukraine was being linked to an investigation into the Bidens. Why don't you ask what did Ambassador Volker said about that? That's a great question. I'm glad that you asked that question. And I will tell you that the reason why that question was so important for you to ask is for many things. Because he [Volker] was in this room for several hours. And during several hours of testimony, he talked about how President Zelensky had no idea there was a hold on aid during the July 25th call.
>
> The next day, Ambassador Volker meets with President Zelensky, and in that meeting there is no reference to a *quid pro quo* or President Zelensky having any idea that there was a hold on aid. Or, over the course of Ambassador Volker's next several weeks engaging with Ukraine, Ukraine makes no reference to there being a hold on aid or there being a *quid pro quo*. And by the way, you know what else Ambassador Volker testified to? This entire time, the aid was getting released. It was going to get released. And guess what happened? The aid got released. And you know what did not have to happen? There was no new investigation that had to get created. This whole thing is a fairy tale. Adam Schiff is misleading you, and you're playing along with it, many of you are. And the American public is then getting deceived.

It was a devastatingly effective moment, made possible by the fact that tight House secrecy rules did not apply to the Volker session. "If

Kurt Volker's interview was a deposition instead of a transcribed interview, we would not have been able to do that," Zeldin recalled later. "That was good for us to be able to communicate."

For Schiff, though, it was very bad. Allowing Republicans to reveal publicly what was said during an interview was not something the chairman wanted to repeat. So Schiff made a change. Subsequent interviews would be formal depositions, subject to those strict secrecy rules. Any member who discussed the contents of the deposition in public could be subject to ethics charges and might have to withdraw from participation in the process. That meant that, after Volker, there would be a tight cover of secrecy on the deposition process. The chairman threatened serious consequences for those who leaked. (As an example, everyone knew the case of Devin Nunes, who in 2017 had to sideline himself from the Trump-Russia investigation after a baseless ethics charge was lodged against him. He was later cleared, but the accusations weakened GOP efforts at a critical time.) Now, when Schiff ordered silence, Republicans fell silent. Look at what happened to Devin, they said privately.

A Rush of Witnesses

The new rules took effect with the next witness on Schiff's list, Marie Yovanovitch, the recalled ambassador to Ukraine. Her October 11 testimony was in the deposition format, under complete secrecy. Her appearance gave Republicans their first look at how the process would work. While they were forbidden from discussing her testimony, someone leaked to the press a copy of Yovanovitch's ten-page opening statement as the deposition was beginning. The leaker could have been on the Yovanovitch side; the witness was free to reveal any or all of what was discussed. Or it could have been Democrats, who knew that, if questioned, they could always point to the witness as the possible leaker. In her statement, Yovanovitch said she had been removed from her position, "as far as I can tell, on unfounded and false claims by people with clearly questionable motives." News stories began appearing immediately, while the deposition was still going on, based on Yovanovitch's statement.

Yovanovitch gave Democrats a witness who could be portrayed as the victim in the story, a career ambassador who was recalled because she might stand in the way of Trump's alleged scheme to pressure Ukraine for an investigation of the Bidens. The weakness in Yovanovitch's testimony was that she knew little beyond her personal experience. She could testify to what happened to her, but she had no contact with the key players in the Ukraine affair and was out of her job before the main events occurred. Was there a *quid pro quo*? Did the Ukrainians feel pressure from Trump? Why was aid withheld? Yovanovitch didn't know the answers to those and many other questions.

Nor did Yovanovitch have any particular knowledge about Burisma—the energy company that granted Hunter Biden a seat on its board—or allegations of corruption. "What do you know about the investigation of Burisma?" asked Republican counsel Steve Castor. "Not very much," answered Yovanovitch.

She also knew little about the efforts of some Ukrainians to disparage candidate Donald Trump in the 2016 U.S. presidential campaign. Indeed, it was during Yovanovitch's testimony that what would become a common misconception—that Republicans were serving Russian interests by alleging that Ukraine, *and not Russia*, interfered in the 2016 election—entered the spotlight. In fact, Republicans fully acknowledged Russian interference but also believed that some Ukrainians made efforts to influence the U.S. campaign—using social media to attack Donald Trump, leaking unverified evidence to discredit Paul Manafort, and supporting Trump opponents in the United States. Republicans readily conceded that none of it was done on the scale or with the governmental direction of the Russian effort; and it frustrated GOP lawmakers no end to hear Democrats accuse them of denying Russian influence and furthering Russian interests. It was, Republicans believed, a Democratic tactic to discredit the GOP defense of the president. Plus, it was not true.

Still, Yovanovitch and others repeated it. "My understanding, again, from the press was that, you know, the allegation that there was Ukrainian interference in our elections in 2016, that it wasn't Russia, it was Ukraine, that that had been debunked long ago," Yovanovitch said, in a classic example of the accusation.

After Yovanovitch, a string of witnesses appeared in rapid succession; things moved so quickly that the main work was done by Halloween. On October 14, former National Security Council aide Fiona Hill testified. On October 15, it was State Department official George Kent; on October 16, State Department official Michael McKinley; on October 17, U.S. Ambassador to the European Union Gordon Sondland; on October 22, William Taylor, a top official at the U.S. embassy in Ukraine; on October 23, Pentagon official Laura Cooper; on October 26, State Department official Philip Reeker; on October 28, former Deputy National Security Adviser Charles Kupperman; on October 29, National Security Council aide Lieutenant Colonel Alexander Vindman; on October 30, foreign service officers Christopher Anderson and Catherine Croft; and on October 31, former senior National Security Council aide Tim Morrison.

Democrats were moving at breakneck speed. With each new witness that appeared, Republicans had the ominous realization that this time, unlike during previous impeachment efforts, Democrats had the organizational strength to make an impeachment happen. What did that mean? It meant Democrats could get witnesses to show up. "What changed everything for us was the fact that they were making progress getting witnesses in the door for depositions," said the senior Republican aide. "Committee chairmen send letters all the time asking for depositions. There's a reason we would think they did not have the wherewithal to pull this off. Nadler sent 80 letters…and never followed up with it. He got zero traction." Schiff, however, was more effective than the hapless Nadler. Plus, the witness list was heavy with foreign policy professionals who were not shy about airing their differences with the president.

The sessions settled into a pattern of secret testimony accompanied by quick leaks of witnesses' opening statements. Taylor's ran fifteen pages; the entire document was given to the *Washington Post* as he testified. Republicans were, however, forbidden from publicly discussing any of the questioning that took place after the opening statement.

Taylor testified that the administration had specifically tied Ukrainian aid to Ukraine's agreement to investigate the Bidens and publicly announce that the investigation was taking place. But Taylor did not know much of that first-hand; his information came from conversations with players like Ambassador Sondland, who later testified that his own information was not rock solid. Still, Taylor was a senior diplomat who accused Trump of a *quid pro quo*, and he became a star witness for the Democrats.

Later witnesses filled in the details. Fiona Hill testified that then-National Security Adviser John Bolton was strongly opposed to the push to persuade Ukraine to investigate the Bidens. Hill quoted Bolton saying, "I am not part of whatever drug deal Sondland and [White House chief of staff Mick] Mulvaney are cooking up." George Kent told the committee that Trump "wanted nothing less than President Zelensky to go to a microphone and say investigations, Biden and Clinton." Gordon Sondland made a mess of his testimony, first testifying that in his mind, he did not think U.S. aid to Ukraine was tied to a Ukrainian announcement of investigations. Then, days later, Sondland changed his testimony to say that his memory had been refreshed by others' accounts, and he now remembered that he *had* thought they were linked. Sondland sent the committee a written correction to his testimony that inadvertently showed how tenuous and tortured the Ukraine allegations were:

> Ambassador Taylor recalls that I told Mr. Morrison in early September 2019 that the resumption of U.S. aid to Ukraine had become tied to a public statement to be issued by Ukraine agreeing to investigate Burisma. Ambassador Taylor recalls that Mr. Morrison told Ambassador Taylor that I told Mr.

Morrison that I had conveyed this message to Mr. [Ukrainian presidential adviser Andriy] Yermak on September 1, 2019, in connection with Vice President Pence's visit to Warsaw and a meeting with President Zelensky.

It was mind-numbingly complex, and in the end never entirely clear. (Just on the example above, Andriy Yermak later said he did not remember Sondland conveying a message to him, making the whole episode even murkier.) The intent of the secret hearings, with their selective disclosure of unanswered allegations, was to use the leaks to build the impression in the public that Trump had committed an impeachable offense, while at the same time using the secrecy to conceal contradictory evidence.

But the secrecy had a much different effect inside the Capitol. There, the effect was to convince even the most wavering Republican that Schiff, Pelosi, and the Democrats had stacked the deck against the GOP. To them, the impeachment inquiry seemed to become more and more unfair every day.

"Process matters"

House Minority Leader Kevin McCarthy had long been convinced that Democrats wanted to impeach the president. Still, when Democrats shifted from the failed Mueller effort to the new whistleblower campaign, it took the GOP a moment to catch up. "When they first started going to impeachment, it kind of took everybody by surprise, about this phone call and this whistleblower," McCarthy recalled. "Nobody really had information." But when McCarthy heard Schiff speak in public about the whistleblower, "that's when I first started saying they're going to do this thing."

McCarthy had been thinking in theoretical terms about how Republicans would respond to an impeachment ever since the GOP lost the House majority in November 2018. Now, he had something specific to consider. He assigned staff to study the Nixon and Clinton impeachments. He examined how Democrats had worked to slow and undermine the GOP Benghazi investigation just a few years earlier. He started thinking about how Republicans could best oppose what he was increasingly convinced Schiff and Pelosi were going to do.

Then, on September 24, when Pelosi announced the impeachment inquiry, McCarthy's planning became a reality. "Once she did her press conference, it was game on—there was no backing off," McCarthy recalled. Pelosi had just announced an impeachment inquiry entirely on her own, with no House vote, ignoring precedent, cutting corners, and denying minority rights. McCarthy understood that that could become a rallying point for Republicans. "The first thing I thought was, if they're going to impeach, process matters," McCarthy recalled.

When McCarthy was home in Bakersfield, California, he would take his dog (Mac, an Australian Shepherd) out for a run and at the same time check in with Republican members by phone. He remembered a specific moment when he realized that Republicans had to frame the impeachment as a matter of fairness. "It dawns on me that the first thing I have to do is set the stage on this," he remembered. He would write a letter to Pelosi outlining the various ways in which she was ignoring precedent and fair play. But even though the letter was addressed to the Speaker, it really wasn't for her. It was for House Republicans, to unite them against the process then getting underway.

It was not as if McCarthy could have taken his concerns directly to Pelosi and talked them out. Their relationship, such as it was, just didn't work that way. When asked whether he talked to the Speaker, McCarthy answered, "Steny and I have real conversations," referring to the number two Democratic leader, Representative Steny Hoyer. With Pelosi, not so much. "Hers is happy talk," McCarthy said of their conversations. "When we're together, she starts talking about the weather. It's embarrassing what we talk about. It's nervous talk." The two never had a substantive talk about impeachment during the entire process.

Was McCarthy able to talk with Hoyer about impeachment? "Yes, but the difficulty was, Hoyer was not having communications with her either," McCarthy responded. "When you talked to other Democrats, they didn't know where she was going."

McCarthy sent the letter to the Speaker on October 3. "I am writing to request you suspend all efforts surrounding your 'impeachment inquiry' until transparent and equitable rules and procedures are established to govern the inquiry, as is customary," McCarthy wrote. There was absolutely zero chance that would happen, but the purpose was for McCarthy to list the procedures—"key historical precedents or basic standards of due process"—that Democrats were bypassing. McCarthy put them in the form of ten questions, among them:

"Do you intend to hold a vote of the full House authorizing your impeachment inquiry?

"Do you intend to involve the full House in each critical step of this inquiry, including defining its scope and establishing its rules and procedures?

"Do you intend to provide the president's counsel the right to attend all hearings and depositions?

"Do you intend to provide the president's counsel the right to cross-examine witnesses?

"Do you intend to refer all findings on impeachment to Chairman Nadler and the Judiciary Committee, as prescribed by Rule X of the Rules of the House, or is Chairman Schiff in charge of leading this inquiry, as has been reported in the press?"

The letter—delivered on the day of the inquiry's first witness interview, with Ambassador Volker—established the position that Republicans would hold throughout the impeachment battle. "I remember Democrats coming to me in the gym, saying you guys are losing because you're talking about process," McCarthy recalled. "And I thought, perfect, keep thinking that. It's like the fruit from the poisonous tree. If you start with something that's poisonous, it's never going to be good."

Pelosi responded almost immediately, telling McCarthy he could forget about his objections. "There is no requirement under the Constitution, under House Rules, or House precedent that the whole House vote before proceeding with an impeachment inquiry," she wrote.

And then Schiff made things worse, angering every single Republican by decreeing that the interviews be conducted in secret. Then he decreed that if a Republican member of the three committees—members of the committees, not just any member of the House—wanted to review a transcript of the interview, he or she had to go to a secure room where a Democratic minder would watch over them at all times. Republicans who were not on the three committees but who wanted to follow developments discovered they were shut out entirely.

For example, Republican Representative Jamie Herrera Beutler of Washington State, not one of the party's firebreathers, tried to go to the room to read the Volker transcript. Democrats turned her away, and a frustrated Beutler made a Facebook video of her experience. "I'm a sitting member of the United States Congress, with top secret clearance," she said in the video. "If impeachment came to the House floor, I would be given a vote. But right now, I'm not being given all of the facts. For instance, yesterday I requested the written transcript of the testimony from the U.S. special envoy to Ukraine, and was denied." The result, Beutler said, was that she had to rely on "media leaks and selected bits of information released by Speaker Pelosi and Chairman Schiff."

Schiff was also free to set and change the rules at any time. And it was all done without the House having passed any resolution to formally begin an inquiry. For Republicans, calling the process one-sided was a gross understatement.

On October 8, a few days after McCarthy's letter, White House counsel Pat Cipollone also took up the issue of fairness. "I write on behalf of President Donald J. Trump in response to your numerous, legally unsupported demands made as part of what you have labeled—contrary to the Constitution of the United States and all past bipartisan precedent—as an 'impeachment inquiry,'" Cipollone wrote in a letter to Pelosi and Schiff. "As you know, you have designed and implemented your inquiry in a manner that violates fundamental fairness and constitutionally mandated due process."

Cipollone accused Democrats not only of wanting to overturn the results of the 2016 election, but also of trying to influence the 2020 election. "As one member of Congress explained, he is 'concerned that if we don't impeach the president he will get re-elected,'" Cipollone wrote. (That member was none other than Representative Al Green, the Democrat who had done perhaps more than any other in the effort to impeach Trump.) Cipollone also noted that Schiff had had some sort of contact with the whistleblower, and then lied about it before delivering his "parody" version of the call at the Maguire hearing. "The American people understand that Chairman Schiff cannot covertly assist with the submission of a complaint, mislead the public about his involvement, read a counterfeit version of the call to the American people, and then pretend to sit in judgment as a neutral 'investigator,'" Cipollone wrote.

Cipollone also argued that the inquiry was constitutionally invalid because Pelosi had gone forward without a vote of the full House to authorize it. "Since the founding of the Republic, under unbroken practice, the House has never undertaken the solemn responsibility of an impeachment inquiry directed at the president without first adopting a resolution authorizing a committee to begin its inquiry." In addition, Democrats denied the president "the right to cross-examine witnesses, to call witnesses, to receive transcripts of testimony, to have access to evidence, to have counsel present, and many other basic rights guaranteed to all Americans." Due process rights were not optional, Cipollone said. "No citizen—including the president—should be treated this unfairly," he wrote, adding that the rushed, partisan nature of the Democrats' inquiry proved that they were acting with political purpose, specifically to weaken the president ahead of the 2020 election.

It is fair to say that Cipollone's objections, like McCarthy's, had 100 percent support among Republicans. And it is also fair to say that they had zero impact on Pelosi and Schiff's conduct of the investigation. So the depositions continued at breakneck speed. Republican questions on the rules were rejected. For example, at the beginning of the Yovanovitch deposition, Representative Zeldin noted that Schiff was not observing the Nixon and Clinton precedents, which allowed the president's counsel the right to participate in the deposition, and asked Schiff how he, as Intelligence Committee chairman, had the authority to question a State Department employee on the issue of U.S. policy toward Ukraine. That was normally under the jurisdiction of the Foreign Affairs Committee, Zeldin noted, and the House had not passed any measure to allow for the change.

Schiff blew him off completely. "We're going to move forward with the deposition rather than address the mischaracterizations of both impeachment history and inquiries and process," the chairman said.

Republican leadership struggled to keep members abreast of what was going on, so they would know something beyond what they read in the press. "When the whistleblower complaint came out, they were alleging all of these sinister things by the president," recalled Representative Steve Scalise, the Republican whip. "A lot of our members started having questions. It was hard to get the facts."

The problem was particularly acute when media reports characterized some new development as a major development in the case. "They'd be building it up as some bombshell," Scalise said, "and the members did not know what was going on." So Scalise and McCarthy started holding members' meetings. They enlisted some of the key GOP players who were in the depositions—Devin Nunes, Jim Jordan, Elise Stefanik, John Ratcliffe, Zeldin, and others—and had them brief the members on what was actually said in the depositions, versus press reports that were often based on leaked opening statements.

The meetings did a great deal to both reduce Republican members' anxieties and to foster unity among them. McCarthy, Scalise, and the other leaders knew that, no matter how much Pelosi and Schiff stretched the rules, votes would eventually come. They had to. And when they did, GOP leaders wanted Republicans to stick together.

Republicans were not only united—they were angry. After three weeks of depositions, party leadership scheduled a group news conference—more of a protest, actually—outside the SCIF where the secret sessions were going on. The event was scheduled for October 17, but everyone awoke that morning to learn that Elijah Cummings, the chairman of the Oversight Committee, had died from a long-term illness. Cummings was respected by Republicans—McCarthy originally thought he would be the one chosen to lead the impeachment effort—and the leadership decided to reschedule the protest/news conference for the next week, October 23.

Laura Cooper, a Pentagon official who tracked U.S. military aid to Ukraine, was scheduled to testify that day. As usual, attendance at the deposition was limited to members of the Intelligence, Oversight, and Foreign Affairs committees. That meant about forty-five Republicans, out of a total of 197 GOP members in the House, were eligible to take part. That exclusion was what the press conference was about. "If behind those doors they intend to overturn the results of an American presidential election, we want to know what's going on," said Representative Matt Gaetz, who along with Scalise was leading the Republican forces.

Gaetz announced from the beginning that it would not be a normal news conference; there would be some sort of action afterwards. "I'm going to have a few of my colleagues give remarks, and then we're going to try to go in there, and we're going to try to figure out what is going on, on behalf of the millions of Americans that we represent." After a long list of speakers, several dozen members headed toward the SCIF. "We're gonna go and see if we can get inside," said Gaetz.

Indeed they could; some were able to simply walk inside the supersecure room. At about that time, Chris Stewart, who as a member of the Intelligence Committee was taking part in the hearings, was headed down to the SCIF. He came upon his colleagues massing outside.

"So I was walking down the stairs to the hearing in the SCIF on Friday and about 30 Republicans were holding a press conference at the bottom of the stairs," Stewart wrote in his journal. "It finished about the time I walked by, and they all just said, 'We're going in there!' I opened the door to let myself in and they followed me into the SCIF and into the hearing room."

Gaetz was the first in. The room had a big table that could seat more than two dozen people, Republicans on one side and Democrats on the other. The witness would be seated at one end, with Schiff to her right and the Republican questioner to her left. Gaetz took the seat directly behind Schiff that would normally be occupied by Schiff's top aide. An awkward scene ensued. Schiff remained motionless in his chair. Republicans across the table tried to suppress laughter as they watched Gaetz loom behind the rigid chairman.

"It was hard not to burst out laughing because Gaetz was just sitting there, and Schiff was just sitting there, the witness was just sitting there, everybody was just sitting there," said one Republican who was in the room. "And nothing is happening. Gaetz looks like he just can't wait to come after Schiff. And Schiff is sitting there with a zombie look on his face."

"It was a long time," the Republican continued. "It was more than just a minute or two. It was like five, six, seven minutes. We're sitting there because we don't control the gavel. And Schiff is silent."

"One of the Democrats asks something, and Schiff says we can't start because people who don't belong in the room are in the room. Then [Jim] Jordan rips into him, and that goes on a while. And when more people pour into the SCIF, you go from 60 people in there to close to 100. You can't even move."

"Schiff went nuts when they came in," Stewart wrote in his journal. "Lots of yelling on both sides."

Finally, Schiff left the room. "We waited around for a while," Chris Stewart wrote, "and then I went into Schiff's office where we congregated to discuss. Schiff wanted us to tell them to leave. I said, 'No way. You're chairman. You go tell them.' Then I told him they weren't going to leave, regardless of who told them. He talked about how they are breaking the rules. I said maybe they are, but you have to decide if impeaching a president in secret is a good idea, and are you going to keep doing it."

Schiff tried the same argument with Representative Jim Jordan. "He told me it was my responsibility to make them leave," Jordan recalled. "I said, 'No, it's not. You're the chairman, I'm not, and I support them being here during this testimony.'"

The bad feelings, which were already high, were intensified by the fact that Schiff had no working relationship with any Republicans. Devin Nunes, the ranking Republican who had joined the crowd in Schiff's office, would not speak to Schiff unless there was a lawyer present. "One of my lawyers says, 'Mr. Schiff would like to speak with you,'" Nunes recalled, "and I say I can't go in there without my general counsel and our top members. I'm not going to engage in any type of conversation with him, especially with no transcriber there."

"[Mark] Meadows is turning all red yelling at Schiff," Nunes recalled. "Eventually Schiff says, 'We're not getting anywhere here,' and we all go back to my office."

The guerilla theater was cathartic for Republicans, but it did not resolve anything. It seemed hard to imagine that relations between the parties on the committee, which had been deteriorating for years, could get any worse. But they could. Just days after the ruckus in the SCIF, Schiff cut off Republican efforts to learn how the Ukraine investigation began. The chairman had moved beyond denying information to non-committee Republicans. He was telling committee Republicans that there were some questions for which they would never receive answers. The frustration level rose.

Lieutenant Colonel Vindman

For Republicans, the hidden identity of the whistleblower was just another part of the excessive secrecy surrounding the Democratic case for impeachment. "These proceedings should be public," Jordan said during the depositions. "Democrats are trying to remove the president 13 months before an election based on an anonymous whistleblower...and they're doing it all in a closed-door process."

For their part, Democrats argued that they were legally required to keep the whistleblower anonymous. "The whistleblower has the right in the statute to remain anonymous," Schiff said in early October, "and we will do everything in our power to make sure that that whistleblower is protected." Later in the month, Schiff repeated that the whistleblower had "a statutory right to remain anonymous."

Schiff was wrong; the whistleblower did not have a "statutory right to remain anonymous." The whistleblower's rights were set out in the Intelligence Community Whistleblower Protection Act, which said: "The inspector general shall not disclose the identity of the employee without the consent of the employee, unless the inspector general determines that such disclosure is unavoidable during the course of the investigation...." The law said clearly that the inspector general was the only official prohibited from disclosing the whistleblower's identity. And even the inspector general could reveal the name of the whistleblower if "such disclosure is unavoidable during the course of the investigation." No one else—not the press, not Congress, not anyone—was prohibited from publicly identifying the whistleblower.

Nevertheless, Schiff went to great lengths to prevent disclosure of the whistleblower's identity. And then he went beyond that. Any testimony on how the whistleblower complaint came to the Intelligence Community Inspector General, Schiff decreed, might reveal information that could lead to the identity of the whistleblower. Therefore, Schiff— who as chair of the committee investigating impeachment, and who, with the Speaker's backing, had unchallengeable authority to limit the investigation and cut off unwanted lines of questioning—would not allow any testimony that in his opinion might lead to the revelation of the whistleblower's identity.

The issue came to a head in the single most important deposition in the entire impeachment investigation—that of Lieutenant Colonel Alexander Vindman, the National Security Council aide who listened to the Trump-Zelensky call and who, along with his twin brother Lieutenant

Colonel Yvgeny Vindman, reported concerns to the NSC's top lawyer, John Eisenberg.

Alexander Vindman was important to investigators because he was the only person listening to the call who believed something improper had happened. He reported it not only to the NSC lawyer but also to an unnamed other person, outside the White House but inside the Intelligence Community. Republicans believed that person, the recipient of Vindman's tip, was the whistleblower, but Schiff forbade discussion of any person in the Intelligence Community with whom Vindman might have discussed the call. Schiff was determined that the process by which the whistleblower complaint came to light remain hidden, and it was that determination that led to tense moments inside the October 29 Vindman deposition.

Vindman arrived in full dress uniform, including the Purple Heart he was awarded after being wounded during service in the Iraq War. The deposition was conducted under the usual rules, with lawmakers forbidden from publicly discussing what was said. But, as had become the practice by then, Vindman's opening statement leaked—he said, "I did not think it was proper [for Trump] to demand that a foreign government investigate a U.S. citizen"—and the news exploded across cable TV even as he answered questions behind closed doors.

In fact, Vindman's extensive testimony—the deposition transcript ran to 340 pages—was more complex than the news reports suggested. Yes, Vindman testified repeatedly that he thought it was "wrong" for Trump, speaking with Zelensky, to bring up the 2016 election and allegations of Ukraine-related corruption on the part of former Vice President Joe Biden and his son Hunter. But the Vindman deposition also revealed a witness whose testimony was filled with opinion, with impressions, who withheld important information from the committee, who was steeped in a bureaucracy that was deeply hostile to the president, and whose lawyer, presumably with Vindman's approval, expressed unmistakable disdain, verging on contempt, for members of Congress who asked inconvenient questions.

The most serious problem with Vindman's testimony was that much of it was based on his personal views. Originally, Vindman had seemed a key witness because he had heard the call, but by the time he testified, the White House had released the rough transcript of the call, and everybody knew what had been said.

Vindman said he was "concerned" about Trump's statements to Zelensky—so concerned that he reported it to NSC lawyer John Eisenberg. Vindman said several times that he was not a lawyer and did not know if Trump's words amounted to a crime, but he repeated that he felt they were "wrong." That was when Republican Representative John Ratcliffe of Texas, a former U.S. attorney, tried to get to the root of Vindman's concerns. What was really bothering him?

"I'm trying to find out if you were reporting it because you thought there was something wrong with respect to policy or there was something wrong with respect to the law," Ratcliffe said to Vindman. "And what I understand you to say is that you weren't certain that there was anything improper with respect to the law, but you had concerns about U.S. policy. Is that a fair characterization?"

"So I would recharacterize it as I thought it was wrong and I was sharing those views," Vindman answered. "And I was deeply concerned about the implications for bilateral relations, U.S. national security interests, in that if this was exposed, it would be seen as a partisan play by Ukraine. It loses the bipartisan support. And then for…"

"I understand that," Ratcliffe said, "but that sounds like a policy reason, not a legal reason."

"I was making a judgment call as a layman," Vindman responded, "thinking that it was wrong."

To Republicans at least, Vindman seemed to be saying that he simply disagreed with what Trump did on the call. Elsewhere in his testimony, Vindman repeated that his greatest worry was that if the Trump-Zelensky conversation were made public, then Ukraine might lose the bipartisan support it had in Congress. That, to Ratcliffe and other Republicans, did not seem a sufficient reason to report the call to the NSC's top lawyer, nor did it seem the basis to begin a process leading to a charge of presidential high crimes or misdemeanors.

At another point, Steve Castor, the Republican counsel, asked Vindman whether he was interpreting Trump's words in an overly alarmist way. Castor pointed to Vindman's use of the word "demand" in his opening statement, saying, "I did not think it was proper [for Trump] to demand that a foreign government investigate a U.S. citizen." Republicans who carefully read the transcript, and who compared it to Trump's general way of speaking, wondered if Vindman had not over-interpreted the president's words.

"The president in the transcript uses some, you know, words of hedging from time to time," Castor said. "You know, on page 3, he says 'whatever you can do.' He ends the first paragraph on page 3, 'if that's possible.' At the top of page 4, 'if you could speak to him, that would be great.' 'So whatever you can do.' Again, at the top of page 4, 'if you can look into it.' Is it reasonable to conclude that those words hedging for some might, you know, lead people to conclude that the president wasn't trying to be demanding here?"

"I think people want to hear, you know, what they have as already preconceived notions," Vindman answered, in what was perhaps the most revealing moment of the deposition. "I'd also point your attention to 'whatever you can do, it's very important to do it if that's possible.'"

"'*If that's possible,*'" Castor stressed.

"Yeah," said Vindman. "So I guess you can interpret it in different ways."

If one could interpret something in different ways, Republicans wondered, then was it a good basis for seeking to remove the President of the United States?

Vindman told the members that he had twice taken his concerns about the call to Eisenberg. He also told his twin brother and Michael Ellis, another NSC lawyer. And he gave what he characterized as a partial readout of the call to George Kent, the State Department official who dealt with Ukraine. That led to an obvious question: Was that everyone

Vindman told about the call? Anyone else, inside or outside the White House? As it turned out, there was someone else. Vindman did speak to one last person, someone in the Intelligence Community. But even though Vindman identified everyone else he discussed the call with, Chairman Schiff would not allow him to reveal who that last person was.

The Republicans' obvious suspicion was that person was the whistleblower. The last person Vindman told, GOP lawmakers believed, consulted Schiff's committee staff and, acting on their advice, wrote the whistleblower complaint that framed the Trump-Ukraine issue in a way that still guided Democrats in their drive to remove the president from office.

Since the person Vindman told was in the Intelligence Community, under normal circumstances, Schiff, as chairman of the Intelligence Committee—which is charged with overseeing the Intelligence Community—might have wanted to know about Intelligence Community involvement in the matter under investigation. But in the Vindman deposition, Schiff strictly forbade any questions about the identity of the person Vindman talked to. "Can I just caution again," Schiff said at one point, "not to go into names of people affiliated with the IC in any way."

That left Republicans struggling to get a foothold. "I'm just trying to better understand who the universe of people the concerns were expressed to," said Castor as Vindman's lawyer refused to let his client answer question after question, each time with the support of Schiff.

"Look, the reason we're objecting is…my client does not want to be in the position of being used to identify the whistleblower, okay?" said Michael Volkov, Vindman's attorney. "And based on the chair's ruling, as I understand it, [Vindman] is not required to answer any question that would tend to identify an intelligence officer."

"Okay," Castor said to Vindman. "Did you express concerns to anybody, you know, that doesn't fall under this category of someone who might be the whistleblower, or is Eisenberg the only…"

Vindman answered that in his "coordination role" at the NSC, he sometimes gave "readouts of relevant meetings and communications" to other officials—"properly cleared counterparts with a relevant need to know."

What did that mean, exactly? Republicans tried on several occasions to get Vindman to explain further. "Some of the other people that you raised concerns to, did you ask any of those folks to do anything with the concerns?" asked Castor.

"I don't think that's an accurate characterization, counsel," Vindman said. "I think what I did was I fulfilled my coordination role and spoke to other national security professionals about relevant substance in the call so that they could take appropriate action. And frankly, it's hard to—you know, without getting into, you know, sources and methods, it's hard to kind of talk about some of these things."

It seemed clear to Republicans that someone was hiding something. Vindman was claiming that he could not tell the impeachment inquiry who he talked to because it might reveal "sources and methods." After several such exchanges, Volkov chastised Republicans, suggesting further inquiries might hurt Vindman's feelings.

"Look, he came here," Volkov said. "He came here. He tells you he's not the whistleblower, okay? He says he feels uncomfortable about it. Try to respect his feelings at this point."

An unidentified voice spoke up. "We're uncomfortable impeaching the president," it said.

"Excuse me. Excuse me," Volkov responded. "If you want to debate it, we can debate it, but what I'm telling you right now is you have to protect the identity of the whistleblower. I get that there may be political overtones. You guys go do what you got to do, but do not put this man in the middle of it."

Steve Castor spoke up. "So how does it out anyone by saying that he had one other conversation other than the one he had with George Kent?"

"Okay," said Volkov. "What I'm telling you right now is we're not going to answer that question. If the chair wants to hold him in contempt for protecting the whistleblower, God be with you.... You don't need this. You don't need to go down this. And look, you guys can—if you want to ask, you can ask—you can ask questions about his conversation with Mr. Kent. That's it. We're not answering any others."

"The only conversation that we can speak to Colonel Vindman about is his conversation with Ambassador Kent?" asked Republican Representative Lee Zeldin.

"Correct," said Volkov, "and you've already asked him questions about it."

"And any other conversation that he had with absolutely anyone else is off limits?"

"No," said Volkov. "He's told you about his conversations with people in the National Security Council. What you're asking him to do is talk about conversations outside the National Security Council. And he's not going to do that. I know where you're going."

"No, actually, you don't," said Zeldin.

"Oh, yes, sir," said Volkov.

"No, you really don't," said Zeldin.

"You know what?" said Volkov. "I know what you're going to say. I already know what you're going to do, okay? And I don't want to hear the Fox News questions, okay?"

Zeldin, perhaps seeking to cool Volkov down, said, "Listen, this transcript is going to be out at some point, okay?"

"I hope so," said Volkov.

Finally Schiff stepped in to stop things. "The gentleman will suspend," he said. "Let's suspend. Counsel has made his position clear. I think his client has made his position clear. Let's move on."

Volkov, representing Vindman, acted with extraordinary derision toward members of Congress taking part in an impeachment inquiry. He got away with it because he was doing precisely what the chairman, Schiff, wanted him to do. In an extraordinary turn of events, Schiff coordinated with a witness to stonewall Schiff's own committee. And he was successful: Republicans were never told the identity of that last person Vindman discussed the Trump-Zelensky call with.

But Republicans did learn the depth of Democratic determination to keep keep the origins of the Ukraine investigation obscure. Two days after Vindman testified, his boss at the NSC, Tim Morrison, came in for a deposition. Morrison had also listened to the Trump-Zelensky call as it happened and did not believe it involved any improper or illegal behavior. Republicans asked Morrison whether Vindman was authorized to discuss a matter as sensitive as the Trump-Zelensky call with others in the government.

"Colonel Vindman, he reports to you," GOP counsel Steve Castor said to Morrison. "What types of officials in the course of his duties would he be responsible for providing readouts to?"

At that point, according to the transcript, the questioning was interrupted for an off-the-record discussion—an indication that a sensitive topic had been broached.

"He may have felt it appropriate to speak to other departments and agencies if they had questions about the call," Morrison answered after a pause.

"Do you know if he did?"

"Yes."

"And do you know who he spoke to?"

"I'm not going to allow him to answer that," Morrison's lawyer, Barbara Van Gelder, interrupted. "It is beyond the scope of this inquiry."

At that point, Schiff broke in. "Again, I want to express my concern that these questions are designed to try to identify and out the whistleblower," he said. "And I would hope that is not counsel's intention. The whistleblower has a right to anonymity."

A short time later, Castor, nothing if not persistent, returned to his line of questioning. "Do you know if Lieutenant Colonel Vindman had communications with any State Department officials like George Kent?" he asked Morrison. That was an established fact; Vindman had testified two days earlier that he talked to Kent.

"We're not going to talk about anybody Mr. Vindman had conversations with," Van Gelder said.

And that was the end of that. Blocked by the chairman, Castor moved on to other questions. Among other things, Morrison testified that Vindman spoke to him about the call but did not say he believed something improper had occurred. Rather, Vindman had two concerns. The first was that "the call did not get into the subject matter we had hoped," Morrison explained. The other was a concern "about the fidelity of the translation." Finally, Morrison said that Fiona Hill, Vindman's boss before Morrison, "had raised concerns about Alex's judgment."

There were other weaknesses in Vindman's testimony. He portrayed himself as an expert on Ukraine but seemed to know nothing about Burisma, and not much about the general issue of corruption. He also appeared to be entirely a creature of a foreign policy bureaucracy that adamantly opposed President Trump. He placed enormous faith in what he called the "interagency"—that is, a group of experts from the State Department, Defense Department, Intelligence Community, Treasury Department, and the White House. He believed the interagency had set a clear U.S. policy toward Ukraine, and he was deeply unhappy that the President of the United States had deviated from the interagency's policy.

"In the spring of 2019, I became aware of outside influencers promoting a false narrative of Ukraine inconsistent with the consensus views of the interagency," Vindman said in his opening statement. The "outside influencers"—apparently Rudy Giuliani, working at the president's direction—were undermining the work of his "interagency colleagues," Vindman said. In the words of the *Washington Post*, Vindman was "deeply troubled by what he interpreted as an attempt by the president to subvert U.S. foreign policy."

Of course, it is the President of the United States, and not the interagency, who sets U.S. policy toward Ukraine and the rest of the world. And Donald Trump was clearly not an interagency sort of man. The president was freewheeling, unbureaucratic, and certainly not always consistent when it came to making policy. But he generally had a big goal in mind, and in any event, he was the president. He, not the interagency, was charged with leading U.S. foreign policy.

Vindman's discussion of the interagency might have contained the key to his role in the Trump-Ukraine affair. In the Trump years, the foreign policy establishment with which Vindman so clearly identified was often at odds, sometimes privately and sometimes publicly, with the president. The conflict went back to the 2016 campaign, when Trump faced the opposition not only of Democratic foreign policy veterans but dozens of members of the Republican foreign policy establishment who signed letters condemning him. In 2019, at about the time Vindman testified, former United Nations Ambassador Nikki Haley published a memoir, *With All Due Respect: Defending America with Grit and Grace*, in which she said two top officials, Secretary of State Rex Tillerson and White House chief of staff John Kelly, sought to undermine the president in order to "save the country."

"It was *their* decisions, not the president's, that were in the best interest of America, they said," Haley wrote. "The president didn't know what he was doing." In the impeachment inquiry, parts of the foreign policy bureaucracy entered into an open war with the president, channeling their grievances through the House Democrats' drive toward impeachment. Vindman was the living embodiment of that bureaucratic war.

The Vindman testimony was both a revelation and a dilemma for Republicans. On the one hand, they all felt confident that Vindman was the original source of the Ukraine investigation. He was the one—the only one—listening to the Trump-Zelensky call who felt something improper had taken place, a judgment he made based on his views of what a proper U.S. policy toward Ukraine should be. And he was the one who contacted the person who became the whistleblower. (At first, Republicans came to that conclusion through circumstantial evidence and a process of elimination, but later, according to Republicans deeply involved in the investigation, someone in Vindman's camp inadvertently confirmed to them, outside of the deposition context, that Vindman did indeed speak with the whistleblower.)

"It was clear, from not just what they were verbalizing but also their body language, that Vindman was the whistleblower source," said Zeldin.

"Vindman was the person on the call who went to the whistleblower after the call, to give the whistleblower the information he needed to file his complaint. It became obvious, not just with what they were saying, but how they were saying it, and how they were acting as they were saying it."

"Ultimately, we know Vindman is the person talking to the whistleblower," said the senior Republican aide. "All the facts point that Vindman here is the coefficient, that he sparked this whole thing. For all intents and purposes, Vindman is the whistleblower here, but he was able to get somebody else to do his dirty work for him."

On the other hand, Vindman was a decorated veteran whom Republicans did not feel comfortable attacking. Some felt he was a villain in the Ukraine matter but a hero in other parts of his life. That posed a conundrum for GOP questioners. "He was someone who was wounded in combat," the senior aide continued. "There were a lot of aspects of his service to the country that are very honorable and deserve respect. We certainly gave him that respect." But for those Republicans, keeping a hands-off posture toward Vindman meant not vigorously pursuing the whistleblower's identity. "Part of the reason that the whistleblower ultimately was never officially confirmed was because Vindman was a decorated military person," the aide said. Republicans felt uneasy about going after him. And of course, Chairman Schiff remained an immovable obstacle to any such questions.

After the Vindman and Morrison depositions, Republicans essentially gave up on their effort to publicly reveal both the whistleblower's identity and the plan that led to the whistleblower complaint. Democrats were barreling ahead with the impeachment, and the fight soon moved to the House floor.

CHAPTER TEN

The Final Rush

The Adam Schiff Empowerment Act—The Search for a
Rationale—The Dilemma of Public Hearings—"Chairman?
Jerry? Chairman?"—Groundhog Day

During the time they conducted the secret depositions—all of October 2019—leading Democrats often likened the process to a grand jury. It was a weak comparison, in part because grand jury proceedings are governed by strict rules, while the House could (and did) set any rules it wanted for the impeachment investigation. Plus, a real grand jury would have involved a prosecutor presenting evidence to a group of impartial jurors. Who would they be, in Schiff's depositions? Nevertheless, Democrats cited the grand jury notion to justify their secrecy, and also to suggest that once they finished the secret phase, they would move on to the public part of their investigation—their indictment of the president.

What was unclear was whether Democrats would also, at some point, get around to authorizing the investigation in the first place. Through September and much of October, Pelosi claimed an authorization vote was not necessary. She made no substantive case, but instead argued that Democrats would not hold a vote because they did not have to. On October 15, 2019, about halfway through the secret deposition process, Pelosi and Schiff held a news conference. "The White House said it's not cooperating in part because there hasn't been a vote to formalize this impeachment inquiry," a reporter asked. "Why not hold a vote and call the White House's bluff?"

"The Constitution is very clear," Schiff answered. "The House shall have the sole power of impeachment. There is no court that's going to find otherwise."

"As the distinguished chairman said, there's no requirement that we have a vote," Pelosi added, "and so, at this time we will not be having a vote.... We're not here to call bluffs."

Still, Kevin McCarthy and House Republicans regularly reminded Democrats, and the public, that Pelosi's predecessors all saw the need to hold impeachment authorization votes. On October 6, 1974, the House voted by the overwhelming margin of 410 to 4 to authorize the Richard Nixon impeachment inquiry; the vote was not only bipartisan but nearly unanimous, except for four exceptionally loyal Nixon Republicans. On October 9, 1998, the House voted 258–176 to authorize the Bill Clinton impeachment inquiry. Thirty-one Democrats broke with the president of their party to support that inquiry—enough to characterize the vote as bipartisan.

Could Pelosi get thirty-one Republicans to break with Trump and support an impeachment resolution? Not in a million years. The speaker did not have a Nixon-like level, or even a Clinton-like level, of support for impeachment. Republicans believed that one of the reasons she put off holding a vote was that she hoped some GOP converts might eventually join her side.

Worse, Pelosi could not meet the standard she herself had created. Back in March, when many Democrats wanted to impeach the president on the basis of the Mueller report, Pelosi created a new benchmark for starting the process. She was firmly against impeachment, she said, because it was "so divisive to the country that unless there's something so compelling and overwhelming and bipartisan, I don't think we should go down that path because it divides the country. And he's just not worth it." With that, Pelosi established her own standard for impeachment: Is it compelling, overwhelming, and bipartisan?

To no one's surprise, the Pelosi standard came back to haunt the Speaker just a few months later. While Schiff, acting with Pelosi's clear approval, drove steadily toward impeachment, Republicans asked: Does it meet the speaker's criteria? Is it compelling, overwhelming, and bipartisan? If not, then drop it. If so, then have a vote. Let's see where people stand.

The Adam Schiff Empowerment Act

The pressure to hold a vote built as October went on. The outcome Pelosi and her fellow Democrats wanted to avoid was to have the vote and end up with an embarrassingly partisan result. There was no way to persuade thirty-one Republicans to join the Democratic impeachment effort. But how about a few? Just enough to call it bipartisan?

The obvious targets were Republican members who represented districts that Hillary Clinton won in 2016. Democrats were keeping a close eye on them; perhaps they might be convinced to vote against the president. The problem was that there were only three such GOP members: Will Hurd from Texas, John Katko from New York, and Brian Fitzpatrick of Pennsylvania. That was a pretty small pool of persuadables. But even they were not, in the end, particularly persuadable. McCarthy paid special attention to each one and felt confident about their votes, despite rumors they might defect.

The highest profile of the three was Hurd, who had received a lot of press attention for occasionally criticizing Trump. (When Trump launched a Twitter attack on The Squad, Hurd called the tweets "racist and xenophobic" and "behavior that's unbecoming of the leader of the free world.") There was a lot of speculation that Hurd might take a stand against Trump. Democrats had high hopes.

"They thought they had him," recalled McCarthy. "Former CIA agent, not going to run again, had made certain comments about Trump. Members came to me and said, 'You should remove him from Intel.' I said, 'Why would I want to remove him from Intel? He's a smart guy. The facts are on our side. He'll be there.' And I was getting pressure—'Oh, you should put in Matt Gaetz, you should put in Meadows'—and I said, 'Why do you assume they're the only people who know something?' And if you watched, some of the great questions came from Will Hurd." In the end, Democratic hopes were dashed; Hurd never voted for any phase of impeachment.

And the others? "Fitzpatrick was an FBI agent," McCarthy continued. "He had worked in Ukraine. He was solid. He knew how corrupt they were. So it wasn't like I had to go convince him."

"Katko was a U.S. attorney," McCarthy added. "He texts me one day, he says, 'When I would use an anonymous person and I'm trying somebody, I had to put them on the stand, they had to face their accuser. Why would we do this here?'"

Hurd, Fitzpatrick, and Katko were supposed to be the most vulnerable Republicans. There was talk of Democrats pouring money into their districts to pressure them to flip. But the manifest unfairness of the Democratic inquiry kept McCarthy and every other Republican—including Hurd, Fitzpatrick, and Katko—united.

McCarthy believed that Republicans' drumbeat of complaints about process eventually forced Pelosi to agree to an authorization vote. The catalyst for changing her mind, Republicans thought, was the brief but highly publicized occupation of the SCIF. Yes, the press criticized Republicans for the action, but it also caused Republicans and some members of the press to ask: why the secrecy? Why is there a secret process going on for this most public of purposes—that is, an inquiry into removing the President of the United States?

"They were never going to bring [the impeachment resolution] up," McCarthy recalled. "It was after we stormed [the SCIF], because...people were asking: Why is this in the basement? Then Pelosi came back."

Asked if he believed Pelosi finally held an authorizing vote because of Republican pressure, McCarthy said, "Yes: 100 percent."

The SCIF incident was October 23. Within days, Democrats were circulating a draft authorization measure. A vote was set for October 31.

Pelosi, Schiff, and the Democratic leadership had other reasons to finally produce an authorization. They realized they needed to sell impeachment to the American people, just as they had tried to sell the Mueller report. They could not do that with a bunch of secret transcripts. They believed, as they had with Mueller, that to win public support they had to turn impeachment into compelling television. Their model was the Watergate hearings, which Pelosi, second-in-command Hoyer, and Whip James Clyburn, all nearing eighty years of age, remembered well. If there could be a John Dean moment—a moment in which a Trump administration insider revealed devastating information about the president's behavior—impeachment might be transformed from a Democratic obsession into a national cause.

But to do that, there had to be hearings. And to have hearings, there had to be rules. And to have rules, there had to be an authorization bill—precisely what Pelosi had delayed for weeks.

The bill's full description was "Directing certain committees to continue their ongoing investigations as part of the existing House of Representatives inquiry into whether sufficient grounds exist for the House of Representatives to exercise its Constitutional power to impeach Donald John Trump, President of the United States of America, and for other purposes." As the lengthy name suggested, Pelosi crafted the resolution not as a new impeachment resolution but rather as a means to continue the existing impeachment inquiry. That way, she could continue to defend her unilateral start while saying a resolution was needed for the inquiry to enter a new phase.

A shorter title for the bill might have been "The Adam Schiff Empowerment Act." The resolution gave the Intelligence Committee chairman far-reaching power over the impeachment process. Pelosi retained ultimate authority, but, like a chairman of the board choosing a chief executive officer, she picked Schiff to run the show and gave him the power to do it.

For the first time, the resolution formally gave the impeachment inquiry to the Intelligence Committee. Until that point, it had been a joint production of three committees—Intel, Oversight, and Foreign Affairs. Under the resolution, Oversight and Foreign Affairs were pushed out of the picture. This would not only streamline the Democratic effort but also cut out of the proceedings some Republicans who were not members of the Intelligence Committee but who had, because of their membership in the other two committees, become thorns in the Democrats' sides.

The resolution also gave Schiff total control over whether to make transcripts of depositions—those already completed and those yet to be done—public. "The chair is authorized to make publicly available in electronic form the transcripts of depositions conducted by the [Intelligence Committee] in furtherance of the investigation," said the resolution. That meant Schiff *could* release transcripts, but was not required to do so.

The bill also gave Schiff the authority to call public hearings and control witnesses. Although there was some discussion about whether Republicans would have the right to call witnesses, the resolution merely gave the ranking Republican on the Intelligence Community, Representative Devin Nunes, the right to *ask Schiff* to call a witness.

"To allow for full evaluation of minority witness requests, the ranking minority member may submit to the chair, in writing, any requests for witness testimony relevant to the investigation," the resolution said. "Any such request shall be accompanied by a detailed written justification of the relevance of the testimony of each requested witnesses to the investigation." Republicans knew they were getting the back of Schiff's hand. It did not matter who they wanted to call as a witness; they could do so only by asking Schiff's permission. What that meant in practice was that they could forget about calling the whistleblower, or Hunter Biden, to testify.

"The rules the Democrats rammed through simply confirm the absolute control Schiff has been exercising this entire time," Nunes said shortly after the text of the authorizing bill was released. "He shouldn't be involved in impeachment at all, since none of this has any intelligence component, but Pelosi obviously thinks [Judiciary Committee chairman Jerry] Nadler is incompetent."

The vote was approaching. For McCarthy, it was the single most important moment in the impeachment to that date. McCarthy, GOP whip Steve Scalise, and the entire Republican leadership had been preparing for the vote since before Pelosi unilaterally announced impeachment on September 24. The whole point of their laser focus on the unfairness of the process was to keep Republicans, no matter what they felt about President Trump, united in opposition to the Democrats' tactics. And if they were united in the belief that the process was inherently unfair, they would not vote to authorize it to move to the next level. "Everything [the Democrats] were doing was solidifying us and showing how it was unfair, which in turn said this whole process is BS," McCarthy recalled.

To dramatize the point, Republican leaders felt it was critical that the authorization receive no GOP votes. Zero. If even one Republican voted to move impeachment forward, the leadership felt that it would allow Democrats to claim broad support for the measure. More important, McCarthy felt a zero-Republicans vote would send an important message to the Republican-controlled Senate that House GOP lawmakers—every single one of them—saw no merit in the Democratic case, and neither should Republicans in the Senate.

The vote happened shortly before noon on Halloween. In the debate that preceded it, Republicans used the words "fair," or "unfair," or "fairness" about forty times. Every GOP speaker pounded the resolution as the codification of the Democrats' unfair procedures. When the votes were cast, 231 Democrats, plus 1 independent—Representative Justin Amash, who had quit the Republican Party four months earlier—voted to authorize the expanded impeachment inquiry. 194 Republicans, along with 2 Democrats, voted against the authorization. Precisely zero Republicans voted for it.

The GOP leadership had achieved its goal, a bit of victory in defeat. From that point forward, McCarthy and his allies could accurately call impeachment a partisan Democratic (or Democrat, as they liked to say) initiative. That was satisfying, but their rhetoric had a higher purpose. The idea was to send a message of Republican unity not only to House Democrats, but to the White House, to the Senate Republicans, who would judge the case if impeachment came to trial, and to the public.

"I think the whole impeachment, internally for Republicans, shifted when we got down to the impeachment inquiry vote," McCarthy recalled. "No one thought we would be 100 percent united, plus we'd get a couple of Democrats. How it came out of the House [determined] what would happen in the Senate. I had a number of senators who told me after that inquiry vote, 'You changed the course.' And a number of people in the Senate told me that what comes out of the House is pretty much what is going to come out of the Senate."

The Search for a Rationale

Part of the Democratic leadership's difficulty in deciding to hold a vote was their confusion about what they proposed to impeach President Trump for. Did he commit a crime? If so, what crime? Did he abuse his power? Did he violate norms? What, precisely, did he do?

The Intelligence Community Inspector General had originally suggested Trump might have broken the nation's campaign finance laws. Under that theory, Trump solicited a thing of value for his campaign—information— when he suggested to Ukrainian President Volodymyr Zelensky that the Ukrainians investigate the business dealings of Joe Biden's son. That might violate the ban on foreign contributions, as well as the money limit for contributions, if one could establish a dollar value for the information.

The theory had all the legal defects that Robert Mueller discovered when he investigated similar charges in relation to the June 9, 2016, Trump Tower meeting—defects that caused Mueller to drop the idea of charging anyone for any actions stemming from the meeting. "I think it's absurd," said Bradley Smith, a former Federal Election Commission chair and a frequent critic of campaign finance laws. "If 'anything of value' were interpreted so broadly, it would mean that foreign governments are consistently violating the ban in foreign spending, whenever they take official actions that may benefit one candidate or another. Similarly, Americans would have to report such activity to the FEC. That is clearly not the law."

In a larger sense, alleging Trump committed a campaign finance violation would be a very difficult sell to the American public. The law is arcane, picayune, and difficult to understand. Candidates and office holders are accused of campaign finance violations all the time, sometimes resulting in their campaigns having to pay a fine. Even if proven— and there is no way Democrats could have proved it—a campaign finance violation was a terribly small thing to propose removing the President of the United States over.

Democrats explored the idea of other charges. Some favored accusing Trump of a *quid pro quo*, which was not a crime but indicated that the president was trying to get something for himself in his dealings with Zelensky. The problem was twofold: 1) The alleged *quid pro quo* never actually happened, and Trump had had some success repeating the mantra "No *quid pro quo*" many, many times; and 2) Many Americans did not know what a *quid pro quo* was. Democrats soon stopped repeating the phrase. "We've got to get off this *quid pro quo* thing," Democratic Representative Jim Himes said November 10. "*Quid pro quo* is one of these things to muddy the works."

Some favored accusing the president of "extortion." For a while, it seemed as if every Democrat was using that word to describe the Trump-Zelensky call. Democrats liked it because unlike *quid pro quo*, extortion was a real crime. It also had a thuggish feel to it, like a mobster demanding protection money. The problem was the Trump-Zelensky call did not sound to the average ear like extortion. "A person commits the crime of extortion when he induces the victim to part with something of value under some kind of duress," George Washington University law professor Randall Eliason wrote during the impeachment battle. To the degree that Americans followed the impeachment issue at all, that did not describe the Trump-Zelensky call.

Campaign finance. *Quid pro quo*. Extortion. Nothing seemed quite right. Then, around mid-November, Democrats began using yet another word to make their case against Trump: "bribery." The *Washington Post* reported on November 14 that the new emphasis on "bribery" was not a coincidence. "The shift came after the Democratic Congressional Campaign Committee conducted focus groups in key House battlegrounds in recent weeks, testing messages related to impeachment," the paper reported. "Among the questions put to participants was whether '*quid pro quo*,' 'extortion' or 'bribery' was a more compelling description of Trump's conduct. According to two people familiar with the results, which circulated among Democrats this week, the focus groups found 'bribery' to be most damning."

So "bribery" it was. The word also had the advantage of actually appearing in the Constitution, which said the president "shall be removed from office on impeachment for, and conviction of, treason, bribery, or other high crimes and misdemeanors." Still, even after focus-grouping "bribery," Democrats grappled with the uneasy sense that whatever the impeachment was about—extortion, bribery, whatever—it was at bottom about Ukraine, and not that many Americans cared about Ukraine, or at least not deeply enough to justify removing a president.

So Pelosi tried yet another pitch. "This isn't about Ukraine," she said. "It's about Russia. Who benefited by our withholding—withholding of that military assistance? Russia. It's about Russia. Russia invading eastern Ukraine. Over 10,000 people [dead], now maybe 13,000, some of them in the absence of our conveying that military assistance that was voted in a bipartisan way by the Congress of the United States. So sometimes people say, 'Well, I don't know about Ukraine. I don't know that much about Ukraine.' Well, our adversary in this is Russia. All roads lead to Putin. Understand that."

With those words, Pelosi and her Democratic colleagues had come full circle. They had been accusing Donald Trump of wrongdoing relating to Russia in 2016 and 2017 and 2018. A long Russia-focused criminal investigation failed to find that wrongdoing. Now, impeaching Trump in 2019, they returned to their old obsession. Impeachment was about Russia. For House Democrats, all roads did indeed lead to Russia.

The Dilemma of Public Hearings

The public hearings, run exclusively by Schiff's Intelligence Committee, began on November 13, two weeks after the impeachment resolution was passed. Democratic leaders got the media setting they wanted. Not only were the hearings covered live, start-to-finish, by the cable networks; they were also televised in their entirety by the broadcast networks. Anchors wore their serious suits to convey the gravity of the moment: for only the fourth time in history, the House was holding hearings to consider impeaching the President of the United States.

A week before, Schiff released most of the transcripts of the secret depositions. (He withheld the transcript of Intelligence Community Inspector General Michael Atkinson, which contained important information about the whistleblower.) The release meant there was very little that would be said in the public hearings that had not already been said behind closed doors. But this time it would be said on television, which was the point.

It was not discussed much at the time, but the hearings created a problem for Democrats. In terms of media coverage, the secret deposition process had worked beautifully. The unanswered allegations in the leaked opening statements made for big headlines and TV coverage, almost all of it negative for Trump and positive for Democrats. What was relatively under-covered, because of the secrecy rules, was the Republican defense of the president that played out in the body of the depositions.

Televised hearings changed that. Although they chafed under Democratic rules, Republicans had equal time at the microphone. They could make their case and explore weaknesses and inconsistencies in the witnesses' testimony. For the first time, there was a semblance of balance in the impeachment process—and just in time for millions of viewers to see.

That meant that both Trump opponents and supporters saw something different than expected. Reporting during the secrecy phase "gave heightened expectations to [the Democratic] base that when the public hearings began, they were going to be hearing the facts as they were presented to them by the media sources they relied on," recalled Republican Representative Lee Zeldin. "As the public hearings unfolded, their own base wasn't able to have their expectations met. Independent-minded observers were receiving a different version than what the media was telling them. And the president's supporters were receiving confirmation that the media was misleading them on a lot of facts."

The committee called twelve witnesses in all, down from the seventeen who gave secret depositions. Most sessions featured a pair of witnesses, beginning with William Taylor and George Kent on November 13. Two days later, Marie Yovanovitch testified alone. On November 19, Lieutenant Colonel Alexander Vindman and Jennifer Williams testified in the morning, and Kurt Volker and Tim Morrison testified in the afternoon. On November 20, Gordon Sondland testified alone in the morning and Laura Cooper and David Hale testified in the afternoon. On November 21, Fiona Hill and David Holmes testified. Packing twelve witnesses into just eight days of hearings, from November 13 to November 21, gave the affair a rushed feel. The public had little time to digest what was said in one hearing before the next began.

For anyone who had followed the impeachment process, the hearings did not reveal much that was new. Taylor made some news when he testified that he had just learned that a member of his staff, David Holmes, had overheard Ambassador Sondland talking with the president on the phone about "the investigations" the day after the Trump-Zelensky call. Sondland made news with a sensational claim of *quid pro quo* that turned out to be less than it appeared.

That gave Republicans an opportunity. They could focus on information that had not been as widely reported as the Democratic allegations. GOP questioners highlighted Volker's testimony that Ukraine had no knowledge of the hold on U.S. aid at the time of the Trump-Zelensky call. They elicited testimony from a number of witnesses that Trump's Ukraine security policy was actually an improvement over Barack Obama's. They explored Vindman's role and found an odd new twist. They tore Sondland apart. In addition, they took care to repeat mantras—most notably, Representative Jim Jordan's "four facts that will never change"—that made the complex story easier to understand.

With Volker, Republican counsel Steve Castor pointed out that the envoy met with Ukrainian President Zelensky on July 26, the day after the infamous call with President Trump. "Were any of these concerning elements that some witnesses have raised about the call, raised in the meeting with President Zelensky?" Castor asked.

"No," said Volker.

"So to the extent there have been assertions that President Zelensky was concerned about demands President Trump had made—"

"I don't recall that."

"You don't recall that?"

"I do not recall being…well, let me turn that around and say he was very positive about the phone call. I don't recall him saying anything about demands but he was very upbeat about the fact of the call."

"And there was no discussion on the part of President Zelensky on how to navigate the various concerns that people have articulated about the call?"

"I don't remember that."

"And…in no way, shape or form in either readouts from the United States or Ukraine did you receive any indication whatsoever or anything that resembled a *quid pro quo*? Is that correct?"

"That's correct."

"And the same would—would go for this new allegation of bribery?"

"I was never involved in anything that I considered to be bribery at all."

"Okay. Or extortion?"

"Or extortion."

Republicans also dug into the idea, expressed by a number of witnesses in the secret depositions, that Trump's Ukraine policy had actually been better for Ukraine than the previous administration's. Three career foreign policy officials—Taylor, Volker, and Yovanovitch—testified that Trump's policy was an improvement over President Obama's.

Speaking to Taylor, Republican Representative Brad Wenstrup said, "In your deposition, you said—and I quote—you were happy with the

Trump administration's assistance. And it provided both lethal and financial aid, did it not?"

"It did, sir," said Taylor

"And you also stated that it was a substantial improvement. Is that correct?"

"That's correct, sir."

Speaking to Volker, Republican Representative Mike Turner noted the Trump aid package to Ukraine included the ability to purchase Javelin anti-tank missiles. "That made a big difference with Ukraine, did it not?"

"A very big difference," said Volker.

With Yovanovitch, Republican counsel Steve Castor asked, "The Trump administration's policy of aid, the aid package to Ukraine, you've testified that, during your tenure as ambassador, America's policy actually got stronger towards Ukraine. Is that accurate?"

"With the provision of Javelins to the Ukrainian military, yes," Yovanovitch answered. "That was really positive."

Lieutenant Colonel Vindman, often described as the "star witness" against the president, testified on November 19. He was paired with Jennifer Williams, a State Department official assigned to work on European affairs in Vice President Pence's office who, like Vindman, listened to the Trump-Zelensky call as it happened on July 25, 2019.

Republicans questioned Vindman extensively about the whistleblower during Vindman's secret deposition. But that did not receive much news coverage, in large part because GOP lawmakers were forbidden from speaking publicly about it. So they used Vindman's appearance in the public hearing to highlight the fact that the entire impeachment saga began with a complaint from an anonymous person—the whistleblower—and that Democrats were still not only hiding the whistleblower's identity but the process through which the whistleblower complaint came to exist. They wanted to ask questions in such a way that it was clear to everyone that Vindman was the whistleblower's original source. As it turned out, Schiff and his fellow Democrats helped them do it.

Representative Devin Nunes, the ranking Republican, asked Vindman, "Did you discuss the July 25th call with anyone outside the White House on July 25th or the 26th? And if so, with whom?"

"Yes, I did," Vindman answered. "My core function is to coordinate U.S. government policy, interagency policy, and I spoke to two individuals with regards to providing some sort of a readout of the call."

"Two individuals that were not in the White House?"

"Not in the White House. Cleared U.S. government officials with appropriate need to know."

"And what agencies were these officials with?"

"Department of State Deputy Assistant Secretary George Kent, who is responsible for the portfolio, Eastern Europe, including Ukraine. And an individual from the Office of—an individual in the Intelligence Community."

Nunes wanted to know which of the seventeen agencies in the Intelligence Community the unnamed individual was from. That is when Schiff interrupted.

"If I could interject here, we don't want to use these proceedings…"

"It's our time, Chairman," Nunes said.

"I know," said Schiff, "but we need to protect the whistleblower. Please stop. I want to make sure there's no effort to out the whistleblower through these proceedings."

Could that have been any clearer? The Republican line of questioning established that: 1) Vindman told two people outside the NSC. 2) One of them was George Kent. And 3) The other was in the Intelligence Community but could not be revealed because Democrats did not want to identify the whistleblower. It did not take a rocket scientist to conclude that that unidentified other person was the whistleblower.

Jordan walked Vindman through essentially the same territory a bit later when Vindman said he discussed the call with only "two individuals" outside the White House.

"Two individuals," said Jordan.

"DAS [Deputy Assistant Secretary] Kent and one other person," Vindman answered.

"And you're not willing to tell us who that other individual is?"

"Mr. Chairman, point of order," interrupted Democratic Representative Eric Swalwell.

"The gentleman will suspend," said Schiff. "This committee will not be used to out the whistleblower."

"Mr. Chairman, I don't see how this is outing the whistleblower," Jordan said. "The witness has testified in his deposition that he doesn't know who the whistleblower is. You have said—even though no one believes you—you have said you don't know who the whistleblower is. So how is this outing the whistleblower, to find out who this individual is?"

"Mr. Jordan, this is your time for questioning," Schiff said. "You can use it any way you like, but...your question should not be addressed to trying to out the whistleblower."

By that time, Republicans believed they had made their point. Vindman was the only person listening to the call who believed he heard something improper, and he was the one who got the whole whistleblower process started by telling the person who would become the whistleblower.

Republicans also briefly explored a bit of information about Vindman that had emerged since his October 29 deposition. A source told the committee that in May 2019, when Vindman traveled to Ukraine with a U.S. delegation for President Zelensky's inauguration, a man named Oleksandr Danylyuk, head of Ukraine's National Security and Defense Council, asked Vindman to become Ukraine's Defense Minister. Danylyuk asked not once, not twice, but three times. Each time Vindman declined.

"At any point during that trip, did Mr. Danylyuk offer you a position of Defense Minister with the Ukrainian government?" asked Castor.

"He did," said Vindman.

"And how many times did he do that?"

"I believe it was three times."

"Do you have any reason why he asked you to do that?"

"I don't know," said Vindman. "But every single time, I dismissed it. Upon returning, I notified my chain of command and the appropriate counterintelligence folks about the offer."

"I mean, Ukraine is a country that has experienced a war with Russia," Castor said. "Certainly their Minister of Defense is a pretty key position…"

"Yeah," said Vindman.

"…for the Ukrainians, for President Zelensky, Mr. Danylyuk to bestow that honor on you, at least asking you, I mean that was a big honor, correct?"

"I think it would be a great honor," Vindman said. "And frankly, I'm aware of servicemembers that have left service to help nurture the developing democracies in that part of the world.… But I'm an American. I came here when I was a toddler. And I immediately dismissed these offers, did not entertain them."

It was unclear what the exchange meant. Vindman said the whole idea was "rather comical," adding he did not know if Danylyuk was joking. Later, Danylyuk himself said it was a joke. But others did not agree. "It was *not* a joke," a senior Republican aide who looked into the matter insisted. Whatever the case, some Democrats accused Republicans of insinuating that Vindman had dual loyalties. It was an unfair accusation; in fact, Republicans saw Vindman as a loyal American who had strong and inflexible views on what U.S. policy toward Ukraine should be and who was offended, and spurred to action, when the President of the United States appeared to change them. In any event, the Defense Minister matter was dropped.

Finally, there was Ambassador Sondland, whose appearance was perhaps the most consequential of the entire hearings. Sondland came in with credibility issues. In his deposition testimony, he had said he "never" thought President Trump attached any precondition to U.S. aid to Ukraine. Then, after others testified that Sondland had, in fact, told Ukrainian officials that there was such a precondition, Sondland submitted a long, carefully worded revision of his testimony.

In addition, at the public hearings another witness, William Taylor, said he had just learned of something he did not know when he testified in his secret deposition: that on July 26, 2019, the day after the Trump-Zelensky phone call, one of his staff said he overheard a telephone conversation in Kyiv between Sondland and Trump. The aide, David Holmes, testified that he was nearby and could hear both sides of Sondland's conversation. He said Trump asked Sondland about "the investigations," and Sondland replied that the Ukrainians were "ready to move forward." Sondland had never mentioned it in his testimony.

So when Sondland walked into the hearing room on November 20, his credibility was a big question mark. "Mr. Sondland is going to have some explaining to do," said Democratic Intelligence Committee member Raja Krishnamoorthi. "Sondland lied under oath to Congress," said Democratic Representative Ruben Gallego. The *Los Angeles Times* published a story headlined, "Is Gordon Sondland credible enough to be a good impeachment witness for either side?" The *New York Times* ran a similar story with the headline, "Why Discrepancies in Gordon Sondland's Testimony in the Impeachment Inquiry Loom Large."

Sondland's answer was not to apologize, or explain, or seek the lawmakers' forgiveness. Instead, he sat down in the witness chair and changed the subject by offering the most sensational soundbite Democrats could ever have wanted. "I know that members of this committee have frequently framed these complicated issues in the form of a simple question: Was there a *'quid pro quo'*?" Sondland said. "As I testified previously, with regard to the requested White House call and White House meeting, the answer is yes."

Sondland added that "Everyone was in the loop. It was no secret." Vice President Pence, Secretary of State Pompeo, White House Chief of Staff Mulvaney—they were all involved.

In an instant, the talk about Sondland lying to Congress vanished. Democrats were absolutely delighted that Sondland, once thought to be a witness friendly to the president, had given them such good material. The media coverage went along. Sondland's testimony was a "bombshell," it was damning, it was devastating, and a "turning point" in the impeachment proceedings.

But the story looked greatly diminished less than an hour later. It started with ostensibly friendly questioning from Schiff. "You've testified that your understanding, it became a clear understanding, that the military assistance was also being withheld pending Zelensky announcing these investigations, correct?" Schiff said to Sondland.

"That was my presumption," Sondland said. "My personal presumption based on the facts at the time. Nothing was moving."

"And in fact, you had a discussion, a communication with the Secretary of State in which you said that logjam over aid could be lifted if Zelensky announced these investigations, right?" Schiff said.

"I did not recall saying the logjam over aid," Sondland responded. "I recall saying the logjam. I don't know that…"

"That's what you meant, right, ambassador?" Schiff said.

"I…I…I meant that whatever was holding up the meeting, whatever was holding up our deal with Ukraine, I was trying to break," Sondland said. "Again, I was presuming."

Republican ears pricked up. Sondland was *presuming* that there was a *quid pro quo*? A few minutes later, Republican lawyer Steve Castor asked Sondland, "I want to turn back to your opener…when you talk about in the absence of any credible explanation for the suspension of aid, [you] later came to believe that the resumption of security aid would not occur until there was a public statement from Ukraine committing to the investigations, correct?"

"Correct," said Sondland.

"And you acknowledge that this is speculation, right?"

"It was a presumption," said Sondland.

Under further Republican questioning, Sondland admitted presumption several more times.

"I made the presumption…"

"I presumed it…"

"Again, that was my presumption…"

Later, another Republican lawmaker, Mike Turner, summed up, "Is that your testimony today…that you have evidence that Donald Trump tied the investigation to aid? Because I don't think you're saying that."

"I've said repeatedly, congressman, I was presuming," Sondland said.

"So no one told you," Turner said. "Not just the president. Giuliani didn't tell you, Mulvaney didn't tell you—nobody—Pompeo didn't tell you. Nobody else on this planet told you that Donald Trump was tying aid to these investigations, is that correct?"

"I think I already testified to that…"

"No, answer the question," Turner said. "Is it correct, no one on this planet told you that Donald Trump was tying aid to the investigations? Because if your answer is yes, then the chairman is wrong and the headline on CNN is wrong. No one on this planet told you that President Trump was tying aid to investigations, yes or no?"

"Yes."

"So you really have no testimony today that ties President Trump to a scheme to withhold aid from Ukraine in exchange for these investigations?"

"Other than my own presumption."

By that point, Sondland's testimony regarding a *quid pro quo*, so exciting just minutes earlier, was in tatters.

Republicans felt confident that they had done some serious damage to the case for impeachment, and they got to do it live on Fox News, CNN, MSNBC, ABC, NBC, CBS, and every other media outlet. More important, they felt that Democrats had only repackaged old revelations—revelations that were not connecting with American voters.

In addition, Republicans had found a way to reduce the extraordinarily complicated case to a quick synopsis. For any microphone in sight, Representative Jordan would recite his "four facts" analysis of the case. "Four facts have never changed and will never change," he said. "We have the transcript; there was no *quid pro quo* in the transcript. We have the two guys who were on the call, President Trump, President Zelensky. Both have said no pressure, no push, no linkage of an investigation to the security assistance money. We have the fact that Ukraine didn't even know the aid was paused at the time of the call. And most importantly, Ukraine took no action, that is, never made any announcement of investigations into anybody, let alone the Bidens, to get the aid released." For Republicans, it was an easy-to-understand substantive defense to go along with the procedural objections they had been raising for a long time.

Republican Chris Stewart wrote two journal entries during the hearings. In the first entry, dated November 18, after the first two days of testimony, he wrote, "They are not going well for the Dems. Boring. Public interest falling rapidly. No bombshells. No surprises. No John Dean to take down the president. Nothing that even comes close to making the American people go holy crap, we've got to remove this president and we need to do it right now. Nothing close to that."

Three days later, on November 21, after the final day of hearings, Stewart wrote, "It's all the same. Really, it is." He predicted that Democrats would soon "kick it over to Judiciary, and we'll be done."

Stewart was right. House rules required that actual articles of impeachment originate in and be passed by the House Judiciary Committee. After the rush of public hearings, that was the next step. For a brief time, the impeachment effort would move from Schiff's control to the unsteady stewardship of Judiciary chairman Jerrold Nadler.

"Chairman? Jerry? Chairman?"

The Judiciary Committee was not going to conduct an all-new investigation into the Ukraine matter. Schiff had already taken care of that. Schiff had also released, on December 3, a 300-page summary of his findings that would serve as the template for the articles the Judiciary Committee would ultimately pass. (In a move that sparked intense Republican objections, it also included the phone records of the president's attorneys, a journalist, and Devin Nunes.) But Nadler had to do *something*. So he planned a hearing, "Constitutional Grounds for Presidential Impeachment," in which friendly law professors would tell

Democrats that they were doing exactly the right thing by impeaching the president.

Democrats picked three professors—Harvard's Noah Feldman, Stanford's Pamela Karlan, and the University of North Carolina's Michael Gerhardt—while Republicans picked George Washington University law professor Jonathan Turley. The plan was simple: the three professors chosen by Democrats would all argue in favor of impeachment, while Turley—who took pains to announce early on that he had not voted for Donald Trump—argued against it.

Back in 1998, House Republicans held a similar hearing during the impeachment of Bill Clinton, although with a lot more professors and more balanced panels. A total of nineteen professors testified, ten called by majority Republicans (one of them was Turley), eight by minority Democrats, and one—it happened to be Michael Gerhardt—chosen by both sides. With so many witnesses, the hearing was an all-day affair.

Nadler announced the law professor hearing just days before it was held. Representative Doug Collins, the ranking Republican on the committee, was at his home in Gainesville, Georgia. He was unhappy with the ratio of three professors chosen by Democrats to one by Republicans. Couldn't there be one more Republican choice? Collins would have been fine had Nadler added another Democrat choice, too, if he just added one more Republican. Returning from running errands, Collins called Nadler to make his case. Nadler said another Republican-chosen professor was not possible. The two went back and forth. Collins made his case again. Nadler again said no.

"I was just asking for one more law professor," Collins recalled. "He said, 'I can't do that, Doug. I can't do that.' I said, 'Mr. Chairman, this is just not inherently fair. Finally, I said, 'I have to say this one more time—' and on the other end, I hear him say, 'That's all I can say'— CLICK. He hung up on me."

"He just flat hung up on me," Collins continued with a laugh. "I remember standing in my front yard, and he hung up and I was saying, 'Chairman? Jerry? Chairman?'"

More than anything else, the conversation illustrated the tension behind the scenes as impeachment headed toward the home stretch. Nadler was under pressure to get the articles done. Republicans remained angry about the process. Schiff and Pelosi's because-we-say-so dash to impeachment created a sense of resentment among GOP lawmakers that would not disappear anytime soon.

One purpose of Nadler's hearing was to test-run different charges against Trump. The Democrats needed a specific charge before they could draft articles of impeachment. But even the charges Nadler focused on— bribery, abuse of power, and obstruction of Congress—were problematic. For starters, the Trump-Zelensky phone call did not fit the contemporary definition of bribery, especially since the Supreme Court had ruled against a "boundless interpretation" of bribery. But Professor Karlan argued that bribery, as the framers of the Constitution understood it, was much more broadly defined, and thus Trump could be charged with something called "constitutional bribery."

Abuse of power was an easier charge to make, because it could mean anything. Professor Feldman made the case that Trump used his office for personal gain and therefore should be impeached for abuse of power. Democratic counsel Norm Eisen then polled the other Democratic witnesses.

"Professor Karlan, do scholars of impeachment generally agree that abuse of power is an impeachable offense?"

"Yes, they do."

"Professor Gerhardt, do you agree that abuse of power is impeachable?"

"Yes, sir."

Turley, however, noted that abuse of power is not a specific crime, and the case for impeachment becomes stronger if a specific crime is alleged. Abuse of power was intolerably vague. "We have never impeached a president solely, or even largely, on the basis of a non-criminal abuse of power allegation," Turley said. "There is good reason for that unbroken record. Abuses of power tend to be even less defined and more debatable as a basis for impeachment than some of the crimes already mentioned."

Finally, there was obstruction of Congress. President Trump had claimed executive privilege, in denying evidence and witnesses demanded by the House, leaving the matter to the courts for resolution. Democrats didn't want to wait for the courts and proposed charging President Trump and impeaching him for allegedly obstructing Congress.

The three Democratic witnesses enthusiastically agreed. Turley did not. "If you impeach a president, if you make a high crime and misdemeanor out of going to the courts, it is an abuse of power," Turley testified. "It is *your* abuse of power."

Republicans were happy to hear it. Turley, with his moderate demeanor, had done serious damage to the Democratic case for any viewers who might still have had an open mind about it. The Democratic impeachment effort was "slipshod," he said, and would "stand out among modern impeachments as the shortest proceeding, with the thinnest evidentiary record, and the narrowest grounds ever used to impeach a president." While that was helpful, GOP lawmakers still viewed the hearing as a worthless exercise, an attempt to apply a gloss of academic credibility to the Democrats' rush to impeachment.

"The law professor hearing, which was a complete and utter waste of time, was the date that impeachment ended and Speaker Pelosi, the next morning, said, just write the articles," Collins recalled. "She couldn't handle it any more."

Indeed, on the day after the hearing, Thursday, December 5, Pelosi held a news conference to announce that she had directed the committee to begin drafting articles of impeachment. "Yesterday...the American people heard testimony from leading American constitutional scholars who illuminated, without a doubt, that the president's actions are a profound violation of the public trust," Pelosi said. "Sadly, but with confidence and humility, with allegiance to our Founders and our hearts full of love for America, today I am asking our chairmen to proceed with articles of impeachment."

It was no accident that Pelosi said "chair*men*"—plural. Her announcement not only gave the go-ahead to writing articles of impeachment. It also signaled that Jerrold Nadler's brief starring role in the play was nearly over. But not without one more fiasco.

Groundhog Day

The Judiciary Committee held its second and final impeachment hearing a few days later, on December 9. Its title was "Presentations from the House Permanent Select Committee on Intelligence and House Judiciary Committee." Basically, that meant Nadler's committee would discuss what Schiff's committee had found about impeachment and declare it sufficient to move ahead. The chairmen—plural—had already prepared articles of impeachment. But first, one last hearing.

The plan for the hearing was unusual in that there were no fact or expert witnesses on the schedule. Again, Schiff had taken care of that. Instead, the committee would hear from two top staff members— Democrat Daniel Goldman and Republican Steve Castor—on the findings of the Schiff investigation, and then from staff—Democrat Barry Berke and Castor again—on the findings, such as they were, of the Judiciary Committee in its consideration of the issue. The plan devolved into weirdness when Berke testified alongside Castor in the morning and then got out of the chair, moved to the dais, and began questioning Castor when Castor was testifying on the Intelligence Committee's findings.

"This committee is not hearing from factual witnesses," Collins objected. "This committee is not doing anything [beyond] hearing from law school professors and staff."

If there were to be a hearing on the Democratic impeachment report, Republicans wanted to have the author of that report, Adam Schiff, testify. But Schiff declined. "Unfortunately, today the witness who is supposed to be the star witness chose to take a pass and let his staff answer for him," Collins said.

It appeared that most members were not terribly interested in what their staff had to say. They preferred bickering with members on the other side. And that is what they did; the arguments that ensued were not about constitutional issues but focused instead on the disputed facts of the Ukraine case. The name "Ukraine" was mentioned 370 times in the transcript, while the name "Zelensky" appeared 262 times. The phrase "obstruction of Congress," on the other hand, appeared once. The hearing was basically one long, and occasionally bitter, quarrel between Republican and Democratic members, who often ignored their employees sitting in the witness chairs.

The discussion was mind-numbingly repetitive. By the time of the hearing, December 9, the same lawmakers had been arguing over the same topics since the Ukraine matter burst into the news in late September. By this hearing, especially hours into this hearing, there seemed to be nothing new to say.

"We heard that over and over and over again…" said one member.

"We hear time and time again…" said another.

"I keep repeating this…" said yet another.

A search of the transcript showed that on twenty-eight occasions one lawmaker or another noted that the committee was hearing the same thing "over and over." Even the condemnations of repetition became repetitious.

"It was Groundhog Day," said Brad Wenstrup.

And then it came to an end, late at night. The hearing went on for fourteen hours and the transcript ran to 116,00 words—longer than most novels.

The next day, December 10, Pelosi and her chairmen unveiled the articles of impeachment. There were two. Article I was for abuse of power, charging that Trump "corruptly solicited" Ukraine to announce an investigation into the Bidens and "with the same corrupt motives" conditioned U.S. aid and a White House meeting on a public announcement of the investigation.

Article II was for obstruction of Congress, charging that Trump directed the White House to "defy a lawful subpoena" from Congress seeking information about the Ukraine matter. "These actions were consistent with President Trump's previous efforts to undermine United States government investigations into foreign interference in United States elections," the article said, in an oblique reference to the Trump-Russia investigation.

Three days later, the Judiciary Committee approved the articles in two votes, both twenty-three to seventeen, along strict party lines. There was nothing left to discuss.

Pelosi set a full House vote for December 18. For House Republican leaders, the vote was a last chance to show unity against what they saw as an impeachment case that was not compelling, not overwhelming, and certainly not bipartisan. Just as they had with the vote to authorize an impeachment inquiry, Republicans felt it was important that no GOP lawmakers, not a single one, vote for impeachment.

McCarthy and Scalise kept in close contact with their fellow House Republicans, especially those thought to have doubts about Trump's defense. Since the end of the secret depositions, they no longer had to hold briefing sessions, but they made sure all Republican House members knew what was going on. And they reminded GOP members of things like this: not too long before, ninety-five Democrats voted to impeach the president for insulting The Squad. This wasn't about Ukraine, they said. This wasn't about U.S. aid. It was about getting Donald Trump, and it had been for a long time.

In a conversation a few hours before the vote, Scalise was confident of the outcome. "We're going to have zero Republicans," he said. When the names of a couple of members thought to be wavering were mentioned, Scalise said he had already spoken to them that day.

Would they vote for impeachment?

"No."

"There's a high confidence level," Scalise explained, "because I communicate with members all the time."

Scalise's confidence was well-placed. The vote for Article I was 230 to 197, with zero Republicans voting in favor. The vote for Article II was 229 to 198, again with zero Republicans.

It was a rushed end to a long process. Just eighty-five days had elapsed between Pelosi's unilateral announcement of an impeachment and the final House vote. But two years and seven months had passed between the appointment of Robert Mueller and the start of the special counsel probe—the *de facto* investigative arm of the House of Representatives—and the final impeachment vote.

About a week before the vote, Pelosi attended an event in Washington called "Women Rule." She did a sit-down interview with a Politico correspondent, Anna Palmer, who naturally began her questions with impeachment.

"One of the biggest criticisms of the process has been the speed at which the House Democrats are moving," Palmer said.

"The speed?" Pelosi answered as the crowd began to laugh. "It's been going on for 22 months, okay? Two and a half years, actually."

"There has been some criticism, though," Palmer continued, "about whether or not you should move forward before the end of the year or wait for the courts. Why do you think now is the time to make the move?"

"I think we're not moving with speed," Pelosi said. "This was two and a half years ago they initiated the Mueller investigation."

Now, that long pursuit had come to an end. The Mueller probe had failed to bring about Trump's impeachment, but it led straight into the Ukraine probe, which did. Pelosi herself said it was all about Russia. The impeachment vote, unthinkable back in 2017, had become a reality.

EPILOGUE

Not Guilty

Pelosi's Game—Trump Fights Back—Nothing Left to Say—
"You're never getting rid of that scar"

The Trump legal team stayed mostly quiet during the impeachment fight in the House. In the first days of the Ukraine affair, they were as surprised as anyone by news reports about a whistleblower complaint they did not know existed. Then, as House Democrats pressed ahead, they were uncertain whether Pelosi would really pull the trigger— whether there would be an impeachment "second chapter," as Jay Sekulow called it.

Of course, they had noticed back in May 2019, when the *New York Times* published a story headlined, "Rudy Giuliani Plans Ukraine Trip to Push for Inquiries That Could Help Trump." The paper said Giuliani planned to look for "information about two matters of intense interest to Mr. Trump."

"One is the origin of the special counsel's investigation into Russia's interference in the 2016 election," the *Times* said. "The other is the involvement of former Vice President Joseph R. Biden Jr.'s son in a gas company owned by a Ukrainian oligarch." After the report, Giuliani canceled the trip.

Trump's lawyers—Giuliani's colleagues—had gotten a heads-up a short time before the story appeared, but otherwise the Ukraine matter was news to them. "We didn't know anything about that until the proposed May trip to Ukraine," said one Trump defense team member. "We knew about that generally before the papers, but not by much. And that was the first we knew that was going on."

The trip was later canceled, and the issue moved off the defense team's radar. And then the matter re-emerged in the form of a whistleblower complaint, blindsiding the team. "It was, 'What's this? A whistleblower?'" the team member said.

Although the team had not officially disbanded—they still would have had more to do even without the Ukraine matter—Sekulow reunited the group to get back to work more quickly than they might otherwise have expected. He asked Jane Raskin to take over what became known as the "Rudy component" of the story—Sekulow knew that Giuliani had become a significant part of the impeachment inquiry and would not be working on the defense. Sekulow established a division of labor between his team and the White House counsel's office, with the White House working more on developing the facts of the case and the outside lawyers working more on the legal issues involved. For its part, the counsel's office was quietly bulking up its staff. And then they all watched Pelosi and the House.

Pelosi's Game

For all of 2019, there was substantial—but minority—public support for Trump's impeachment. On the day Mueller testified before the House, the FiveThirtyEight polling average showed that 36.9 percent of the public would support Congress beginning the process of impeachment, while 52.5 percent would oppose it. Nancy Pelosi's unilateral announcement of an impeachment inquiry on September 25 raised support for impeachment significantly. By October 3, the day the secret depositions began, support had risen to 45.2 percent while opposition had fallen to 44.5 percent. (By that time, the polling questions were not whether

Congress should start an inquiry—one was underway—but whether the public supported impeaching the president.)

After that, nothing changed much. On November 13, the day the public hearings began, polls showed 47 percent in favor of impeachment versus 44.7 percent against. On November 21, the day the public hearings ended, support was split almost evenly, with 45.6 percent in favor and 45.5 percent against. On December 18, the day the House voted to impeach Trump, it was 47.2 percent in favor versus 46.6 against.

The numbers seemed almost set in stone. From the day the public hearings began to the day of the impeachment vote, support for impeachment went up all of two-tenths of one percentage point, from 47 percent to 47.2 percent. It was a solid number—but short of a majority. Months earlier, Pelosi had set the requirement that impeachment be "compelling and overwhelming and bipartisan." But the support she could muster never reached that level.

Nevertheless, by the end of December 18, impeachment day, a Senate trial for the president was a certainty, whether a majority of the public wanted it or not. At least that is what everyone thought until Pelosi threw another curveball.

The vote on the second and final article of impeachment was finished at 8:50 p.m. on the 18th. In the only recent precedent for such an event, the Bill Clinton impeachment, the next step was that the House majority appointed impeachment managers who would prosecute the case before the Senate. The newly appointed managers then physically walked the articles over to the Senate. It all happened within a few hours after passage of the articles.

But just as she had at nearly every previous step in the impeachment process, Pelosi chose to do things differently.

The Speaker held a news conference shortly after the vote. "I view this day, this vote, as something that we did to honor the vision of our Founders to establish a republic," she said. That was precisely the kind of boilerplate any observer would expect. But then: "We cannot name managers until we see what the process is on the Senate side.... So far, we have not seen anything that looks fair to us, so hopefully it will be fair, and when we see what that is, we'll send our managers."

What? The House would not appoint managers? "You would wait to send the articles until you understand what the Senate is going to do?" a reporter asked.

"We will make a decision as a group, as we always have, as we go along," said Pelosi.

"Could you presumably withhold the articles of impeachment until you get what you consider to be a fair trial?"

"Well, again, we will decide what that dynamic is, but we hope the resolution of that process will be soon in the Senate."

"Would you never send the articles?"

"We are not having that discussion," Pelosi said. "We will make our decision as to when we will send it when we see what is happening on the Senate side. But that is a decision we will make jointly."

The room buzzed as reporters began to understand what Pelosi was saying. This impeachment would again break with precedent. Pelosi asked for quiet. "Don't shout, okay?"

"Can you guarantee that the impeachment articles will be, at some point, sent to the Senate?"

"That would have been our intention," Pelosi said. "But we will see what happens there."

"So, you may not?"

"You're asking me, are we all going to go out and play in the snow?" Pelosi said, clearly becoming irritated. "That has not been part of our conversation."

"That is why we are asking," a reporter said. "We need clarification, since you have raised the prospect of not sending the articles over."

"No," said Pelosi. "I never raised the prospect. You asked the question. I never raised the prospect. I said we are not sending it tonight because it is difficult to determine who the managers would be until we see the arena in which we will be participating. That's all I said. I never raised the prospect."

With that, Pelosi cut off the news conference. On what was surely the most historic night of her speakership, Pelosi had taken a momentous event—impeaching the president—and turned it into a confusing mess. What had appeared to be a clear path of action—appointing managers, sending the articles to the Senate, preparing for trial—immediately became the subject of uncertainty.

Pelosi had apparently gotten the idea of withholding the articles from John Dean, the convicted Watergate felon whom Nadler had invited to testify before the Judiciary Committee. "Pelosi, according to an aide, had been mulling the tactic since she heard former Nixon White House counsel John Dean float the idea on CNN on Dec. 5," reported *Time* magazine. In that appearance, Dean suggested that Pelosi might hold on to the articles for months, even beyond the 2020 presidential election. "I think Nancy Pelosi has some real leverage in this," Dean said. Another person who commanded respect in the Democratic world, Harvard law professor Laurence Tribe, concurred, and even suggested withholding the articles indefinitely, since a Senate trial run by Republicans under Majority Leader Mitch McConnell "would fail to render a meaningful verdict of acquittal."

It was a terrible idea. The Constitution gave the House the "sole power" of impeachment. That gave Pelosi, as Speaker, great leverage over everything that happened in the House. But the Constitution also gave the Senate the "sole power" to try all impeachments. The speaker of the house had no leverage at all over what happened in the Senate trial.

Republicans were stunned by the move. "After months of Pelosi acting like this was the most important thing in the world," recalled GOP whip Steve Scalise, "saying how time was of the essence, and it was somber and important that they move this through...she holds the papers, literally doesn't deliver them to the Senate."

"It totally undercut her argument that the investigation had to be rushed because this was some sort of supposed emergency," recalled Lee Zeldin, "and it extended the division and pain this whole process she created was causing our country."

Theories emerged. Most Republicans believed Pelosi was hoping that some mysterious new witness or evidence would pop up, allowing Democrats to announce a breakthrough in the case against Trump before a Senate trial. A well-connected observer, A.B. Stoddard of *The Hill*, said there was "a lot of pressure on Democrats to wait this out until there is more to throw at the president." It was not clear what "more" might be—perhaps some new development coming from an investigation of Giuliani associates by prosecutors in the Southern District of New York. What was clear was that Democrats felt there was a good chance new evidence would emerge, if they could only delay the impeachment trial a bit.

Republicans also believed Pelosi was doing exactly what she said she was doing, trying to dictate to the Senate how it should conduct the trial. Or perhaps she did not have much faith in the case and was uncertain about how to proceed.

On that last point, Republicans noticed something odd. During the delay, Pelosi began to discuss the completeness and finality of the House impeachment all by itself. No matter what the Senate did, she stressed, Donald Trump had been impeached, and nothing would change that. "This president is impeached for life," she said on ABC on January 12. It was a way of both claiming victory and acknowledging defeat in the Senate ahead of time.

Contrary to John Dean's notion, Pelosi had no leverage at all with McConnell. In fact, McConnell seemed amused by the whole thing. Senate Republicans did not want to impeach the president, he noted, so they would not be crushed by the prospect of not having to impeach the president. "I admit I'm not sure what leverage there is in refraining from sending us something we do not want," McConnell said drily.

McConnell discussed Pelosi's gambit with fellow Republicans at their weekly GOP lunch. Afterward, one senator texted a one-word description of his Republican colleagues' reaction to Pelosi: "Laughter." "Mitch was literally laughing as he was sharing this with the group," the senator recalled. "'So your leverage over us is, you're not going to send us something that we don't want to begin with?'"

Humor aside, McConnell wanted to dispel any confusion about who would be running the Senate trial. "There will be no haggling with the House over Senate procedure," he tweeted on January 8. "We will not cede our authority to try this impeachment. The House Democrats' turn is over."

Trump Fights Back

"They've been trying to impeach me from day one," Trump told a campaign rally in Battle Creek, Michigan, the night the House voted on impeachment. "Crazy Nancy Pelosi's House Democrats have branded themselves with an eternal mark of shame." In the days that followed, Trump talked about impeachment frequently, and tweeted about it even more. He attacked the unfairness of the Democrats' process. He mocked Pelosi and Schiff. He made a Clintonesque vow to keep doing his job for the American people, no matter what his opponents in Congress might do.

But while the president was talking, his legal team remained remarkably silent. Sekulow and White House counsel Pat Cipollone were watching and preparing, but they were not talking publicly.

The preceding two months had been a time of intense uncertainty for the team that weathered the Mueller investigation. "I'm monitoring the statements being made by the House members," Sekulow recalled. "I came to the conclusion that if there was an opportunity, they would take it, to try an impeachment. But even as late as November, they were still very much undecided."

"By mid-November, we start thinking hmmm, they may go there. Then, all of a sudden, you could tell this was going to be the second chapter. By December, we had a team together."

The "second chapter" meant the next step in a continuing Democratic effort to impeach the president. Sekulow had been fighting it since June 2017, shortly after the appointment of Mueller. To the president's lawyers, the impeachment of late 2019 was part of one long campaign. The subject matter changed slightly—from Russia to Ukraine—but the goal was always the same: remove Donald Trump from office.

The legal team worked with the White House counsel's office on dividing responsibilities—which lawyers would handle which issues? Who would be prepared to stand up in the well of the Senate and answer if Issue A or Issue B were raised? The team worked quietly, away from the public fray. They would speak when the time came to defend the president in the Senate, and not before.

Their silence allowed a number of Democrats and their allies in the media to suggest that the White House had no defense. The president could complain about process all he wanted, they said, but he had no defense on the substance of the case.

"They can't contest the facts," said lead Democratic impeachment manager Representative Adam Schiff.

"The case is uncontested," said House manager Representative Hakeem Jeffries.

"Trump has no defense at all," tweeted Professor Tribe.

The criticism grew after the House managers released a forty-six-page trial memorandum summarizing arguments for the Senate. It was essentially a cutdown of the 300-page report that Schiff produced for the Intelligence Committee. The sheer volume of unanswered accusations led to concerns among Republicans. When would the White House defend itself?

"They wanted a substantive defense before the trial," recalled Jay Sekulow. "Let me give you the answer to that: Never try your case before you try your case. You can always attack process beforehand, but don't try your case before you try your case."

When the team finally released its defense, a 110-page memorandum, it was the first time the president systematically addressed the accusations against him. It was an across-the-board defense, questioning the constitutional validity of the articles, the fairness of the House's impeachment process, and the evidence for Article I (the abuse of power accusation) and Article II (the allegation that the president obstructed Congress).

First came the constitutional validity of the articles. "The articles fail to state impeachable offenses as a matter of law," the memo said. The

Trump team argued that Article I's abuse of power charge was an offense made up by House Democrats to cover for their failure to discover any legitimately impeachable offense. The standard for impeachment in the Constitution was, of course, "treason, bribery, or other high crimes and misdemeanors." That standard, the Trump lawyers said, "requires a violation of established law to state an impeachment offense." But in the articles, Democrats "have not even attempted to identify any law that was violated," the memo said. "Moreover, House Democrats' theory in this case rests on the radical assertion that the president could be impeached and removed from office entirely for his *subjective motives*—that is, for undertaking permissible actions for supposedly 'forbidden reasons.'"

The argument over whether impeachment requires an actual crime was long-running and had never been settled. But the Trump team had raised a compelling point about the Democrats' motive-based analysis of Trump's actions, which was, of course, a continuation of Mueller's motive-based analysis of the Trump-Russia matter. House Democrats considered, but rejected, charging Trump with an identifiable crime, like bribery, and instead chose an abuse of power charge that relied heavily on investigating the president's motives. Of course the president had the authority to do X or Y, the Democrats appeared to be saying, but what were his motives in doing it? Adopting the motive standard could play havoc with future presidencies, the defense lawyers argued. "That standard is so malleable that it would permit a partisan House—like this one—to attack virtually any presidential decision by questioning a president's motives. By eliminating any requirement for wrongful conduct, House Democrats have tried to make thinking the wrong thoughts an impeachable offense."

On Article II's obstruction of Congress charge, the Trump team argued first that the president had been "extraordinarily transparent" about the Ukraine matter. In an unprecedented act of openness, he released the transcript of the July 25 conversation with President Zelensky. "That should have put an end to this inquiry before it began," the lawyers wrote. "The president was not 'obstructing' when he freely released the central piece of evidence in this case." Then, when Trump refused to honor some Democratic demands for more information, he invoked privileges fundamental to the operation of his and future presidencies. House Democrats obviously disagreed—but at the same time, they had not been willing to wait for a court to settle the dispute.

"Invoking constitutionally-based privileges and immunities to protect the separation of powers is not an impeachable offense," the memo said. Perhaps Democrats thought otherwise, the lawyers wrote, but "the president cannot be removed from office based on a difference in legal opinion."

The memo objected to the secret depositions, which Trump lawyers were forbidden to attend, saying they "deprived the president of the fundamentally fair process required by the Constitution." It objected to the House's decision to delay passing an impeachment authorization measure until after the secret depositions had been completed. And it objected to the "show trial"—the public hearings held by the Intelligence Committee—in which Trump's lawyers were also forbidden to participate. Pelosi often cited the Constitution's grant of the "sole power of impeachment" to the House, but Trump argued that did not mean the House had no obligation to create fair procedures. "The Supreme Court has made clear that independent constitutional constraints limit otherwise plenary powers committed to one of the political branches," the memo said. For example, even though the Constitution allows each house of Congress to set its own rules, it "may not by its rules ignore constitutional restraints or violate fundamental rights." (The quote was from an 1892 Supreme Court case.)

Then the defense memo addressed the evidence behind the Democrats' Ukraine allegations. "The evidence squarely refutes the made-up claim that the president leveraged security assistance in exchange for Ukraine announcing an investigation into either interference in the 2016 election or the Biden-Burisma affair," the lawyers wrote. The primary piece of evidence, they argued, was the transcript of the Trump-Zelensky call.

When Trump raised burden-sharing with Zelensky—"Germany does almost nothing for you"—he was discussing a "consistent theme in [his] foreign policy," the lawyers wrote, about the need for Europe to take a more active role in its own defense. As for the Biden-Burisma matter, there were legitimate concerns about the Bidens' activities in Ukraine, the lawyers argued, and Zelensky "has publicly confirmed that he understood President Trump to be talking precisely about corruption." Whatever Vice President Joe Biden did in Ukraine, he had, given his son's business involvements there, acted with a "monumental conflict of interest." In addition, "there was *no* discussion of the paused security assistance on the July 25 call." Plus, "President Trump asked President Zelensky to 'do *us* a favor,' and he made clear that 'us' referred to '*our country*'—as he put it, 'because *our country* has been through a lot.'"

The memo went on to argue that not only did Trump not link security assistance to investigations on the call, Zelensky did not perceive any such link, and "other high ranking Ukrainian officials confirmed that they never perceived a connection between security assistance and investigations." Plus, they did not even know the security assistance had been paused.

"There are only two people with statements on record who spoke directly with the president about the matter," the memo continued. One was Ambassador Gordon Sondland and the other was Republican Senator Ron Johnson of Wisconsin, who discussed the aid issue with Trump at the time. "Both have confirmed that the president expressly told them there was no connection whatsoever between the security assistance and investigations." Given that, the Democrats' case rested "entirely on witnesses who offer nothing but speculation. Worse, it is speculation that traces back to one source: Sondland." Some of the testimony involved "chains of hearsay" that ultimately traced back to Sondland, who, as Republicans had shown so effectively in the public hearing, based his testimony on his own presumption of events.

Then, the memo noted, security assistance flowed to Ukraine without the announcement of any investigations. In addition, a number of witnesses testified that Trump had a strong record of supporting Ukraine. As far as pausing aid was concerned, Trump had paused aid to other countries in the past, given his general belief that foreign aid was not always spent wisely. The memo mentioned pauses in aid to Afghanistan, South Korea, El Salvador, Honduras, Guatemala, Lebanon, and Pakistan, in just the previous year. Pausing aid to Ukraine was not a rare or unprecedented act. Finally, the memo said, Zelensky got a meeting with the president without any preconditions.

Of course, no Democrat would be swayed by the Trump defense memo. The Democratic Party, in both House and Senate, was firmly committed to removing the president from office, and nothing would change that. But the defense memo was not aimed at Democrats. It was aimed at Republicans, who had until that time objected mostly to the process of impeachment. Behind the scenes, they were anxious to have a substantive response to the specific allegations Democrats had been making for months. With the defense memo, they got one.

Nothing Left to Say

Pelosi gave up her effort to withhold the articles on January 10. She got nothing from the holdout. No dramatic new evidence emerged, and McConnell did not make any concessions to her demands for a "fair" trial in the Senate. But she had, for what it was worth, extended the period of public discussion about impeachment. "I believe she finally ran out of options and realized there was no political gain anymore," Representative Doug Collins, ranking Republican on the House Judiciary Committee, said in a text exchange the day of Pelosi's decision. "The case never changed, and the outcome has not been altered, but it appears to have allowed them to talk more about it and try to influence public opinion away from the show in the House and the inevitable result in the Senate."

The House voted on January 15 to appoint managers and formally send the articles to the Senate. That same day, the new managers—Schiff, Nadler, Jeffries, Zoe Lofgren, Val Demings, Jason Crow, and Sylvia Garcia—solemnly walked the articles from the House to the Senate.

The trial formally began the next day, January 16, when Supreme Court Chief Justice John Roberts arrived to preside and all one hundred senators took an oath as jurors. The clerk read the articles of impeachment and then senators knocked off for four days to observe the Martin Luther King Jr. holiday.

The trial resumed on January 21 with an impassioned twelve-hour debate on the Senate's rules. The issue under consideration was whether the Senate would call new witnesses in the trial. Democrats, who on the one hand claimed that their case against the president was overwhelming, nevertheless wanted to call new witnesses to provide unspecified additional evidence. Republicans noted that House Democrats had full control over the calling of witnesses and the gathering of evidence during the impeachment inquiry. The Democrats had made a choice to end the inquiry when they did, and they had voted on a specific set of articles to send to the Senate. Now, as the trial began, it was the Senate's job to make a judgment on those articles—not to re-open the investigation.

Republicans prevailed on all the evidence questions, winning a series of votes by a party-line margin of fifty-three to forty-seven. The session lasted until nearly 2:00 a.m.

There was also a fight about the timing of the arguments. Each side had twenty-four hours to make its case, which McConnell wanted done over two twelve-hour days. It would have been a grueling schedule, particularly for the many senators in their 70s and 80s. After some debate, the Senate changed the schedule to three eight-hour days. That meant Democrats took Wednesday, Thursday, and Friday, January 22, 23, and 24, to make their presentation. They used about twenty-one of their allotted twenty-four hours. Then the Trump team took over with a shortened session on Saturday, January 25. Everybody took Sunday off and the Trump team resumed its defense on Monday, January 27. The defense came back for a third day on Tuesday, January 28, but wrapped up early. In the end, the defense used about half of its twenty-four hours.

After that, the Senate had sixteen hours for questions, which took place on Wednesday and Thursday, January 29 and 30. On Friday,

January 31, the Senate held a final debate on motions to allow new witnesses. There was much drama around the question of whether any Republicans might defect to the Democratic side and support witnesses. Four defectors were needed for Democrats to prevail, but in the end, only two, GOP Senators Susan Collins and Mitt Romney, changed sides. The witness motion was defeated on a 51–49 vote.

After that, the Senate did not quite know what to do next. Planning was complicated by the fact that the president's State of the Union address was scheduled for the next Tuesday, February 4. So the Senate decided to take the weekend off, come back on Monday, February 3 for closing arguments, and then take Tuesday off for the State of the Union. A final vote was set for Wednesday, February 5. On that day, the Senate gathered in the morning and acquitted Trump on both articles before noon.

The acquittal was entirely expected. The only unexpected news was Romney's decision to vote to convict Trump on Article I (abuse of power) while voting to acquit him on Article II (obstruction of Congress). Romney thus became the first senator ever to vote to remove a president of his own party.

In the end, the vote on Article I was 48 for and 52 against. (It would have required 67 yes votes to convict the president.) The vote on Article II, with Romney back in the Republican fold, was 47 for and 53 against.

Coverage of the trial featured breathless discussion of the controversies of the moment. Who might vote for witnesses? Would Republicans angrily rebuke Nadler, who accused them of covering up for the president? Would Justice Roberts intervene in the partisan disputes? And what about former national security adviser John Bolton, who had turned on Trump and might possibly testify against him? (He didn't.)

It was enough to keep news coverage going for hour after hour, but it wasn't much. The fact was, by the time the Senate trial came around, there was nothing new to say about impeachment. No minds were changed, no new arguments were made, no ground was broken. The event that some saw as the climax of the impeachment battle was in fact the anticlimax. The real news had been made in the months before, as the House lurched toward impeaching the president. By the time the Senate convened, it was all over.

"You're never getting rid of that scar"

The drive to remove Donald Trump from office had stretched from the moment he was sworn in on January 20, 2017, to the moment the Senate acquitted him on February 5, 2020. The formal mechanisms of impeachment—a nascent movement in the House, coupled with a special counsel to serve as its investigative arm—started with the appointment of Robert Mueller on May 17, 2017. By any counting, the attempt to bring Trump down went on for a long time.

During that time, some Democrats worked themselves into a seemingly permanent state of hysteria over Russia. There was breathless (and endless) discussion of each new revelation out of the Mueller probe. There were serious people who, with a straight face, called the president a Russian agent. There were serious people who accused him of treason. There were serious people who believed the allegations in the Steele dossier. Reason, proportion, and critical thinking virtually disappeared from the daily debate.

The public discussion of the Russia matter continued long after Mueller, working behind closed doors, had given up on finding conspiracy or coordination—collusion—between Russia and the 2016 Trump campaign. And when, after the release of the Mueller report in May 2019 and Mueller's Capitol Hill testimony in July, it became impossible to allege collusion any longer, support for impeachment still *grew* among House Democrats. More than half of them supported impeachment when, in the sixty days or so after Mueller's appearance, impeachment over Russia began to morph into impeachment over Ukraine.

Nancy Pelosi, who had earlier acted as a moderating force among the members of her party eager to impeach the president, became the face of impeachment when she decided not to wait until the release of the Trump-Zelensky transcript or the whistleblower complaint before announcing an impeachment inquiry. The antipathy between the Speaker and the president, already high, reached stratospheric levels. In mid-October 2019, with the debate raging on Capitol Hill, she stormed out of a White House meeting with Trump, accusing him of a "meltdown" during a discussion about Syria. Republicans in the meeting sensed that she was the one close to melting down. Their fight had become personal.

In January, after the House voted to impeach, Pelosi taunted Trump by saying he was "impeached for life." On February 6, the day after the Senate acquittal, Pelosi wagged her finger at the president during a news conference. "You're impeached forever," she said. "You're never getting rid of that scar."

When Trump delivered the State of the Union in the House chamber, it was Pelosi's job to sit on the platform behind him. When he arrived, he handed her a paper copy of the speech and she reached out to shake his hand. He did not respond. There was some question of whether he saw her gesture or not, but the fact was, he did not shake her hand. Throughout the speech, Pelosi's every expression and move could be seen as the president, his back to her, delivered the address. When Trump finished and Republicans were applauding, Pelosi picked up a few pages of the speech and ripped them in two. Then she picked up a few more pages and ripped them up, too. She did that until the entire speech was in pieces, and then she tossed the shreds of paper onto the desk.

It was a moment in which the anger and frustration of the preceding three years simply boiled over. Democrats had tried everything they could to remove Trump from office. They tried using a special counsel. They tried not using a special counsel. They tried secret hearings. They tried open hearings. They tried to enlist Republicans in their work. They tried going it alone. In the end, nothing worked. Trump was still standing.

There was, though, a last resort available to them. There always had been. A presidential election was coming in November 2020. Trump would stand for the voters' judgment, as he had in 2016. Elections were the way Americans delivered their verdict on sitting presidents, and judgment would come for Trump as it had for his predecessors. The Founders made it exceedingly difficult to remove a president from office, but they required all presidents who desired a second term to stand for re-election after four years. That would be Trump's test. Had Democrats not lost their heads in a years-long fit of anger and passion, they would have seen that all along.

Acknowledgments

I would like to thank the many people who spoke to me and gave me information during the reporting for this book from 2017 to 2020. Sometimes off the record, sometimes on, they helped me understand what was going on at times when hysterical reports from some news outlets obscured, rather than revealed, the true nature of events.

I also owe a debt to the *Washington Examiner*, which gave me the freedom to pursue the story, and to Fox News, which allowed me to discuss it at all of its various stages.

Many thanks also to Park MacDougald, who gave the manuscript a sensitive and helpful reading. Also thanks to Regnery's Harry Crocker, who first approached me about the book, and who edited it, and Tom Spence, who approved the project.

One evening, as I was nearing the completion the book, I was discussing with my wife Marty the things that remained to be done. Among them was the Acknowledgments. "Are you going to do a dedication to your wife, without whom you couldn't have done *blah blah blah*?" she asked.

Yes, I am. With love and eternal gratitude.

Index